T0329425

CAMBRIDGE STUDIES IN ECONOMIC HISTORY

PUBLISHED WITH THE AID OF THE ELLEN MCARTHUR FUND

GENERAL EDITOR

M. M. POSTAN, M.A.

Professor in Economic History in the University of Cambridge

THE

THEORY AND PRACTICE

OF

CENTRAL BANKING

1797–1913

THE
THEORY AND PRACTICE
OF
CENTRAL BANKING
1797—1913

by

E. VICTOR MORGAN

CAMBRIDGE
AT THE UNIVERSITY PRESS
1943

CAMBRIDGE UNIVERSITY PRESS
Cambridge, New York, Melbourne, Madrid, Cape Town,
Singapore, São Paulo, Delhi, Mexico City

Cambridge University Press
The Edinburgh Building, Cambridge CB2 8RU, UK

Published in the United States of America by Cambridge University Press, New York

www.cambridge.org
Information on this title: www.cambridge.org/9781107690868

First published 1943
First paperback edition 2013

A catalogue record for this publication is available from the British Library

ISBN 978-1-107-69086-8 Paperback

Contents

CONTENTS

TABLES

CHARTS

Editorial Preface

Discerning readers will not fail to notice the pioneer quality of Mr Morgan's essay. They will also observe that its novelty lies not so much in its matter as in its theme. It is not that the matter is in any way hackneyed or stale. There are many things in the book which at least one reader found wholly new, and which other and more expert readers may find at least interesting. Yet the principal characteristic of the book is not the information which it contains, but the purposes for which the information is employed. Mr Morgan has set out to do what in the writing of modern economic history has so seldom been done. His study is both historical and theoretical, and though many students before him tried to marry economic history to economic theory, few of them ever achieved the union on Mr Morgan's terms.

Economic studies combining theory with history fall, as a rule, into two interrelated groups. They are conceived either as exercises in "applied economics" in which a few historical facts are used to illustrate the few economic theories which are capable of being illustrated; or else as "historical revisions" in which certain well-known episodes of economic history are re-told in terms of modern theory. Examples of the former will be found embedded in most of the better known economic treatises from Adam Smith to Marshall and Keynes. Examples of the latter have been lately produced by economists and historians alike: *vide* Bresciani-Turoni's book on the German inflation, Rostow's articles on the Great Depression, or Fisher's article on the commercial policy of the Tudors.

Mr Morgan attempts none of these things. While his debt to modern economic theory and more especially to Keynes will be obvious to all (and economic theories are an avowed part of his subject) he treats the theories themselves as historical facts and subjects them to historical analysis. At the same time the book is no mere "history of economic doctrine". It pays an equal if not a greater attention to the banking policies, the monetary changes and the movements of prices, which sometimes influenced theoretical discussion and were often themselves affected by contemporary doctrines. The two topics are run on concurrent lines, which often intersect, but are never merged or confused.

For the same reasons the book is also something more than an economic history of economic theory. It is not the kind of essay on the economic determinism of economic thought which the Marxists of the older dispensation would like to have written had they known how. The parallel treatment of monetary events and monetary theories reveals not only the connections between the facts and the theories, but also the occasional gaps between them. Some of the gaps will be noticed in Mr Morgan's treatment of the bank restriction period, for the experiences of the time apparently failed to generate new economic ideas. In the author's own words the period "produced only a restatement of theories all of which had been stated before, and many of which were a century old". Similarly, it does not appear as if the second half of the nineteenth century, and more especially the period between the Bank Charter Act and the passing of the Great Depression—an epoch of great changes in prices, great developments of investment, and at least two complete business cycles—witnessed any great or illuminating departures in monetary theory. In these fifty-odd years Mill and Marshall produced their great syntheses of economic doctrine, and Jevons very nearly revolutionised the theory of value. Yet the theory of money, prices, credit and business cycles made relatively little progress in spite of continuous accumulation of highly relevant evidence. Giffen's essays, Jevons's index number, Bagehot's description of the money market, and Newmarch's history of prices were perhaps the only specialised writings on currency worth Mr Morgan's commendation, and yet even they were out of scale, and perhaps even out of touch, with the lessons of capitalist finance in the most boisterous and turbulent stages of its growth. To his own credit and to his readers' edification Mr Morgan does

not fail to note the "autonomous" phases in the development
of economic thought, and from this point of view few passages
in the book are more suggestive than those dealing with the
genesis of the controversy between the banking and the currency schools. Mr Morgan makes it clear that the controversy
owed more to its own antecedents than to the lessons of the
contemporary banking practice.

The reader will not fail to note that this preface, like all prefaces, does little justice to the book. In spite of his specialised interests even the editor found his attention diverted and his interest
stimulated by several "purely historical" passages. The summaries of railway finance and of the Great Boom can profitably
be read for their own sakes, but the other historical summaries,
though laconic in the extreme, are also sufficiently illuminating
to attract the attention of those economic historians who do
not happen to be interested in Mr Morgan's main themes.

M. M. POSTAN

PETERHOUSE

Author's Preface

Most of the work for this book was done while I held a research studentship at Christ's College, and the first debt which I have to acknowledge is, therefore, one of gratitude to the Master and Fellows. I should like to thank the Managers of the Ellen McArthur Fund for their permission to make slight alterations to chapters I to VII as originally submitted to them, and to add chapters VIII to XI. Others to whom my grateful thanks are due are Mrs J. V. Robinson and Mr P. Sraffa, who have given me valuable criticism and advice, and enabled me to correct a number of mistakes (though the responsibility for the mistakes which remain is, of course, entirely my own); the staff of the University Press who, in spite of their own difficulties at this time, have always been willing to help with mine; and my wife, who has given me constant assistance from the preparation of rough notes to the compilation of the index.

E. V. M.

November 1942

Chapter One

BANKS AND BANKING IN THE EARLY NINETEENTH CENTURY

THE BANK OF ENGLAND

When John Horsley Palmer, Governor of the Bank in 1832, was asked what were its chief functions, he replied:

> To furnish the paper money with which the public act around them, and to be a place of safe deposit for the public money, and for the money of individuals who prefer a public body like the Bank to private bankers.[1]

It will be noticed that Palmer stresses the action of the public with the notes provided by the Bank, for throughout the first half of the century the Bank was earnestly disclaiming any active role in determining the quantity of money.

But already the Bank's functions had ramifications which are hardly suggested in Palmer's simple outline. The functions of a modern central bank are fourfold: to act as manager of the National Debt and banker to the government; to regulate the currency; to be a banker's bank, and to act as lender of last resort. Even at the beginning of the nineteenth century we can find important traces of all these functions.

The Bank and the National Debt had grown up together, and critics of both said that the prosperity of the Bank depended on the Debt. The Bank kept the books in which transfers of stock were recorded, and made the dividend payments, for which services it received a commission prescribed by the terms of the charter. The Bank also handled the government account. The revenue was received and accumulated as government deposits, on which, in accordance with the Bank's usual rule, no

1 Committee of Secrecy on the Renewal of the Bank of England Charter, 1832, Q. 181.

interest was paid. When payments exceeded revenue, the government was allowed to overdraw its account by means of deficiency bills and special advances. After their formation in 1826 the branch banks assisted in the collection of the revenue, by receiving it from the commissioners in the provinces, and crediting it to the government account in London. The very complex machinery of the Exchequer was somewhat simplified by an act of 1834, by which payments formerly made to the Tellers of the Exchequer were now made direct to the Bank.

The amount which the Bank could lend to the government was fixed by law, but during the French wars Pitt had the restriction removed, after the directors had questioned the legality of the advances which he required. It was the demands of Pitt which eventually led to the restriction of cash payments in 1797, and, when it came to a question of resumption, the directors insisted on the repayment of £10 mn. of their advances to the government. The repayment was accompanied by a new restriction on lending, but the deficiency bills still remained, and the Bank was left free to deal in the Exchequer bill market to any extent which it thought fit.

Government finance in the 1820's was a notorious mixture of complexity and incompetence. For instance, the sinking fund was obstinately maintained, even in years when there was a budget deficit, and when money for the fund had to be borrowed at a higher rate than was being paid on the stock redeemed. By a similar muddle, deposits were allowed to accumulate in one account, while another was paying interest on deficiency bills. These deposits were very useful to the Bank, as it knew exactly when they would be required, and so could re-lend a very high proportion of them, but the profit thus gained brought with it a great deal of unpopularity.

So much for the Bank's relations with the government. The regulation of the currency will form one of the main themes of this book, and here it is intended only to clear up a few technical points.

Until 1826 the Bank was the only body of more than six partners which might issue notes in England, but an act of that year restricted the monopoly to an area within sixty-five miles of London. In practice, the Bank enjoyed a complete monopoly of issue in London, as the London private bankers had all given up issuing notes before the end of the eighteenth century. Bank of England notes also circulated generally in Lancashire, but elsewhere there were only a small number, most of which were held by country bankers in order to facilitate transactions with London, and by way of a reserve.

There circulated in the provinces a great number of notes of private banks having less than six partners and, after 1826, of a growing number of joint-stock banks. These notes formed the principal currency of the agricultural districts, but a great deal of industry and commerce was financed by bills of exchange. The bill of exchange was at its most important in domestic trade during the Napoleonic wars, but then it suffered a decline, relatively, though not yet in absolute volume. In 1819, S. J. Lloyd says that the circulation of bills in Lancashire is ten times that of notes, but in 1832 G. C. Glynn states: "I think a great deal of that which was formerly done in bills of exchange is now done in cash." This is only natural, as bills of exchange had arisen before there was a reliable paper currency, and the conditions which had given rise to the system were now rapidly passing.

Until the end of the eighteenth century the Bank had issued no notes of less value than £10, but shortly before 1797 £5 notes, the lowest denomination allowed by law, were issued. At the time of the Restriction Act, the law was modified to allow the issue of £1 and £2 notes, and during the war these were issued both by the Bank of England and the country banks. The act of 1819 provided that the small notes should cease in 1822, but as one of its measures for the relief of the depression, the government prolonged their life until 1833. The Bank, however, stopped issuing the small notes, save for the forgotten million which were so opportunely discovered during the crisis of 1825. After that crisis the small notes received much of the blame, and the law was again amended, so that they finally disappeared from circulation in 1829.

There were four channels through which Bank of England notes might come into circulation: in exchange for bullion bought by the Bank, in advances to the government or to individuals, through the purchase of securities in the market, and through the discount of commercial bills. Advances to individuals were made only at the end of the quarter, of which more later. During the Restriction Period the Bank occasionally bought gold in the market at substantially above the mint price, and after the resumption it acted as agent for the mint, and was prepared to buy, on its own account, any gold which might be offered to it at the mint price.

As between government securities and bills of exchange, there was a marked change of policy between 1819 and 1832. In 1819 the directors were clamouring for the repayment of £10 mn. of their advances to the government, though no one anticipated so large a contraction in the liabilities of the Bank. It was said that the replacement of government advances by commercial bills would give the Bank greater control over its issues. Governor Dorrien put the point thus:

In the case of the government advances, the Bank has no control over its issues; but when the money is lent upon discounts the directors are enabled to check any improper speculations, or any circumstances that they think injurious to the country. This will tend to bring the issues upon a level with the circulation that is required for the commerce of the country.

But this does not imply any forcible contraction of issues, for he adds:

The Bank is always ready to lend on commercial paper that is legitimate in its origin, and is not carried to too great an extent by the parties that apply for discount.[1]

This policy was a natural consequence of the principle which governed the Bank's conduct during the wars, namely that notes ought to be issued to whatever extent was necessary in

1 House of Commons Committee on the Resumption of Cash Payments, 1819, Dorrien's evidence, p. 26.

order to satisfy "the legitimate needs of commerce", as measured by the demand for discounts of good bills at 5%. That this policy was to be continued is clear from the above quotation from Dorrien, and from Deputy-Governor Pole's assertion that the repayment of the government advances would result in no reduction of the circulation so long as market rate of discount did not fall below 5%.

But before 1832 the idea of "the legitimate needs of commerce" had been replaced by Horsley Palmer's principle of "keeping the securities even", and allowing the liabilities to vary according to the influx or efflux of bullion. Moreover, the purchase of Exchequer bills in the market, or the easily calculable and limited advances on deficiency bills, are a very different thing from the importunate demands of a government at war, or only just recovering from a war. Finally, the experience of the post-war years taught the Bank that it might often be very difficult to obtain good commercial discounts without a great reduction of interest rates. Consequently, when a 4% rate produced little demand, the Bank refused to take part in a scramble for discounts, and turned to government securities instead.

Palmer tells the Committee of 1832 that he thinks Bank rate should normally be above market rate, so that there should be but little demand for discounts, which tend to interfere with private bankers, and to cause an undue enlargement of the circulation. He says:

As an exclusive bank of issue in the capital, it appears to me that it (the Bank) cannot beneficially conduct a discount account to any great extent with individuals except in times of discredit. When the circulation is full, a competition with private bankers would, in all probability, lead to an excess, in addition to the other difficulties which would occur in the attempt on the part of the Bank of England to regulate their issues by this channel.

In pursuance of this policy, government securities were increased from about £13 mn., after the completion of the repayment promised in 1819, to £20·8 mn. in August 1832. It is interesting to note that, at the very time when Bank rate was conceived as an instrument for the regulation of credit, it was destined to be effective only in times of pressure.

There was a brief return to the views of Dorrien and Pole shortly after the passage of the act of 1844, when Bank rate was reduced to $2\frac{1}{2}$%. But even this reduction left Bank rate higher than market rate, as Gurney's were charging only 2%, and the new policy earned a great deal of condemnation while only achieving moderate success.

At the beginning of the century market dealings in securities were confined to Exchequer bills, and their object was less the regulation of the currency than the assistance of the government, by supporting the market in time of weakness. But with the decline of the Bank's commercial discounts after the wars, the Exchequer bill market assumed major importance. During the depression of the early 1820's the Bank also bought stock in the market; the practice was condemned at the time, and there were no more purchases until 1830. Even then dealings were small, and were shortly discontinued again until 1837. It is not until 1840 that large-scale dealings in Consols take place, and by that time Exchequer bills were becoming less marketable and "open market operations" in general were being superseded for the time by a more flexible Bank-rate policy.

One of the problems of post-war finance was the quarterly payment of the dividends on the enormously increased National Debt. Before each payment large government deposits accumulated in the Bank; on the appointed day payments were made to stockholders throughout the country, and only gradually, through the recipient's own banks, did the money find its way back to the circulation of the metropolis. This produced a scarcity of money, and a rise in interest rates quite unconnected with the normal course of trade. During the Restriction Period the Bank acted as a rough and ready stabiliser by automatically supporting the Exchequer bill market whenever it showed serious weakness.[1] In 1829 the Bank first offered to make ad-

1 W. T. C. King, *The History of the London Discount Market*, p. 84, footnote 2.

vances, at market rate, on bills of exchange, Exchequer bills and East India bonds, during the "shuttings", the time in which the books were closed for the transfer of stock.[1]

The transaction appears in the books of the Bank, first as an increase in government deposits, and a decline in the circulation; then an increase in the securities and the circulation as advances were made, a decline in deposits as the dividends were paid, and finally a decline in the circulation as the money returned and the advances were paid off. The initial decline in the circulation is not noticeable, as advances were taken in anticipation of the scarcity which it was known would otherwise occur. In the weekly returns, the increase in the circulation is seen to follow, as we should expect, the increase in deposits, but the monthly averages which we have compiled for 1832-40 telescope the two so that they coincide. The advances were generally made for a minimum period of ten days and a maximum of six or seven weeks.

In connection with the establishment of the branches, the Bank made an attempt to extend its circulation. Any private banker who offered to abandon his own note issue, and work with Bank of England notes, was given a limited amount at 3% on the security of bills of exchange. The amount depended on the banker's previous circulation, and there was a minimum which he must take, and a maximum which he could only exceed by discounting in the normal way. The difference between the two was about 14%. This was a general offer made to all private banks, and the Bank maintained that it never made overtures to any particular firm. A number of banks availed themselves of the offer, but the majority jealously clung to their own issues.

The third function we mentioned was that of being a banker's bank. London bankers, in growing numbers, were opening accounts with the Bank during the Napoleonic wars. Its strict rules were discouraging to private accounts, but after 1825 facilities for payment by cheque were considerably extended. Until the crisis of that year the London banks held only small

1 Palmer's evidence, Committee of 1832, Q. 255.

balances with the Bank, and relied on rediscounting to meet any sudden demand, but the crisis led to the keeping of somewhat larger reserves and to a growing reluctance to re-discount. In 1832 G. C. Glynn states that "It is our practice, and I believe it so likewise, now with nearly every banking house, to keep a large deposit in the Bank of England".[1] But even so, bankers' balances remained very small, both by modern standards and in relation to their liabilities, and in the years immediately before 1844 the total seldom exceeded £1 mn.

In its modern interpretation, the Bank's action as lender of last resort implies that its funds must not be largely employed in the market in normal times, but that they must always be available in time of pressure. The change from commercial bills to government securities as the backing for the note issue, and the maintenance of Bank rate above market rate, set the Bank apart from the market. The distinction was emphasised by the rise of the specialist discount houses and the cessation of re-discounting by the London banks. In fact, we may say that, by 1832, the Bank was in very nearly its modern position in this respect.

The realisation of its responsibilities to provide cash in time of emergency was delayed by the action of the government in issuing Exchequer bills to merchants in distress during the crises of 1793 and 1811. The demand for such aid was renewed in 1825, and it was only after Liverpool had very firmly refused that we hear the last of it. The evil consequences were twofold, for the Bank was blinded to its natural responsibility, and the public was encouraged to look to the government for aid, instead of seeing to the liquidity of its own position.

The crudest reaction of the Bank to a crisis was in 1795, when it was simply announced that a certain proportion of all bills sent for discount would be returned. The usury laws, of course, prevented the raising of Bank rate above 5%, so that the only way of limiting discounts was either by restricting the usance of bills, or by some form of rationing. The announcement of 1795, however, created general outcry, and we know of no

1 Committee of 1832, Q. 2870.

instance of general and indiscriminate rationing since that date. During the wars the Bank was, in general, prepared to discount any good paper brought to it, but the directors reserved the right, of course, to discriminate against names which were thought to be taking up too large commitments.

The first post-war test was the crisis of 1825. During the autumn the Bank was restricting discounts by discriminating against what were believed to be the less sound firms. There was no general rationing, but there are individual complaints of bills being returned. In December, when the crisis had already become acute, the restrictive policy was reversed, and the Bank lent very freely. In February 1826, at the instigation of the government, advances were even made on the security of merchandise, but this is the only known instance of its kind.

The repeal of the usury laws made it possible to restrain the demand for accommodation by raising its price, but in 1836 and 1839 the directors showed themselves shy of imposing too high rates, while in October 1840 they chose to restrict the usance of bills rather than raise the rate above 5 %.

Advances, other than by way of discounts, were made to the Northern and Central Bank in 1836, and to merchants in the American trade in 1837. Thus, gradually, and in spite of some opposition from the theorists, it was coming to be established that the Bank had a duty to provide the greatest possible amount of credit in an emergency to those who were most in need, and that the best way of so doing was by way of discounts regulated by a changing Bank rate.

In passing we may note that the Bank first allowed discount accounts to bill brokers in 1830 and, later in the decade, began to discount London bills on each weekday instead of on Thursdays only. Partly in defence of cautious banking principles, and partly from reluctance to assist a possible rival, the Bank refused to discount any bill bearing the name of a joint-stock bank.

We have already referred to the branch banks, set up, at the instigation of Liverpool's government, in 1826 and the following years. Besides the offer to private bankers which we have mentioned, the branches also offered discount facilities, though these were circumscribed by the strictness of the rules imposed. Discounts were only made for those having a discount account, and not only had each account to be approved by headquarters, but so also had each bill brought for discount, before its value could be credited to the customer's account. One way in which the branches competed with existing banks, however, was in not charging any commission; other bankers, too, gradually abandoned the practice, and often blamed the Bank for forcing them to do so.

But if the country bankers suffered through the loss of commission, they gained in increased facilities for transmitting money to London. On the whole, we may accept Palmer's contention that the branches were founded as a source of convenience to the government and the public, and were not intended either to compete with the country banks, or to make any great profits for the Bank.[1]

THE LONDON PRIVATE BANKERS

The London private bankers were a body of men of great wealth and repute, containing names famous in banking history, some of which survive and preserve their separate identity to this day. "There are Barclays and Bosanquets and Curries; Dorriens, Frys, Glynns and Grotes; Hanbury and Hankey and Hoare; Jones Lubbock and Masterman; Smith and Spooner, Whitmore and Williams."[2] In spite of, and indeed because of their great position, these men went their way almost untouched by the spotlight of publicity which shone on other banking activities. Enquiries were mainly concerned with the issue of notes, and the causes of bank failures; these firms had long ceased to issue notes, and failures among them were extremely rare. Consequently when London bankers gave evidence, as did Sir Coutts Trotter in 1819 and George Carr Glynn in 1832, they were asked not about their own business, but their opinion of the conduct of the Bank of England and the country banks.

1 Committee of 1832, Q. 481.
2 J. H. Clapham, *An Economic History of Modern Britain*, vol. I, p. 283.

These banks worked with Bank of England notes, receiving deposits, discounting bills, lending on securities, and doing a profitable agency business for the country banks. At the beginning of the nineteenth century, however, the London banks ceased to pay interest on bankers' deposits, and one consequence of this was the increased disposition of the country banks to lend short money to the discount market.

The bankers' clearing house dates from the eighteenth century, and in 1827 there were thirty-two members, including most of the big firms, though one or two, such as Coutts, whose connections were mainly West End, remained outside. Its premises were in Lombard Street, "Adjoining the banking house of Messrs Smith, Payne and Smith, whose property it was", and there each member had a drawer. Clerks came twice a day, and dropped into each drawer bills and cheques payable by the owner. These were added up and cancelled out by two salaried inspectors, and the balance settled at the end of the day. As late as 1844 balances were still settled in banknotes, but soon afterwards this method was superseded by cheques on the Bank of England.[1]

THE PRIVATE COUNTRY BANKS

When we come to describe the private banks of the provinces we are met with a bewildering variety, from which any generalisation must be misleading, and we can only quote a few examples.

The law imposed no restriction on banks of less than six partners, save the obligation to register at the Stamp Office, and pay a stamp duty on notes. As Lord Liverpool said: "Any petty tradesman, any grocer or cheesemonger, however destitute of property, might set up a bank in any place."[2] Many of these banks went under in every crisis from 1793 to 1825, but on the other hand there were large firms, such as Gurney's of Norwich or Stuckey's of Somerset, which were owned by men of great

1 Clapham, op. cit. pp. 283–4, and The Bankers' Magazine, Nov. 1844.
2 Hansard, 17 Feb. 1826, p. 462.

wealth, and run on unexceptionable principles. After the crisis of 1825, which took toll of eighty banks, the system was settling down; only the fitter were surviving, and failures in future were much fewer. But there still remained a great variety of practice.

Except in Lancashire, almost all these banks issued notes, but the amount of the issues, like the reserve held against them, was very variable. Most of the country circulation was in agricultural districts, and in 1841 H. W. Hobhouse asserts that only half a million was in industrial areas, but this would probably not have been at all true for the beginning of the century.[1] Speaking of the resumption of cash payments in 1819, Hudson Gurney said: "The amount of our circulation compared with our deposits is so small that it would not enter into our calculations, either the one way or the other."[2] William Becket of Leeds stated in 1832 that his circulation was "not one-fourth of the deposits", and Charles Smith Forster of Walsall said that notes formed one-sixth of his total liabilities. On the other hand J. P. Wilkins of Brecon, whose dealings were largely with Welsh cattle drovers, had nearly half his liabilities in notes, and Vincent Stuckey tells the Committee of 1841 that he derives half his profit from notes, though they are rather less than half his liabilities.

The issue of notes lent prestige to a bank. Thus Forster says:

I think there are advantages attending the circulation of country bank notes which are not obvious to all country bankers; I think it gives a sort of éclat to the establishment; it answers the purpose of the address card of the tradesman; it makes the bank notorious, and makes it the subject of conversation, and brings deposits and customers....I conceive that when a banker abandons his circulation he degrades into a bill broker.[3]

Though a few banks accepted the offer of the Bank of England, the official policy of the Country Bankers' Committee was very hostile to any extension of the Bank's circulation.

On the subject of reserves against notes there is a very wide

1 Select Committee on Banks of Issue, 1841, Hobhouse's evidence.
2 Commons Committee of 1819, p. 251.
3 Committee of 1832, QQ. 1503-4.

difference, and it is seldom clear whether the reserve mentioned is against notes only, or notes and deposits. Presumably the latter was the general rule. Attwood thinks that a Birmingham banker would keep Bank of England notes to about a quarter of his circulation.[1] Beckett keeps gold to the extent of one-seventh, and gold and Bank of England notes combined to the extent of one-half of his circulation. Stuckey keeps a cash ratio of one-twentieth only; he does not say whether this is in gold or notes, but he made no change after Bank of England notes became legal tender in 1833. On the other hand, he states that, in time of uncertainty, the reserve may rise to three- or four-twentieths, and before the crisis of 1825, he says, he took down enough Bank of England notes to pay three-quarters of his circulation.[2] The only generalisations which we can make about reserves are: first, that they were small; secondly, that they were very variable; and thirdly, that, small as were total reserves, gold reserves were much smaller. Especially after 1833, the Bank of England had become practically the sole keeper of the country's gold reserve.

According to Hobhouse the number of note-issuing private banks was 430 in 1833 and 270 in 1840, the decline being largely due to amalgamations and absorptions by joint-stock banks. In some years before 1833 the number must have been even higher. Despite the stamp duty, no accurate estimate of the amount of the country circulation can be made before the re-forms of 1833. Notes were stamped, whether they were actually issued to the public or held in reserve by the banker; notes once stamped might be re-issued any time up to three years, and there is no means of knowing the actual life of a note. The general view was that there was a great deal of fluctuation in the amount of issues, and hence arose the importance of the discussion as to the relationship between these notes and the price level. But the only scientific investigation, that made by Burgess for the Committee of 1832, rather contradicts this im-

1 House of Lords Committee on the Resumption of Cash Payments, 1819, p. 12.
2 Stuckey's evidence in 1819, 1832, 1836 and 1841.

pression. He compiled an index number showing fluctuations from year to year, and based on the returns of 122 banks. This index, which we quote elsewhere, shows a quite remarkable constancy. It is true that the evidence may have been selected to support the case of the country bankers, but even so we must allow far more weight to this investigation than to the mere guesses which are the alternatives.

There was a fairly regular seasonal fluctuation, the circulation rising in the autumn and spring, and falling in the summer and winter.

Notes were generally made payable at sight either at the place of issue or by the London agent. At the beginning of the century some were payable subject to a few days' notice, and some bore interest, but neither of these practices was common, and both soon died out.

It was the general view of country bankers that their issues depended on prices, that they had no causal influence either on price movements or the exchanges, and therefore that they had no need to concern themselves with such things. An exception is Stuckey, who tells the Committee of 1832:

The first thing we enter at every quarterly meeting, is the price of gold and silver, and the exchange with Paris and Hamburg; that is to serve as a beacon for the general management of our business.[1]

But even he does not think that an increase in country issues has any important effect on the exchanges, or that they ought to be regulated in exact conformity with exchange fluctuations.

The minutes of all the parliamentary committees are packed with denials that the country banks have any responsibility in this matter, ranging from J. P. Wilkins's blunt "Exchange has no more to do with us than last year's snow",[2] to this reasoned statement of Hobhouse:

The amount of the ordinary local dealing and expenditure is the principle which at any and all times limits and determines the amount of those various circulations. Whatever increases the dealing and expenditure increases the circulation, and vice versa. Therefore the

1 Committee of 1832, Q. 1016.   2 *Ibid.* Q. 1605.

country bankers are perfectly passive in the matter; no competition on their part can increase the circulation beyond this amount; no artificial management can reduce it under this amount.[1]

It is notable that the legal tender clause in the act of 1833 is interpreted by the country bankers as throwing the sole responsibility for the maintenance of the gold reserve on the Bank of England, and absolving them from any duties which they might have had in the matter.

From the beginning the country banks had accepted deposits as well as issuing notes, and now the deposits were generally the greater in value. At first interest was paid on all deposits, but with the growth of the cheque system the practice was changed. As early as 1832 Stuckey comments on the use of the cheque:

A great portion of the taxes of the County of Somerset are now paid in the same way. In these cases there is very little circulating medium used compared with what it formerly was.[1]

Some bankers stopped giving interest on deposits at all, and in 1841 Hobhouse says that this is the general rule. If so, there were a number of exceptions, and the distinction between current and deposit accounts was already being made, among others by Stuckey's.[2]

The third source of funds, besides notes and deposits, was, of course, the banks' capital. Of this little or nothing is known. It consisted of the personal fortune of the banker, and this he could not, according to the standards which then governed public enquiries, be expected to disclose. Often it must have been small, and often, too, the banker was engaged in some other form of business, and the capital employed in the two would not be clearly separated.

So much for the liabilities side of the balance sheet. How were these funds employed? Of cash reserves we have already spoken, and call loans were not yet a general method of employing funds for banks at any distance from London. It is strange, to those brought up in modern banking traditions, that

1 Committee of 1832, Q. 978.   2 *Ibid.* Q. 968.

long-term government securities were regarded as a good form of investment, and it was the most cautious bankers, such as Stuckey, who specially preferred them. The strength of the prejudice is shown with regard to joint-stock banks, for there was a strong school of thought in favour of compelling them by law to hold a certain proportion of such securities. Besides Consols there were, however, Exchequer bills, and there was much discussion as to whether these were more or less marketable than bills of exchange.

The most popular asset was, however, the commercial bill. But though increasing in volume, the bill was becoming relatively less important in the post-war period. William Leatham, a Wakefield banker who made extensive researches, gives the following figures for drawings of bills:

1815	1824	1835	1839
£650 mn.	£405 mn.	£405 mn.	£528 mn.

Such a growth must have less than kept pace with the growth of banking assets, and bills must have formed a smaller proportion in 1839 than in former years.

Advances to customers other than by discounts came later, but as the cheque superseded the bill, they increased rapidly in importance. In agricultural districts advances were made to farmers on the security of stock; Stuckey issued almost all his notes in advances to farmers, and Wilkin's bank made advances to Welsh drovers on promissory notes at 5%. Advances in commercial districts soon followed, and Beckett told the Committee of 1832 that he often made advances on personal security at 4%. A conventional rate for advances was being established at about the time that the conventional rate for discounts was being undermined, and Hobhouse speaks of "a practically uniform rate" on advances of 5%.

Bankers in agricultural districts found that they habitually had surplus deposits which they could not employ, while those in industrial districts were faced with greater demands for discounts than they could meet. So it came about that these banks habitually sent bills for discount in country districts, either directly or through the agency of the London discount market. There was also much abuse of re-discounting by banks which were working on an altogether too small cash basis, but the complaints against the habit tended to confuse its harmful with its innocent and useful form.

During the war there was a practically conventional 5 % discount rate both in London and the country, but in the years immediately after the peace London brokers began to cut rates. The conventional 5 % lingered for some time in the country, and longest of all in those districts in which deposits and demands were about equal and there was, therefore, no need for re-discounting. It was only during the 1830's that the establishment of the branch banks, and the extension of the scope of the discount market, resulted in the establishment of approximately uniform rates, at any one time, throughout the country.

THE JOINT-STOCK BANKS

The beginning of joint-stock banking is associated with the name of Thomas Joplin, who, before 1826, urged the advantages of the system, and suggested that the existing law did not preclude the establishment of banks having more than six partners, provided that they did not issue notes. The act of 1826 permitted the formation of note-issuing joint-stock banks, outside a radius of sixty-five miles from London, and the act of 1833 contained a declaratory clause making clear that non-issuing banks were legal even within that radius. By 1833 there were 32 English joint-stock banks, at the end of 1836 there were 79 issuing and 20 non-issuing banks, and by 1841 the total had grown to 115.[1]

The state of the law, both in what it said and what it left unsaid, was still chaotic. Notes might not be made payable in London, and bills payable in London might not be drawn for less than £50, though Stuckey's continued to pay its notes in London with impunity after it adopted the joint-stock form. A case brought by the Bank against the London and West-

1 Clapham, *op. cit.* pp. 511–12.

minster established that a London joint-stock bank might not accept a bill for less than £50, a dog in the manger act, as the Bank did not accept such bills itself. Neither could a joint-stock bank accept a bill of less than six months' date. The Committee of 1837 found that the common law forbade one partner to sue another while the concern had any outstanding debts, which made the sums owing by the directors of the Northern and Central Bank quite irrecoverable at law. This was duly altered, but the following year a further act was found necessary to remove a provision in common law which prevented a firm recovering any debts due to it because one of its shareholders was a clergyman.

Liability was unlimited, and the companies had no corporate status; at law they were simply a partnership, and actions had to be brought in the name of every single member, though these might number hundreds. The London and Westminster sought an act to enable it to sue and be sued in the name of its officers, but the bill was rejected in the Lords, after the Lord Chancellor had given his opinion that it would constitute an infringement of the government's agreement with the Bank. Gilbart, therefore, got round the law by making all his contracts through trustees.[1]

The Committees of 1836 and 1837 pointed out a number of other gaps in the law, some of which we should now regard as matters to be regulated by the force of public opinion, rather than by legislation. Among them were the lack of any control over the amount of capital, or the denomination of shares, the size of reserve funds, or the relationship between dividends and genuine profits.

The joint-stock banks had to face opposition both from the Bank of England and the private bankers, and Gilbart was refused a discount account by the former, and denied admission to the clearing house by the latter.

A few of the joint-stock banks, and notably the Northern and Central, justified all the evil which was spoken of them. The Northern and Central had its headquarters at Manchester, and

1 Clapham, *op. cit.* p. 510.

branches scattered over the North country. The chairman, Henry Moult, confessed that neither he nor his colleagues on the board had any previous knowledge of banking. When he was asked, with respect to the reckless advances of the bank:

Did you attempt to apply any principle by which the amount of your business should bear a certain proportion to the amount of your capital and deposits?

he feebly answered:

At the board we did so, but we could not carry it out at all...we could not bring some of our managers to bear on these points.

The directors were not only feeble and ignorant, but actively dishonest. The London and Westminster allotted the bank some of its shares, in order to secure its London agency, and the directors distributed these shares among themselves at par, though they commanded a substantial premium in the market. They allotted shares to themselves at less than their market price, and then accepted these shares as security for the very advances by which they were paid for. Directors were allowed huge overdrafts on very slender security. One Agnew, a picture dealer, whom the chairman said he would trust with £500, owed £23,903, while Mr Hardy, "who was very much involved in shares", was overdrawn by no less than £70,000. These transactions were entered in a private ledger, and when the Bank of England was asked for assistance this ledger was concealed from it. And yet Moult has the brazen impudence to lay the blame for his failure on the Bank:

When I came to London, I found the true cause of our distress; it was that the Bank of England had set its face entirely against discount of any of our paper, or the paper of any joint-stock bank of issue, in consequence of which we could not get any discount. They would not do anything for joint-stock banks of issue.[1]

But such mismanagement was quite exceptional. Some other banks committed errors of judgement, but in the main they were staffed by men of previous experience in private banking,

1 Select Committee on Joint Stock Banks, 1837, Moult's evidence.

men of undoubted honesty and high ability, and apart from the
Northern and Central there were no other big failures until
1847.

The joint-stock banks were, of course, in just the same line
of business as the private banks, and what we have said of the
one will go for the other too. Two important criticisms were
made of them in the early days. They were accused of unduly
expanding their issues in 1836, and so of promoting the speculation of that year, and they were accused of excessive re-discounting. For the first, they replied that, if allowance were
made for the private issues which they absorbed, the net increase was small. Figures bear them out in this, and there can
be no doubt that the main responsibility for the expansion of
credit in 1836 must rest not with the joint-stock banks, but with
the Bank of England. The second accusation contains an element of truth, but one reason for the joint-stock banks discounting more, on an average, than the private ones, was that
they were almost all situated in industrial districts, where, as
we have seen, re-discounting was necessary. In any case, the
practice was by no means universal.

The greatest change which the joint-stock banks were to
bring about was the development of branch banking. This met
with much opposition, and the Committees of 1836 and 1837
favoured some restriction on the number of branches, and their
distance from the parent bank. Some joint-stock banks were
unitary establishments, and some had only a few branches;
Stuckey, for instance, confined his branches to Somerset, as he
had done when the bank was a private firm, and used the joint-
stock form merely so that he could have a partner in charge of
each branch. The lead in the bold extension of branch banking
was, however, given by the National Provincial, which already,
by 1836, had branches scattered over Wales, the South-West,
the Midlands, and East Anglia.

THE LONDON DISCOUNT MARKET

We have still to speak of the institution which, until the amalgamation movement of the 1890's, formed an essential link between London and country banks, and between country banks in various districts. The bill market, in its nineteenth-century form, arose out of the rapid extension of country banking, and the inequality between districts, whereby some banks had a permanent surplus of funds available for discount, and others a permanent deficiency. Those banks with a surplus employed their London agent, himself a banker, to procure them bills for discount. At first the agent charged a commission to the lender, but by the end of the eighteenth century this had been generally abandoned. But the firm of Smith and Holt, London agents for Gurneys, insisted on retaining their commission, and their conservatism eventually cost them their connection, and led to the formation of the first specialist bill-broking firm.

In 1802 Thomas Richardson, a clerk of Smith and Holt, left that firm, and began sending bills to Gurneys on his own account, and without charging a commission. Thus began the firm which, as Richardson, Overend & Co., and later Overend, Gurney & Co., was to be the dominant influence on the discount market until 1866.

The new business developed rapidly, and other firms of less importance began to take their share. The decision of the London banks not to pay interest on deposits led the country banks to seek a fuller employment of their funds through the discount market. The arrival of the joint-stock banks, with their practice of extensive re-discounting, brought a further expansion of business, as their endorsement rendered negotiable a great mass of bills drawn on small tradesmen, which would not otherwise have been discountable in the London market.

These two changes also had another effect, the creation of a supply of "call money" which could be borrowed from day to day at very low rates of interest. The bill brokers negotiated these loans independently of their other business, and, from running the two side by side, it was but a short step to combining them, by themselves financing bill dealings out of their capital resources supplemented by call loans. When this was first done, we do not know. There is an account of Richardson, Overend & Co. which suggests that they may have been carrying their own bill portfolio as early as 1814, but, if so, it must have been on a very small scale. An essential preliminary to any large-scale dealings was the existence of re-discount facilities, which were not available until the Bank gave discount accounts to the brokers in 1830.[1]

The effect of all these changes was, of course, to increase the velocity of circulation of money, and in this connection the following figures, quoted by Liverpool, are of interest:

AVERAGE PERIOD OF CIRCULATION OF
BANK OF ENGLAND NOTES

Denomination	In 1792	In 1818
£1000	22 days	13 days
£300–500	24 „	14 „
£100	84 „	49 „
£10	236 „	157 „

So much for the institutional framework within which the Bank of England was operating in the early nineteenth century. We can now pass to our main theme, the detailed study of its working.

1 This section is based chiefly on W. T. C. King, *The History of the London Discount Market.*

Chapter Two

THE BANK RESTRICTION PERIOD
1797–1821

CAUSES OF THE RESTRICTION

War with France, which was declared in January 1793, produced a severe commercial crisis, in which the government intervened with advances of Exchequer bills to traders in distress. But events soon resumed a fairly normal course, and it was not until 1795 that serious banking difficulties began. These difficulties fall into two phases, a foreign drain of gold and then, after this had been stemmed, a run on the banks at home.

The demands for bills on foreign centres created by our military and naval activities were accentuated by a guaranteed loan of £4 mn. to Austria. A further demand for gold was created by the collapse of the French assignats, and the return of France to a completely metallic standard. The exchanges began to fall in March 1795, were below gold export point in May, and so continued until December 1796, by which time the reserve of the Bank had been greatly depleted.

The government continued to raise large sums by loan, and to demand advances from the Bank in spite of the protests of the directors. In December 1795 the directors decided to ration private discounts, a policy for which they were severely censured. Meanwhile, with trade recovering, and prices rising, there was a general demand for money, and that which the Bank of England would not provide was supplied by the country banks, often with very inadequate reserves. The final cause of the suspension of cash payments was the landing of a small French force at Fishguard; this caused a panic run on the country banks, who, in turn, presented their Bank of England notes for payment.

By an order in council of 27 February 1797 the Bank was forbidden to make any payments in specie except for the armed forces abroad, and except that it might repay half of any sum of over £500 subsequently deposited in gold with it. The suspension was confirmed by Parliament on 3 May, and the act was successively renewed, so that it did not finally expire until 1821. Three days previously another act had authorised the issue of notes of less value than £5.

The suspension act applied only to the Bank of England, but in fact the country banks had no option but to refuse to pay in gold and tender Bank of England notes instead, and these were generally accepted without question. Writing in 1803 Sir William Forbes notes only one attempt to enforce payment in coin. This was a case brought against the firm of Oakes & Son of Bury St Edmunds, "by a Mr Grigby, whose conduct was severely reprobated by Mr Baron Hotham, who tried, and apparently managed to shelve the case".[1] Following Lord King's famous circular to his tenants, demanding payment of their rents in gold, or in such an amount of notes as would buy the amount of gold due in the market, an act of 1811 made it illegal to take a higher price in notes than in gold. Bank of England notes thus became in fact, though not in law, legal tender.

BANK OF ENGLAND POLICY

Before 1797 the directors were beginning, however uncertainly, to appreciate the importance of the international balance of payments, and to regulate their note issue with reference to the state of the exchanges, and to their bullion reserve. This implied that discounts must be limited to the difference between notes issued in other ways, and the maximum which was thought desirable by reference to outside circumstances. In other words, the Bank must have a conscious discount policy.

J. Raikes, then Deputy-Governor, told the Committee of 1797 that "the real supply of cash can only be obtained by the

1 Quoted by Prof. Cannan, *The Paper Pound*, p. xvii.

effect of the general balance of trade in our favour".[1] His rather crude ideas of how a reduction of the Bank's circulation would operate appear in a subsequent answer, when he says that, had it not been for its advances to the government, it might have avoided suspension by the reduction of its notes, and that reducing the notes "below what the convenience of commerce required", "might probably have obliged merchants to bring their property from abroad and, amongst other property, gold and silver".

S. Bosanquet, a director and member of the Committee of Treasury, further explains the connection between the balance of payments and the Bank's reserve.

The Governor, D. Giles, gives his opinion on discount policy as follows:

Do not the Bank directors regulate their issues upon discounts by an attention to the proportion of cash in their coffers, and the amount of their outstanding notes? They ought to do so; and generally do regulate their conduct in consequence.

Would any circumstances which should occasion a diminution in the amount of their cash, and an increase in their outstanding notes, therefore, generally speaking, induce them to issue less in the way of discounts? Certainly.

But we must add that Giles later says: "We should never be hurt by discounts if we had no other advances to Government", and that, in December 1795, he thought it sufficient that discounts should be prevented from rising above what they had been in June, though the reserve had been reduced by half.

Whatever its responsibilities when compelled to pay its notes in gold, Giles thought that the Bank was released from them by the suspension. He justifies the increase in discounts which took place, on the plea that it was necessary to prevent commercial distress, and adds:

It is also obvious that, as the Bank did not pay in money, no inconvenience could arise from the issue of notes for that purpose.

1 This and the following quotations are taken from the Report of the Committee of Secrecy on the outstanding demands on the Bank, House of Commons 1797, reprinted in *Parliamentary Papers*, 1826, vol. III.

This marks the beginning of the change, which we see in its full consummation in the evidence of Whitmore and Pearse before the Bullion Committee.[1] No attention is paid either to the state of the exchanges or the market price of gold, and Whitmore declares that:

It is my own opinion, I do not know whether it is that of the Bank, that the amount of our paper circulation has no relevance at all to the state of the exchanges.

On the other hand, it was claimed that discounts were regulated with reference to the total amount of the note issue:

I should wish it to be understood that they (the directors) do now set limits to their advances, according to circumstances, as their discretion may direct them.

And again:

The attention of the Court being constantly drawn to the amount of our notes in circulation, certainly does operate upon us, either to the reduction or the increase.

But when we go on to ask to what the total amount of the note issue is related, we find that it is to nothing else than the demand for discounts. Whitmore says:

I have always stated that we never forced a note into circulation, and the criterion by which I judge of the exact proportion to be maintained is by avoiding as much as possible to discount what does not appear to be legitimate commercial paper. The banknotes would revert to us if there were a redundancy in circulation, as nobody would pay interest for a banknote that he did not want to make use of.

Pearse agreed with this, and added:

In discounting bills which are sent to us for that purpose, for which discount is taken at the rate of five per cent per annum, if

1 Report of Select Committee on the High Price of Gold Bullion, *Parliamentary Papers*, 1810, vol. III.

there was with the public an excess of banknotes, those bills would be fought for for discount by the public at a reduced rate, and would not make their appearance at the Bank.

Both agreed that the security against over-issue would be un-impaired if the rate of interest were reduced to 4, or even 3 %, and Whitmore concludes this part of the enquiry as follows:

In my view of the subject, nobody would pay three per cent interest even, or indeed any interest of money, unless it were for the purpose of employing it for speculation, and provided that the con-duct of the Bank is regulated as it now is, no accommodation would be given to a person of that description.

In other words, however low the rate of interest may be driven, and however large the Bank's issues may become it cannot produce an over-expansion of credit so long as it does not discount accommodation paper.

This is the "legitimate demands of commerce" theory, by which the policy of the Bank was regulated throughout the Restriction Period.

THE BALANCE OF PAYMENTS AND THE FOREIGN EXCHANGES

The evidence on which to base a complete study of the balance of payments is quite inadequate, and the lack of exact figures is made the more confusing because of the dislocation to trade caused by the Continental System and the American boycott.

The figures for imports and re-exports are given only in official values fixed in 1696. The correction for government payments abroad is not difficult, but the even more important one for shipping earnings, and interest payments, is practically impossible.

In evidence before the Bullion Committee, Inspector-General Irving estimates the balance of payments, but he admits that he places little reliance on the figures. He calculates real values on the basis of prices supplied to him by merchants, and deducts from the imports the value of imported fish, which is the produce of British labour and capital, and the excess of imports from India and the colonies, which he assumes to represent interest payments. He thus obtains the following figures (in £ millions):

Year	1805	1806	1807	1808	1809
Imports ...	53·6	50·6	53·5	45·7	59·9
Deduction ...	9·1	8·0	8·9	8·2	8·7
	44·5	42·6	44·6	37·5	51·2
Exports ...	51·1	53·0	50·5	50·0	66·0
Active balance	6·6	10·4	5·9	12·5	14·8[1]

I have made a further calculation based on the parliamentary returns, itemised by commodities after 1805, the official values as quoted by Irving[2] and the quotations transcribed from price currents by Prof. Silberling.[3] Selecting the commodities common to the three, I obtained a list of nineteen imports, forming a proportion of the total, by official value, varying from 37 to 53%, and ten re-exports, forming from 22 to 37% of the total. I have converted these into current values by dividing by the official price, and multiplying by the average yearly price derived from Prof. Silberling's figures. From the totals thus obtained, and assuming the ratio of real to official values to be the same for the whole as for the sample, I have estimated total imports and re-exports by the formula

$$\text{Total real value} = \frac{\text{Total official value} \times \text{Real value of sample}}{\text{Official value of sample}}.$$

To form an estimate of the balance of payments I have added the declared value of exports on the credit side, and Prof. Silberling's account of government payments abroad on the debit side. The latter is rather an under-estimate, as it is based on payments by the war office only, and does not take account of the navy or ordnance. The estimate takes no account of shipping earnings or interest payments, on both of which we probably had a favourable balance, and in taking the same prices

1 Bullion Report, Appendix.
2 *Parliamentary Papers*, 1826, vol. XXII, p. 47.
3 "British Prices of Thirty-five articles": MS. in the library of the London School of Economics.

for imports and re-exports it ignores the profits of merchants in the re-export trade. It is thus exaggeratedly unfavourable, but it may serve for a rough measure of changes from year to year (Tables I, II and III).

At first sight, the results are startling. They show an adverse balance for every year save 1803, 1812 and 1821, and a very large one for 1810, 1814 and 1818. If, however, we deduct the average amount of Irving's correction from the imports, and add 10% to the exports for merchants' profits, we get a positive balance for 1805–8, 1812, 1816 and 1820–1, and this leaves shipping receipts still unaccounted for. It is rather disturbing that there should be so great a divergence from Irving's estimate for 1810. The surprisingly unfavourable balance of the post-war years is due partly to the fact that our estimate may have been distorted by the great increase in the import of cotton.

Table I

ESTIMATED IMPORTS, 1805–21

Col. A. Proportion of sample to total imports by official value.
 „ B. Official value of sample.
 „ C. Current value of sample.
 „ D. Official value of total imports.
 „ E. Estimated current value of total imports.

Col. A in %, others in £ millions

Year	A	B	C	D	E
1805	39	11·8	23·6	30·1	60·0
1806	41	11·7	22·1	28·8	54·5
1807	44	12·6	24·9	28·8	56·7
1808	37	10·9	24·0	29·6	65·2
1809	42	14·0	30·7	33·8	73·8
1810	44	18·2	40·2	41·1	91·0
1811	46	13·1	25·6	28·6	54·8
1812	49	11·2	21·6	23·0	44·2
1813	—	—	—	—	—
1814	39	13·6	40·5	36·6	108·4
1815	37	13·2	33·3	36·0	90·5
1816	42	12·7	28·7	30·1	68·3
1817	41	14·0	31·4	34·0	76·0
1818	42	17·1	39·4	40·1	92·5
1819	45	15·2	32·9	33·7	72·6
1820	51	16·1	25·5	31·5	49·7
1821	53	15·8	23·0	29·7	43·3

Table II

ESTIMATED RE-EXPORTS, 1805–21

Col. A. Proportion of sample to total re-exports by official value.
" B. Official value of sample.
" C. Current value of sample.
" D. Official value of total re-exports.
" E. Estimated current value of total re-exports.

Col. A in %, others in £ millions

Year	A	B	C	D	E
1805	22	2·2	3·1	10·0	14·1
1806	22	2·0	3·4	9·1	15·6
1807	28	2·7	3·2	9·4	11·3
1808	26	2·5	2·7	9·7	10·2
1809	25	3·7	4·4	15·2	17·9
1810	29	3·5	5·4	10·9	17·1
1811	34	2·8	3·2	8·3	9·4
1812	29	3·3	4·9	12·0	17·7
1813	—	—	—	—	—
1814	28	5·7	11·9	20·5	39·2
1815	31	5·2	8·5	16·9	27·7
1816	32	4·6	6·5	14·6	20·6
1817	33	3·8	6·0	11·5	18·1
1818	35	3·8	6·9	10·8	19·7
1819	36	3·6	6·4	9·9	17·8
1820	36	3·8	4·7	10·5	12·9
1821	37	4·0	4·8	10·7	12·9

Also, all the items of which the estimate does not take account would be increased by the coming of peace.

As an example of exchange rates I have taken that with Hamburg, as quoted by Tooke and Newmarch (Table IV). The only point to notice is that, since England was in law on a gold standard, and Europe on a silver one, the par of exchange depends on the market price of the one metal in terms of the other. In the eighteenth century, the ratio of gold to silver was 14·8 : 1, but during our period it rose to 15·5 : 1, as fixed by law in France, so parity rose to 36 schillings to £1.

In 1805, when our estimate shows a fairly large deficit, the exchange was low. The positive balance of 1806 was attended by a recovery, which was continued in 1807 when, after allowing for corrections, the balance was probably not large in either direction, and in 1808, in spite of a renewed adverse balance.

Table III

ESTIMATED BALANCE OF PAYMENTS, 1805–21

Col. A. Declared value of exports of British produce and manufactures.
 „ B. Estimated value of re-exports.
 „ C. Estimated value of imports.
 „ D. Professor Silberling's estimate of extraordinary government payments abroad.
 „ E. Estimated balance of payments.

£ millions

Year	A	B	C	D	E
1805	41·1	14·1	60·0	4·5	−9·3
1806	43·2	15·6	54·5	1·8	2·5
1807	40·9	11·3	56·7	2·6	−7·1
1808	40·5	10·2	65·2	6·6	−21·1
1809	50·2	17·9	73·8	9·1	−14·8
1810	50·0	17·1	91·0	14·1	−38·0
1811	34·9	9·4	54·8	13·8	−24·3
1812	43·7	17·7	44·2	14·8	2·2
1813	—	—	—	—	—
1814	47·9	39·2	108·4	23·1	−44·4
1815	53·2	27·7	90·5	11·9	−21·5
1816	42·9	20·6	68·3	2·9	− 7·7
1817	41·8	18·1	76·0	4·4	−20·5
1818	46·6	19·7	92·5	8·9	−35·1
1819	35·2	17·8	72·6	2·2	−21·8
1820	36·4	12·9	49·7	0·7	− 1·1
1821	36·7	12·9	43·3	—	6·3

The adverse balance of 1809–10 is followed by a great fall in the exchange, culminating in 1811, when the balance is already on the mend; in 1812 the effect of exchange depreciation is seen in a positive balance, and this leads to a recovery in the exchange. The records for 1813 were destroyed in the famous customs house fire. Most of the adverse balance of 1814 came at the beginning of the year, and the exchange was then very low; it later recovered, but it was not until 1816, when the balance had probably become positive again, that it rose to par. The adverse balance of 1818–19 was followed by a further decline, and it was only after the positive balance of 1820–1 that parity was again reached. Always, an adverse balance is followed by a fall in the exchange; this fall of itself tends to correct the adverse balance, and so the exchange recovers again.

Table IV

THE EXCHANGE WITH HAMBURG, 1797–1821

Flemish schillings to £1: old par, 34/3½, new par, 36.

Date	Rate	Date	Rate
24/2/97	36/0	28/2/09	31/0
25/8/97	37/7	22/8/09	29/4
23/2/98	28/0	27/2/10	29/0
24/8/98	37/3	28/8/10	30/9
22/2/99	37/7	26/2/11	25/0
23/8/99	34/0	30/8/11	25/6
28/2/00	31/4	28/2/12	28/0
22/8/00	32/2	28/8/12	28/9
27/2/01	31/7	26/2/13	30/0
25/8/01	31/6	27/8/13	26/6
26/2/02	32/2	22/2/14	29/0
27/8/02	33/2	23/8/14	32/0
25/2/03	34/4	28/2/15	32/2
26/8/03	32/10	25/8/15	32/6
24/2/04	34/8	27/2/16	34/8
31/8/04	35/10	27/8/16	36/9
19/10/04	35/8	28/2/17	36/7
26/2/05	35/8	22/8/17	35/0
27/8/05	35/5	27/2/18	34/0
26/11/05	32/9	25/8/18	34/6
25/2/06	34/2	19/2/19	33/11
26/8/06	34/5	3/8/19	35/11
27/2/07	34/10	3/3/20	36/4
28/8/07	34/2	1/8/20	37/6
26/2/08	34/6	27/2/21	38/2
26/8/08	35/2	28/8/21	38/2

It will be noted that all the years of adverse balance were years of exceptional foreign payments; if these be subtracted, as well as the other items we have mentioned, we have a positive balance for the whole period, except 1814 and 1817–19.

GOVERNMENT EXPENDITURE, AND ITS EFFECT ON ACTIVITY

Accounts of national income and expenditure are contained in Table V. Column A shows total national expenditure. Columns B and C show interest and capital charges respectively. The latter represent chiefly funding operations. The former are transfer payments, and they will have an inflationary or de-

Table V

NATIONAL INCOME AND EXPENDITURE, 1790–1816

Col. A. Total national expenditure.
  „   B. Interest charges.
  „   C. Capital charges.
  „   D. Government payments abroad.
  „   E. Net "active expenditure".
  „   F. Income from taxes.
  „   G. Income from borrowing.
  „   H. Difference between total borrowing and transfer payments, col. G
        −cols. B and C.

£ millions

Year	A	B	C	D	E	F	G	H
1790	26·2	9·4	9·4	—	7·4	17·0	8·9	− 9·9
1791	28·6	9·4	10·6	—	8·6	18·5	10·5	− 9·5
1792	27·6	9·3	10·6	—	7·7	18·9	8·5	−11·4
1793	30·6	9·2	8·8	0·6	12·0	18·5	12·4	− 5·6
1794	42·7	9·8	15·9	2·3	14·7	19·3	23·0	− 2·7
1795	51·4	10·5	12·7	4·4	23·8	19·1	32·5	9·3
1796	52·5	11·6	14·3	1·0	25·6	19·4	35·6	9·7
1797	71·6	13·6	24·6	0·2	33·2	21·5	53·1	14·9
1798	64·2	16·0	14·9	0·2	33·1	27·2	37·0	6·1
1799	79·1	16·9	29·6	1·3	31·3	32·5	43·6	− 2·9
1800	98·6	20·7	31·2	1·1	45·6	42·6	56·2	4·4
1801	91·1	19·1	32·7	1·7	37·6	35·9	59·7	7·9
1802	76·7	19·6	28·3	0·6	28·2	38·5	42·5	− 5·4
1803	69·7	19·9	22·4	0·2	27·2	40·4	30·9	−11·4
1804	76·5	19·8	19·1	0·1	37·5	48·1	32·9	− 6·0
1805	102·5	21·5	35·2	0·8	45·0	53·2	53·0	− 3·7
1806	106·2	22·4	39·6	0·7	43·5	58·0	51·0	−11·0
1807	106·3	23·0	39·4	1·7	42·2	62·3	50·0	−12·4
1808	120·1	22·3	49·0	3·9	44·9	65·2	59·3	−12·0
1809	121·7	23·4	47·1	5·6	45·6	66·5	58·7	−11·8
1810	128·5	23·7	50·3	6·8	47·7	72·3	59·3	−14·7
1811	131·5	23·9	49·3	11·6	46·7	70·4	65·0	− 8·2
1812	147·9	25·6	56·2	13·0	53·1	70·2	80·7	− 1·1
1813	174·1	26·4	67·9	17·9	61·9	76·7	105·3	11·9
1814	163·7	29·1	56·4	15·5	62·7	78·0	88·9	3·4
1815	173·4	31·4	73·9	7·0	61·1	82·8	95·5	− 9·8
1816	122·3	32·2	57·5	1·3	31·3	69·9	55·8	−33·9

Note. In 1800 the end of the financial year was changed from 10 October to
5 January. The financial year 1800 thus contains 15 months. Column F is net
before 1800, gross afterwards.

flationary effect according as the proportion spent on consumption exceeds or falls short of the proportion financed by taxation. Column D is government payments abroad, which will
produce no direct effect on activity. Columns F and G show

receipts from taxation and borrowing respectively, and column H the difference between total borrowing and transfer payments, i.e. column B plus column C.

If receipts from taxation balance the part of expenditure which produces a direct effect on activity—"active expenditure" we shall call it—an increase in total expenditure will have an inflationary effect only in so far as taxation is met by a diminution of saving. If, as is generally assumed, taxation is met out of consumption, such an increase will merely involve the transfer of resources from one occupation to another, and the only effect on prices would be through frictions in the transfer. An excess of "active expenditure" over taxation represents a net increase in demand, and an excess of taxation over "active expenditure" a net decrease, unless the excess taxes are offset by the parts of interest payment which are spent on consumption. Thus, so long as borrowing balances only interest and capital charges, and payments abroad, it will have no directly inflationary effect.

In the first five years of the war taxation failed to keep pace with active expenditure; in 1792 taxes had produced 18·9 mn., while active expenditure had been only £7·7 mn., but by 1795 the latter had risen to 23·8 mn. and the former to only £19·1 mn., a deficiency which continued to 1799. In that year there was a very slight excess of taxes over "active expenditure", but in 1800 and 1801 there was again a deficiency. From 1793 to 1801, therefore, government financial policy was, without doubt, inflationary. From 1801 to 1811, however, we have an excess of taxation over "active expenditure" greater than the normal pre-war excess. Interest payments and foreign remittances have greatly increased, but even after allowing for the effects of these, there can hardly have been an inflationary tendency. Thirdly, there was a renewed inflationary period in 1812–14, which was markedly reversed in the post-war years.

The increases in prices from 1793 to 1801 and from 1812 to 1814 can, therefore, be largely attributed to the effects of war finance, but no such explanation will suffice for the movements of 1801–11.

CURRENCY, WAGES AND PRICES, 1797–1801

We have seen that government financial policy was causing a rise in prices in this period. At the same time an adverse balance of payments, only in part a consequence of this rise, was causing a depreciation of sterling, and this in itself made our imports dearer, and so produced a secondary rise in the domestic price level. We have also seen that the Bank repudiated any responsibility in the matter and, rightly or wrongly, adopted a policy which gave free play to these forces. We have now to trace the results of this policy.

For general prices I take the index number compiled by Prof. Silberling.[1] For the price of wheat, which varied much more than general prices and was of paramount importance, I have compiled an index from the *Gazette* averages quoted by Tooke. Tooke gives these figures only from 1793, so the index is based on that year, whereas that of Prof. Silberling is based on the year 1790 (Table VI).

I give quarterly averages of Bank of England notes and also what Silberling calls "total advances", i.e. commercial discounts and the holding of Treasury bills combined.[2] For the country banks, I give figures of notes stamped, but, for reasons which we explained in the last chapter, very little reliance can be placed on these. There remains the gold coinage, estimated at from £20 to £40 mn. Most of this disappeared in the course of the war, but it is impossible to say when, as one cannot know the premium necessary to induce people to break the law against melting. We shall, therefore, confine our discussion to Bank of England notes and advances, bearing in mind that the country notes and gold coinage are very uncertain quantities.

By the first quarter of 1797 the general index had already risen to 143, while the wheat index stood at 111. The general

---

1 Prof. N. J. Silberling, "British Prices and Business Cycles", *Review of Economic Statistics*, Oct. 1923.
2 Silberling, "Financial and Monetary Policy of Great Britain during the Napoleonic Wars", *Quarterly Journal of Economics*, vol. XXXVI.

Table VI

A. PROFESSOR SILBERLING'S INDEX OF GENERAL PRICES, AVERAGE OF 1790: 100

B. *GAZETTE* AVERAGE PRICE OF WHEAT, 1ST QUARTER OF 1793: 100

	A				B			
Year	1	2	3	4	1	2	3	4
1790	97	99	102	101	—	—	—	—
1791	99	99	97	101	—	—	—	—
1792	103	101	101	102	—	—	—	—
1793	109	112	108	108	100	108	107	102
1794	109	106	105	108	108	109	111	112
1795	115	125	129	135	124	140	193	175
1796	135	134	135	138	202	172	156	126
1797	143	142	136	144	111	106	115	120
1798	148	148	149	152	107	110	108	103
1799	152	157	158	155	106	126	153	189
1800	154	156	161	164	216	249	240	255
1801	173	172	164	155	312	291	246	159
1802	147	144	141	141	159	143	144	127
1803	149	156	159	158	120	125	120	115
1804	156	151	149	156	108	110	126	165
1805	169	161	158	158	191	191	197	167
1806	159	160	155	153	159	174	174	165
1807	155	153	150	149	163	161	156	144
1808	156	164	169	175	147	159	175	191
1809	183	173	169	178	201	194	201	220
1810	184	182	173	166	216	236	241	212
1811	166	159	152	157	201	187	193	221
1812	161	160	162	168	229	278	307	252
1813	178	180	183	198	256	252	233	181
1814	211	203	190	189	165	152	156	155
1815	170	169	165	157	158	149	142	120
1816	142	134	130	135	115	149	172	208
1817	142	140	141	149	218	228	190	171
1818	153	150	148	150	180	184	177	174
1819	146	138	132	130	169	154	157	142
1820	128	126	123	120	140	148	149	121
1821	120	118	116	116	114	111	120	116

index fell to 136 in the third quarter, but then rose steadily to 156 in the second quarter of 1800; the pace then quickened, and a peak of 173 was reached in the first quarter of 1801. One of the main reasons for this quickening of the pace was the very bad harvests of 1799 and 1800, which caused a rise in the wheat index from 106 in the first quarter of 1799 to no less than 312

Table VII

A. QUARTERLY AVERAGE OF BANK OF ENGLAND NOTES OUTSTANDING

B. QUARTERLY AVERAGE OF THE BANK'S "TOTAL ADVANCES"

£ millions

Year	A				B			
	1	2	3	4	1	2	3	4
1790	10·2	11·2	11·3	11·5	—	—	—	—
1791	11·6	12·1	11·8	11·2	—	—	—	—
1792	11·3	11·8	11·4	11·2	—	—	—	—
1793	12·0	12·2	11·0	11·1	—	—	—	—
1794	11·4	10·5	10·4	11·0	11·5	11·3	9·4	9·8
1795	12·4	10·9	11·0	11·6	12·0	14·3	12·7	13·0
1796	10·8	10·8	9·7	9·6	14·4	13·7	11·6	12·7
1797	9·8	11·7	11·0	11·4	12·6	13·6	12·3	11·1
1798	12·9	13·0	12·2	12·2	13·3	14·2	13·2	13·5
1799	13·0	13·8	13·4	13·8	14·4	15·3	15·4	16·3
1800	15·0	15·0	15·1	15·5	18·8	19·4	18·7	19·0
1801	16·4	15·8	15·3	15·7	22·1	21·6	19·4	19·4
1802	15·6	16·8	17·0	17·4	21·0	22·8	20·8	17·3
1803	15·7	16·2	16·8	17·3	19·5	23·1	24·6	23·5
1804	17·6	17·6	17·1	17·2	24·9	25·8	24·0	23·1
1805	17·6	16·9	16·5	16·5	26·2	26·1	23·3	22·5
1806	16·8	17·0	16·7	16·6	24·5	28·2	26·0	23·3
1807	16·6	16·8	17·0	16·4	25·3	27·7	27·5	26·0
1808	16·6	17·2	17·2	17·4	26·7	27·0	28·0	27·6
1809	17·8	18·5	19·6	19·9	29·2	30·8	31·1	30·1
1810	20·4	21·3	24·2	24·2	32·4	35·4	37·8	35·2
1811	23·3	23·6	23·3	22·9	32·6	34·2	35·0	33·8
1812	23·3	22·9	23·5	23·3	35·4	36·8	37·0	36·2
1813	23·9	23·9	24·0	24·2	37·3	39·2	38·4	39·1
1814	25·2	25·9	28·6	28·0	38·7	43·0	46·4	43·6
1815	27·3	27·0	27·2	26·1	42·0	45·6	43·7	38·6
1816	26·6	26·4	27·2	26·1	34·8	36·5	36·3	30·3
1817	27·1	27·5	29·5	28·9	28·4	28·2	27·7	25·7
1818	28·4	27·5	26·9	26·0	28·0	29·1	30·1	28·8
1819	25·8	25·4	25·5	23·9	29·0	28·1	28·5	25·1
1820	24·1	23·8	24·5	23·3	25·1	22·8	22·2	18·9
1821	24·2	22·9	20·7	18·5	19·9	18·2	18·9	14·8

in the first quarter of 1801. The scarcity made necessary abnormal imports from the Continent, and this contributed to the depreciation of the exchanges.

Prof. Bowley's index of agricultural wages[1] shows a rise

1 "Statistics of Wages in the U.K. during the past 100 years", *Journal of the Royal Statistical Society*, 1898–9.

Table VIII

QUARTERLY VALUE OF £1 AND £5 COUNTRY
BANK NOTES STAMPED, 1806–21

£ millions

Year	1	2	3	4
1806	—	13·6	10·7	11·9
1807	12·5	9·2	11·0	11·6
1808	13·3	12·3	14·9	25·0
1809	20·2	26·3	23·1	20·1
1810	17·8	13·9	13·1	10·8
1811	10·8	14·8	18·7	17·2
1812	16·2	17·6	15·3	25·6
1813	21·6	18·7	17·5	23·2
1814	16·4	17·7	14·5	15·0
1815	12·4	9·7	9·0	9·0
1816	10·7	11·2	8·9	13·1
1817	14·6	14·4	17·7	22·3
1818	20·4	16·5	20·2	18·6
1819	11·1	6·4	6·8	7·2
1820	5·8	6·1	7·6	7·4
1821	7·6	7·2	9·5	10·5

from 52 in 1790 to 58 in 1793, 74 in 1797, and 83 in 1801. It will
be noted that the rise in the early years was considerably more
than that of prices. The few figures available for industrial
earnings show a wide variation, but generally the rise was
neither so large nor so early as in agriculture.

The rise in prices was accompanied by a rise both in the note
circulation and in the advances of the Bank. Both reached a
peak in the first quarter of 1801, at the same time as the price
indices, but the detailed comparison can most easily be made
by reference to Chart I.

CURRENCY, WAGES AND PRICES, 1802–10

We have seen that, during this period, the inflationary financial
policy of the government was completely changed. Neither
were there the famine conditions which characterised 1800 and
1801. The harvests of 1801–3 were abundant, and the wheat
index fell as low as 108 in the first quarter of 1804. Thenceforward harvests were variable, and prices fluctuated con-

siderably, the index rising as high as 241 in the third quarter of 1810.

The general index fell to 141 at the end of 1802, but then jumped to 159 in the third quarter of 1803. For the next four years fluctuations were narrow, but there was then another sharp rise to 183 in the first quarter of 1809. This rise was accompanied by a fall in the exchanges to the lowest point they had yet reached, and by a corresponding rise in the market price of bullion.

Neither the rise of 1803 nor that of 1808–9 can be attributed to government borrowing; the former took place at a time of abundant harvest, and that factor was only of moderate importance in the latter. Nor is it convincing to argue that the exchanges were depreciated by payments abroad, and that the price rise was a secondary effect of this. The argument could not apply to 1803 at all. In 1808–9 foreign payments were increasing, and trade was hampered by the Continental System, but new markets were being developed in America. We must remember that Napoleon's boycott was only partially effective, and that the serious fall in the exchanges did not begin until two years after its inception. We are, therefore, forced to the conclusion that these movements could have been only normal cyclical fluctuations, aided by the liberal policy of the Bank, and the position of the Bank becomes, therefore, all the more interesting.

The index of agricultural wages rose a further twenty points to 103, and rises in industrial wages seem to have been larger, and more general than in the previous period.

There is no very close correlation between the price indices and either the issues or the advances of the Bank, but, as will be seen from the chart, there is a marked tendency for both to follow price movements. Thus the price peak of 1803 is followed by one in notes in the first quarter, and of advances in the second quarter of 1804. During the next five years advances increased largely, and notes remained more or less constant. In the renewed price rise of 1808–9, the tendency of notes and advances to follow prices is even more marked, the peak in both not being reached until the third quarter of 1810.

CURRENCY, WAGES AND PRICES, 1810–15

In the autumn the state of prices and the foreign exchanges was giving rise to general alarm, and in August Ricardo wrote his letters to the *Morning Chronicle*. Horner, expressing Ricardo's views in the House, secured the appointment of a Select Committee to enquire into the causes of the high price of bullion. The Committee produced its report, written by Horner, Huskisson and Thornton, in June 1810, but it was not published until August, and the House did not discuss it until the following May. Horner then introduced sixteen resolutions, one of which declared it to be the duty of the Bank directors to take account of the price of bullion and of the foreign exchanges so long as the suspension should last, and another stated that cash payments ought to be resumed after two years, whether the war was over by that time or not.

All these resolutions were defeated, and an opposite set, moved by Vansittart, was carried in their stead. One of these declared that

> The promissory notes of the Bank of England have hitherto been, and are at this time, held in the public estimation to be the equivalent to the legal coin of the realm, and generally accepted as such in all transactions to which such coin is legally applicable.[1]

Thus the House repudiated the findings of its Committee, and it was decided that the suspension should continue.

The bad harvest of 1808–9 was the beginning of a run of lean years, and the wheat index rose to 307 in the third quarter of 1812. It was not until after the good harvest of 1813 that prices again fell sharply. The increased intensity of the war led to a great increase in borrowing, and government finance again becomes an inflationary force. Further, foreign remittances greatly increased, amounting to over £10 mn. in each of the years 1811 to 1815, and to no less than £17·9 mn. in 1813. Such payments, combined with abnormal imports of grain, inevitably tended to a further depreciation of the pound.

1 Quoted, Cannan, *op. cit.* p. xxvi.

Prices maintained their high level until the autumn of 1810, when there was a crisis precipitated by the failure of large firms in the South American trade, and accompanied by considerable unemployment and distress. The general price index dropped thirty points to 152 in the third quarter of 1811, and it was not until two years later that the high level of the spring of 1810 was again passed. The highest point of all, 211, was reached in the first quarter of 1814, but there was again a rapid decline to 157 at the end of 1815.

The exchanges reached their lowest point in 1811, after the fall in prices had begun, and recovered in 1812 and the beginning of 1813, in spite of a renewed rise in prices. This strongly suggests that the dominant influence was the level of foreign payments, and not domestic prices.

Agricultural wages remained practically constant, the index having fallen only to 100 by the end of 1815. Industrial wages showed differences from one industry to another, but the general level seems to have been fairly stable.

Bank accommodation again shows a marked tendency to follow price movements. The increase in accommodation in the autumn of 1810 has its parallel in other crises, and represents the satisfaction of an increased liquidity preference rather than an addition to the active circulation. In 1812 both notes and advances were at a slightly lower level, but in 1813 both rose, though the movement was most marked in advances. The peak for both, however, was not reached until the third quarter of 1814, six months after prices had reached their highest point.

THE END OF THE RESTRICTION PERIOD, 1815–21

With the end of the war the impediments to our foreign trade were removed, the government no longer remitted large sums abroad, and expenditure was no longer financed by means of inflationary borrowing. The fall in prices continued until the index reached 130 in the third quarter of 1816, a drop of 81 points in two and a half years. The price fall was accompanied by a fall in the circulation and a rise in the gold stock of the Bank, a recovery of the exchanges and a fall in the mint price of gold. The reform of the currency and the return to cash payments thus became practical politics again.

The first point was dealt with by Liverpool's Currency Act of 1816. Gold was made the sole standard of value, and silver was to be legal tender only for sums up to two guineas. At the same time silver was revalued, the troy pound being coined into 66 shillings instead of 62. It was further provided that the government might fix by royal proclamation a time after which the mint should be open for the coinage of silver, 62 of the light shillings being given for the pound. This proclamation was never issued, and the mint continued to buy its silver in the market, and to keep the issues of silver small.

The ratio of the two metals in France had recently been raised from 14·8 to 15·5 to 1, and England, instead of raising the ratio proportionately, had lowered it. It was therefore argued that there must be a profit on the export of gold to France in return for silver, and the act was therefore blamed for the failure of the Bank's first attempt at resumption. Had the full intention of the act been carried out, such an effect would probably have resulted, but as it was, the future showed that the restriction of the amount of silver in circulation and the sum for which it was legal tender afforded a sufficient safeguard.

The restriction of cash payments should have come to an end six months after the end of the war, but it was prolonged successively by three acts until July 1818.

By August 1816 gold had fallen to £3. 19s. 0d. per oz., and it would have been even lower had the Bank not been buying at that price, for the exchanges were above par, and gold was being imported in large quantities. In November 1816, with gold at £3. 18s. 6d. per oz. and the Bank stock at £8 mn., the directors made an experiment in resumption by offering to pay in cash all £1 and £2 notes issued before 1812. In April 1817 the price of gold had risen to £3. 19s., but the Bank stock had increased to £10 mn., and the offer was extended to all £1 and £2 notes dated before 1816. There was very little demand for gold, as the exchanges were still above par and notes were preferred for domestic circulation. The treasure continued to grow and, in September 1817, though the price of gold had risen to £4. 0s., the Bank held £12 mn., and extended its offer to all notes issued before the beginning of 1817.

Meanwhile the note issue reached a new high level in the third quarter of 1817, of £29·5 mn. There was a general fall in interest rates and, as the Bank maintained a constant rate, its discounts declined, but this was offset by increased holdings of government securities. In the autumn of 1817 Vansittart borrowed £14 mn. from the Bank, which brought the Bank's total loans to the government to a level which had only once been exceeded during the war.[1]

Already the exchanges were beginning to fall and the price of bullion to rise. There was a revival of trade and a rise in domestic prices; the failure of the harvest of 1816 caused a great rise in corn prices and made necessary large imports; there was the usual speculative import of raw materials, and total retained imports rose from £11,306,000 in 1816 to £23,019,000 in 1819; large loans were negotiated in London for France, Russia and other powers, and the low rate of interest prevailing created an inducement to employ money abroad.

The result was that the exchanges fell, the market price of gold rose, and the notes which the public had formerly been so willing to hold were now presented for payment. The Bank's apparently ample reserve was reduced to little over 4 mn. by the spring of 1819. The circulation declined by some 4 mn., but this was not a conscious act of the Bank, but merely the result of the continued decline in commercial discounts, and the repayment of some £5 mn. of government advances. Harman tells the Committee of 1819 that "we did not make any reduction (of issues) with a view to checking the export of gold and silver".[2]

The resumption was postponed for a further year from July

1 Feavearyear, The Pound Sterling, p. 202.
2 House of Lords' Committee on the Resumption of Cash Payments, 1819, p. 217.

1818. In the spring of 1819 a further postponement was being considered, but the directors passed the resolution:

That it appears preferable to submit to the consequences of a parliamentary enquiry rather than pass a bill for a time inadequate to the circumstances in which the country might be placed.[1]

Accordingly both Houses appointed Committees, and on the strength of the preliminary report, resolutions were passed in April requiring the Bank to make no further payments in cash until Parliament had further considered the matter.

The Committees found almost universal agreement on the need for the resumption of cash payments, but great difference of opinion as to the difficulty of the operation and the time which should be allowed. The Bank directors took the view that resumption must depend on circumstances affecting the exchanges and that, as these could not be foreseen, resumption ought to be left to their discretion, without the fixing of any time limit. Samuel Gurney thought that resumption should be postponed for two or three years. Ricardo thought that only a small reduction in the note issue would be necessary to close the gap between the market and the mint price of gold: "I should think to the amount of about five or six per cent; I measure it by the difference between the market and the mint price of gold."[2] William Haldimand, a director, on the other hand thought it necessary that issues should be reduced "forcibly" by three or four million, and explained:

By the term "forcibly", I mean a reduction not arising from three or four millions less being demanded, but from three or four millions being demanded and refused by the Bank to the public or the government.[3]

There was general agreement that the advances of the Bank to the government should be repaid, not so much that the Bank might reduce its issues, but that it might hold them in more liquid form.

1 House of Commons Committee of 1819, Report.
2 *Ibid.* p. 137.
3 *Ibid.* p. 54.

The Bank made representations to both Houses suggesting that they should be allowed to pay in gold at the market price and stating:

It is incumbent upon them to consider the effect of any measure to be adopted, as operating upon the general issue of their notes, *by which all the private banks are regulated*, and of which the whole currency, exclusive of the notes of private bankers, is composed. They feel themselves obliged, by the new position in which they have been placed by the Restriction Act of 1797, to bear in mind not less their duties to the establishment over which they preside, than their duties to the community at large, whose interests in a pecuniary and commercial relation have in a great degree been confided to their discretion.[1]

This affords an interesting contrast with most of the other official utterances of the Bank, in which the principal concern has been to repudiate the powers and responsibilities which are here so frankly accepted.

The protest and suggestion of the directors were, however, ignored. By the bill which Peel introduced, complete suspension was to continue until 31 January 1820; from 1 February 1820 to 1 October the Bank was to pay in gold bullion at £4. 1s. per oz.; from 1 October to 1 May 1821 at £3. 19s. 6d., and from then until 1 May 1823 at £3. 17s. 10½d., the former mint price. On the latter date payment in sovereigns was to take the place of payment in bullion. Ricardo submitted a plan by which the Bank should always pay in bullion, so that gold would not circulate, but would be available as a safeguard against a fall in the exchanges. Questions put to other witnesses showed a general approval of the plan, but it was only adopted for the period of transition. The act also removed the restriction on the export of the precious metals.[2]

A further act made it unlawful for the Bank to lend to the government for longer than three months without the sanction of Parliament, and at the same time the government resolved to repay £10 mn. of the Bank's advances.

1 Hansard, vol. XL, p. 602. My italics.   2 59 Geo. III, c. 49.

The boom of 1818 came to an end at the close of that year, and Peel's bill, as the act of 1819 was called, was followed by a sharp fall in prices. The general price index touched 153 at the beginning of 1818, and remained at 150 at the end of the year, but it then fell to 130 at the end of 1819, to 120 at the end of 1820, and to 118 in the second quarter of 1821, when cash payments were resumed. The balance of payments again turned in our favour and, by August 1819, the exchanges were nearly at par, and the price of gold was down to £3. 18s. By the beginning of 1820 gold was being imported in large quantities at the market price, and by February 1821 the Bank's gold stock had risen to nearly £12 mn. For once the government was as good as its word in repaying the advances, and government securities fell from £22 mn. at the beginning of 1819 to £12 mn. at the beginning of 1822. This decline was offset partly by an increase in the bullion, and partly by a decrease in the circulation, which dropped from £25·8 mn. in the first quarter of 1819 to £22·9 mn. in the second quarter of 1821. In these circumstances, with a ratio of gold to notes of about a half, and with gold still coming in, the Bank asked Parliament for a bill enabling it to resume cash payments in full from 1 May 1821, and so the restriction came to an end two years earlier than had been intended.

CONCLUSIONS ON THE RESTRICTION PERIOD

We are now in a position to form an opinion on the extent and nature of the influence exercised by the Bank; on whether it played an active or passive role in relation to price changes or, in the rather confusing terminology of the time, "whether gold increased or notes declined in value".

We have seen that almost all the major changes are associated with important non-monetary factors; either inflationary budgets, a rising cost of living due to bad harvests, exchange depreciation due to artificial payments, or commercial speculation consequent on the development of new markets. We have also seen that there is little correlation between price movements and the notes or advances of the Bank, and that, so far as this correlation exists, there is a marked tendency for accommodation to follow prices.

Contemporary critics, with the notable exception of Tooke, attacked the Bank for having actively caused the price rise. But if this was so, surely we ought to find some trace of it in the statistics, instead of which the fact that the note issue always increases after prices rise suggests that the Bank played a passive role. If we disabuse our minds of "quantity theory" notions, this seems the more likely sequence. We know that the directors were willing to discount all good commercial paper at a uniform rate, and that they believed themselves thereby to be giving free play to non-monetary forces. Obviously, then, any stimulus to such a system must be a non-monetary one; as such a stimulus took effect incomes, and eventually prices, would rise, and more banknotes would be required. Notes would be freely available to meet this need, but the Bank would be only a passive agent in the matter. This is not, of course, to say that a refusal on the part of the Bank to allow any expansion of its issues would not have checked the rise in prices; obviously it must have done so; but such a check could have operated only by a rationing of credit equivalent in effect to a rise in the rate of interest, and would have been regarded by the Bank as a violent and unjustifiable interference with the natural course of events.

When we come to consider whether or not it was wise of the Bank to pursue the policy which it did, we must distinguish between the war and the post-war period.

During the war Parliament had recognised the existence of special circumstances to the extent of absolving the Bank from the obligation to pay in cash, and the directors were entitled to modify their policy accordingly. There were three courses open to them: to act as they did; to aim at stabilising domestic prices and to allow forces outside their control to produce their natural effect in the depreciation of the pound; or to act as they must if they had been paying in cash, to contract credit, and force down prices to whatever level might have been necessary to restore the balance of payments, and keep the exchanges at par.

The latter course was the one recommended by the Bullion Committee, but it would have involved a great reduction in domestic prices, and such a reduction can only be effected at a cost of disorganisation, unemployment, and wastage of national resources, which a nation at war cannot afford. This was the point which the Bullion Committee overlooked.

With the coming of peace, however, the position was quite different; the Bank was now bound by law so to conduct its affairs as to be able to resume cash payments as soon as possible, and to maintain them thereafter. But the directors held the policy of accommodating the legitimate demands of commerce to apply not only to wartime, but to the normal workings of a central bank operating a gold-standard currency. The result was the failure of the first attempt at resumption, which demonstrated in fact, as clearly as the Bullion Report had demonstrated in theory, that a central bank paying its notes in cash must have a conscious and active policy for the regulation of credit.

Chapter Three

MONETARY THEORY OF THE BANK RESTRICTION PERIOD

MONETARY AND REAL ECONOMICS

The Bank Restriction Period is the earliest time at which we can accurately speak of monetary theory as a separate branch of economics; the beginning of a separation which was to be very much emphasised in the later nineteenth century, with unfortunate consequences.

It is true of the Mercantilists, if a body of writers holding such diverse opinions may be grouped together under a common label, that they attached too much importance to the precious metals. They thought of a gold reserve as a potential war chest, and they were thinking "power economics" in states which were playing a game of "power politics". It was necessary to develop, as an antidote to this, a system of "real economics", the economics of human effort and human happiness, just as utilitarian political theory was a necessary antidote to the totalitarian political practice of the eighteenth century. But the change which came with the Physiocrats and Adam Smith was loss as well as gain.

Smith begins his work with a statement of the labour theory of value. He says:

The real price of everything, what everything costs to the man who wants to acquire it, is the toil and trouble of acquiring it. What everything is really worth to the man who has acquired it, and wants to dispose of it, is the toil and trouble which it can save to himself, and impose upon other people. What is bought with money or with goods is purchased by labour, as much as what we acquire by the toil of our own body....It was not by gold or by silver, but by labour, that all the wealth of the world was originally purchased; and its value, to those who possess it, and who want to exchange it for some new productions, is precisely equal to the quantity of labour which it can enable them to purchase or command.[1]

Smith follows this with a very modern statement of an "equilibrium theory" of money prices, but he does so only in parenthesis, before returning to the discussion of how the natural price, or labour value, is divided between wages, profits and rent.

Ricardo re-states the labour theory of value in his *Principles of Political Economy* almost as a truism. In his preface, he says that "the principal problem in political economy" is "to determine the laws which regulate the distribution of the whole produce of the earth between landlords, capitalists, and labourers".[2]

Thus we have economists who specialise in "real" economics, and who regard money as a complication to be eliminated before getting down to the important problems of the subject, and others, such as Thornton, Blake and Wheatley, who are strictly monetary theorists. Even those writers, such as Ricardo and Malthus, who dealt with both branches of the subject, did so at different times, and tended to treat the two as watertight compartments.

The immediate consequence was a much too superficial examination of the mechanism by which the quantity of money affects prices, accompanied by a facile acceptance of a crude form of the quantity theory, and a neglect of the frictions and injustices associated with a large change in prices. The two more permanent legacies, both associated with Ricardo, were the assumption of full employment, and the theory that interest is determined by the marginal yield of capital.

We have now to examine this very specialised monetary branch of economics in more detail, and in its relation to the special problems of the Bank Restriction Period.

1 Smith, *Wealth of Nations*, World's Classics edition, p. 33.
2 Quoted, Cannan, *Theories of Production and Distribution*, p. 189.

CURRENCY AND PRICES: THE QUANTITY THEORY

It was recognised that the functions of money were both to act as "the great wheel of circulation", as Adam Smith put it, and to act as a standard of value, but the circumstances of the time naturally led to a great emphasis on the latter. The first essential in a standard of value is constancy, and during the eighteenth century it seemed that good gold coin afforded a standard as constant as was necessary for practical purposes. But this foundation was shattered by the suspension of cash payments and the rise in the market price of gold, and men were plunged back into the days of the great currency depreciations and the medieval arguments about "valor intrinsicus" and "valor impositus". Should the standard be a disc of precious metal, containing its own value in the esteem men set upon it, and carrying the image and superscription of the sovereign merely as a guarantee of its weight and fineness? Or was there not some unique and invariable measure of value, independent of the varying esteem in which men held metal, which could be imposed by the sovereign and maintained constant by him? Ricardo, and the authors of the Bullion Report, ridiculed the idea of an ideal and immaterial standard, and maintained that the legal standard of value was gold; if gold rose above its mint price in coin or notes, that could only be because coin or notes were depreciated. Yet practical men saw changes in the price of gold which had nothing to do with the currency, and were not convinced. Hence the groping for an ideal standard, and the haggling over the meaning of the word "depreciation", which so complicate the discussions of the period; hence Bosanquet's pound, which was "the interest on £33. 6s. 8d. at 3%", and Thomas Smith's "abstract pound", on which Sir Robert Peel heaped so much contempt in 1819.

The "quantity theory" of money and domestic prices had descended from Bodin, through a long line of Mercantilists, to Locke and Hume, and it was accepted by most writers on both sides of the Restriction controversy.

The crude view that changes in prices are proportional to

changes in the quantity of money was qualified, in theory at least, by the concept of velocity of circulation, which also had been recognised by Hume.

Thornton gives a very careful analysis both of differences in velocity between different kinds of currency, and between the same kind at different times. In this connection he gives special attention to the state of confidence, and sets out a "liquidity preference" theory:

In general it may be observed that a high state of confidence tends to quicken the circulation (of Bank notes), and this happens upon a principle which shall be fully explained. It must be premised that, by the phrase a more or less quick circulation of notes, will be meant a more or less quick circulation of the whole of them upon an average. Whatever increases that reserve, for instance, of Bank of England notes which remains in the drawer of the London banker as his provision against contingencies, contributes to what will here be termed the less quick circulation of the whole. Now a high state of confidence contributes to make men provide less amply against contingencies. At such a time, they trust, that if the demand upon them for a payment, which is now doubtful and contingent, should actually be made, they shall be able to provide for it at the moment; and they are loth to be at the expense of selling an article or getting a bill discounted, in order to make provision so much before the period at which it shall be wanted. When, on the contrary, a season of distrust arises, prudence suggests that the loss of interest arising from a detention of notes for a few additional days, would not be regarded.[1]

We could go on quoting from many writers to show that they appreciated the importance of the velocity of circulation; yet these same people, even including Ricardo, often slip into neglecting it, and talk of prices rising and falling in exact proportion to changes in the quantity of money. The reason is probably that they did not see any reason why changes in the quantity of money should affect velocity, and so thought that this could conveniently be tucked away in the assumption of *ceteris paribus*. The effect of changes in the quantity of money on confidence, and so on velocity, was not generally realised.

1 *Paper Credit*, ed. Hayek, pp. 96–7.

A more serious weakness was the neglect of the mechanism by which changes in the quantity of money were transmitted to prices. A contributory cause of this was that most of the leading students of the subjects were either landowners or City men, for the price of agricultural products is subject to so many influences quantitatively more important than a moderate change in the amount of money, while on the stock exchange the adjustment takes place very much more quickly and easily than elsewhere.

Again, Thornton's analysis is so striking an exception as to be worth quoting at length:

Let us suppose, for example, an increased number of Bank of England notes to be issued. In such case the traders of the metropolis discover that there is more than usual facility of obtaining notes at the Bank by giving bills for them, and that they may, therefore, rely on finding easy means of performing any pecuniary engagements into which they may enter. Every trader is encouraged, by the knowledge of this facility of borrowing, a little to enlarge his speculations; he is rendered, by the plenty of money, somewhat more ready to buy, and rather less eager to sell; he either trusts that there will be a particular profit on the article which is the object of his speculation, or else he judges that, by extending his general purchases, he shall at least have his share of the ordinary profits of commercial business, a share which he considers to be proportional to the quantity of it.... Thus an inclination to buy is created in all quarters, and an indisposition to sell. Now, since the cost of an article depends upon the issue of that general conflict between the buyers and the sellers,... it follows, that any circumstance which serves to communicate a greater degree of eagerness to the mind of one party, or to that of the other, will have an influence on price.[1]

Perhaps because he was a merchant and not a stockbroker or a farmer, Thornton was vividly conscious of the pains attending a reversal of the process, the contraction of notes and the forcing down of prices:

The manufacturer, on account of this unusual scarcity of money, may, even though the selling price of his article should be profitable,

1 Thornton, op. cit. p. 195.

be absolutely compelled by necessity to slacken, if not to suspend his operations.... But secondly that very diminution of the price of manufactures, which is supposed to cause them to be exported, may also, if carried very far, produce a suspension in the labour of those who fabricate them. The masters naturally turn off their hands when they find their goods selling exceedingly ill. It is true that, if we could suppose the diminution of Bank paper to produce permanently a diminution in the value of all articles whatsoever, and a diminution, as it would then be fair that it should do, in the rate of wages also, the encouragement to future manufacture would be the same, though there would be a loss on the stock in hand... (but) the rate of wages, we know, is not so variable as the price of goods.[1]

Thornton is the only writer in the Restriction Period who recognised this rigidity of money wages and inferred from it that a reduction in general prices, consistent with full employment, could only be obtained after a period of unemployment sufficient to overcome this resistance.

Other writers, notably Malthus and Mushet, were very conscious of the evils attending a rise in prices, but did not pay much attention to those involved in a fall. Malthus, alone, remarks that an expansion of the currency causes not only an expansion of trade along the lines suggested by Thornton, but also an increase in capital:

Whenever, in the actual state of things, a fresh issue of notes comes into the hands of those who mean to employ them in the prosecution and extension of a profitable business, an addition to capital results.

But an increase in currency is not thereby justified:

The grand and paramount objection to the stimulus which is applied to the productive power of a country by an excessive increase of currency, is that it is accomplished at the expense of a manifest injustice. The observations we have may afford a natural explanation of the facts, that countries are often increasing in riches amidst an increasing quantity of individual misery; that a rise in prices is often found conjoined with national prosperity, and a fall

1 Thornton, *op. cit.* pp. 118-19.

in prices with national decline. But whatever phenomena they may assist to explain, they cannot alter the foundation of right or wrong, or give the slightest sanction to unjust transfers of property.[1]

Malthus here hints at an association of falling prices and national decline, but that is all he says of it, and in another place he implies that he takes quite a facile view of the process of contraction:

In the case of a diminished supply from the mines, or a greater consumption of the precious metals in some of the principal countries in Europe, an immediate demand would be felt in the rest for bullion to be exported; the market price of bullion would rise for a time above the mint price; the notes of different banks would be returned upon them to be exchanged for coin which would be sent abroad. The consequence would be that the whole currency, consisting of the same proportion of paper to coin, would be diminished in quantity and raised in value; the exchanges, which had been unusually unfavourable, would be restored to their accustomed level, *and no other effects would be felt than a general fall in prices* throughout the commercial world.[2]

Most of the other writers, including Ricardo, considered the quantity equation as a sort of balance, adjusting itself automatically, painlessly, and very nearly instantaneously.

The natural consequence was that the sponsors of the Bullion Report failed to see the inconvenience which would be caused by a drastic reduction of issues, even in time of war, and underestimated the dislocation which would be produced by the eventual return to cash payments in 1819. Their opponents, however, were prevented from striking what should have been their most telling blow by the fact that they held much the same view of the essential nature of the mechanism connecting currency and prices. Hence the futility of many of the arguments by which men opposed something which they instinctively felt to be wrong, but against which they could make out no logical case.

1 *Edinburgh Review*, Feb. 1811, pp. 364–5.
2 *Ibid.* p. 355. My italics.

THE RATE OF INTEREST

Of less immediate practical importance, though of great consequence for the future development of economic theory, was the turn given to the theory of the rate of interest during these years. This followed from the neglect of the price mechanism, which we have discussed, for the importance of the theory which regards the rate of interest as being the price of money is that it provides the link in the connection between money and prices. Since this connection was assumed to be automatic, it was natural to seek an explanation of the rate of interest elsewhere.

The later Mercantilists had been trying to develop a theory of the rate of interest in terms of the supply and demand for money, but they were vigorously attacked by Hume, who held that the abundance or scarcity of money could affect only prices; interest must be determined by the profits on capital. The same line was taken by Adam Smith.

Nevertheless, Thornton still clung to the old view, though he never followed up its implications. For instance, he told the House of Lords Committee of 1797:

I should conceive that the high rate of interest for money, amounting to eight, ten, or even eighteen per cent, which has been evident in the price of Exchequer bills, India bonds, and other securities soon convertible into Bank Notes, has arisen in a great measure from the scarcity of Bank Notes, the price paid, if I may so express it, for the purchase of Bank Notes naturally increasing in proportion as those notes are few in number and in great demand.[1]

Ricardo, however, follows Smith and Hume:

It can, I think, be made manifest that the rate of interest is not regulated by the abundance or scarcity of money, but by the abundance or scarcity of that part of capital not consisting of money...if the Bank had an issue of twenty millions, and were subsequently to increase it to fifty or a hundred millions, the increased quantity would all be absorbed in the circulation of England, but would, in

1 Reprinted in Hayek's edition of *Paper Credit*, pp. 296–7.

all cases, be depreciated to the value of twenty millions.... Profits can only be lowered by the competition of capitals not consisting of circulating medium. As the increase of Bank Notes does not add to this species of capital... it cannot add to our profit, nor lower interest.[1]

This passage, apart from its theory of interest, is an example of the facile way in which Ricardo viewed the process of price adjustment, for he even rejects Malthus's contention that there will be a forced transfer of wealth.

Among theoretical economists, the last word lay with Ricardo, and economic theory was committed for a hundred years to regarding interest as determined by the marginal yield of capital.

MONEY, FOREIGN TRADE AND EXCHANGE RATES

The idea of an equilibrium distribution of money, the precious metals being divided among all the nations of the world in exact proportion to their needs, so that there is no inducement either to import or to export them, was one which had already been worked out by the Mercantilists, and by Hume.

This is how the process is described by Ricardo:

The precious metals were divided into certain proportions among the different civilised nations of the earth, according to the state of their commerce and wealth, and therefore according to the number and frequency of the payments they had to perform. While so divided, they preserved everywhere the same value, and as each country had an equal necessity for the quantity actually in use, there could be no temptation offered either for their importation or exportation.[2]

He continues:

Excess of currency is but a relative term; if the circulation of England were ten millions, that of France five millions, that of Holland four millions, etc., whilst they kept their proportions, though the currency of each country were doubled or trebled, neither country would be conscious of an excess of currency.[3]

1 Ricardo, *High Price of Bullion*, pp. 50–6.
2 *High Price of Bullion*, p. 1.   3 *Ibid.* p. 7.

This original equilibrium is rather like an act of creation, and we are given no very clear idea of how it came about.

But once in equilibrium, all were agreed that the balance of payments, taken over any period of time, must balance. Thornton, for instance, says:

It may be laid down as a general truth, that the commercial exports and imports of a state (that is to say the exported and imported commodities, for which one country receives an equivalent from another) naturally proportion themselves in some degree to one another, so that the balance of trade, therefore (by which is meant the difference between these commercial exports and imports), cannot continue for a very long time, to be either highly favourable or highly unfavourable to a country.[1]

The Bullion Committee deduce the same fact, for an inconvertible paper currency, as follows:

The price of bills being regulated in some degree by that of British commodities, and continuing to fall until it becomes so low as to be likely to afford a profit on the purchase and exportation of those commodities, an actual exportation nearly proportional to the amount of bills drawn can hardly fail to take place. It follows that there cannot be, for any long period, either a highly favourable or a highly unfavourable balance of trade.[2]

But with regard to the mechanism by which the balance was maintained under a system of gold or convertible paper currency, there was some difference of opinion. One school, including Ricardo, Malthus, and most of the supporters of the Bullion Report, believed that adjustment came about through the effect of the quantity of money on prices; another, including Thornton and Wheatley, believed that it happened rather through each individual adjusting his expenditure to his income.

The former explanation is of respectable antiquity having been first advanced by Mun in his controversy with Malynes, accepted by many of the later Mercantilists, and completed and

1 Thornton, *op. cit.* p. 141.   2 Bullion Report, p. 29.

systematised by Hume. If any country exceeded its due proportion of the precious metals, prices in that country would rise, while prices in the countries from which the metals had been drawn would have fallen. Thus the first country would find itself selling less to foreign countries and buying more from them, until gold or silver again flowed out, and the proportions of the precious metals, and so the price levels, again came into equilibrium.

Ricardo and the Bullion Report follow closely the doctrine of Hume, though without his distrust of convertible banknotes. On the contrary, Ricardo welcomes such a currency, as it serves all the purposes of a gold one, and, at the same time, allows the country using it to employ a greater proportion of its resources with profit. The working of the system is thus described. If in France gold were dearer (i.e. prices were lower) than in England, English gold would be exported for French goods, and

The Bank might continue to issue notes, and the specie to be exported with advantage to the country, so long as their notes were payable on demand, because they could never issue more notes than the value of the coin which would have been issued had there been no Bank.[1]

If, on the other hand, the price of gold bullion rises above the mint price:

The Bank will contract its issues till they should have increased the value of the remainder to that of gold bullion, and consequently to the value of the currencies of all other countries. All advantage from the exportation of gold bullion would then cease, and there would be no temptation to exchange Bank notes for guineas.[2]

The distinction between a purely specie system, one of specie and convertible paper, and one of inconvertible paper was made less clearly than it might have been. The doctrine as formulated by the Mercantilists and Hume applied only to a purely metallic currency, and here the adjustment was obviously automatic and self-regulating. As appears from the

1 Ricardo, *op. cit.* p. 8.   2 Ricardo, *op. cit.* p. 11.

passage quoted above, Ricardo thought that the introduction of convertible paper made little difference, and under-estimated the degree of artificial regulation necessary to ensure convertibility, a lesson which was to be learnt at much cost in the generation after the resumption. So far as an inconvertible system was concerned, it was recognised that artificial control of the volume of currency was necessary; the principles on which such control was to be based we shall have to discuss later.

The doctrine that equilibrium is preserved through changes in the quantity of money, and so in prices, has associated with it an interesting and important heresy. It originated long ago in a confusion between the individual and the state. The individual made a profit by buying cheap and selling dear, and it seemed that a favourable trade balance for a nation was analogous to the profit of an individual, and could likewise be increased by buying cheap and selling dear. This view dates back to Hales, who argued against a reduction of prices in England that foreign merchants would not reduce their wares proportionately:

They be strangers, and not within obedience of oure soveraigne lord, that dve buy and sell such wares; as yron, tar, flax and other. Then consider me, if you cannot compell them, whether yt were expedient for vs to leue strangers to sell theire commodities deare, and we oures good cheape; yf it were so, then were yt a greater enrichinge of (other countries) and impourishinge of oure owne, for they should have much treasure for theirs, and haue oure commodities (from vs) for a very lyttl; except ye coulde devyse to make one price of oure commodities amonst oureselves, and another outwarde, which I cannot see how yt may be.[1]

The same view was taken by Malynes and a number of the Mercantilists. It reappears in Boyd's *Letter to William Pitt*, where it produces much confusion, and later in the writings of Vansittart, Atkinson, and other opponents of the Bullion Report. In modern parlance, we might describe it as a con-

1 *Discourse of the Common Weal*, ed. Lamond, p. 40.

fusion between the balance and the terms of trade. It is, of course, true that the balance of trade would be made more favourable by a rise in the price of exports if foreign demand for them were inelastic. Vansittart and Atkinson do not use that word for it, but they probably make such an assumption tacitly, for it was a habit to take demand very much for granted, to think of people requiring a certain amount of a commodity and setting out to get it whatever the cost.

The orthodox theorist never confuted the heretics with reasoned argument, but relied on the repetition of what to them seemed obvious facts. They also placed themselves in a weak position in concentrating on the effect of currency contraction in reducing prices and increasing exports, and neglected the effect on imports which had already been noticed by Hume. Had they analysed this, they might have replied that, even if foreign demand for exports were inelastic, a sufficient degree of currency contraction would still redress the balance of trade by reducing money incomes at home, and so reducing imports.

We turn now to the income theory of adjustment. I know of no antecedent for this before the Restriction Period, and it seems to have been an original contribution of Thornton, though later taken up by Wheatley.

Thornton believed in the efficacy of adjustment through prices up to a point, but distrusted it for two reasons. So far as the effect on imports was concerned—and he was one of the few who paid any attention to this—he believed that our imports consisted largely of food and raw materials, which it would be harmful to cut down. As to exports, he did not subscribe to the inelasticity heresy, but he was very conscious of the frictions involved in a sudden contraction of the currency, and believed that, by creating unemployment, it would diminish "that exportable produce, by the excess of which above imported articles, gold is brought into the country", and so frustrate its own object.

He therefore fell back on the view that, quite independently of changes in the currency, there is an automatic tendency for exports and imports to adjust themselves through each individual adjusting his expenditure to his income:

The equalisation of the commercial exports and imports is promoted not only by the unwillingness of the richer state to lend to an unlimited extent, but by a disinclination to borrow in the poorer. There is in the mass of the people, of all countries, a disposition to adapt their individual expenditure to their income. Importations conducted with a view to the consumption of the country into which the articles are imported (and such perhaps are the chief importations of a poor country) are limited by the ability of the individuals in that country to pay for them out of their income. Importations with a view to subsequent exportation, are in a like manner limited by the ability to pay which subsists among the individuals of the several countries to which the imported goods are afterwards exported. The income of the individuals is the general limit in all cases. If, therefore, through any unforeseen circumstance, if through war, scarcity, or any other extensive calamity, the value of the annual income of the inhabitants of a country is diminished, either new economy on the one hand, or new exertions of individual industry on the other, fail not, after a certain time, in some measure, to restore the balance. And this equality between private expenditure and private incomes tends ultimately to produce equality between the commercial exports and imports.[1]

This theory had no great influence at the time, but it is an interesting foreshadowing of the income theory of transfer which was later developed by Wicksell.

In connection with their views on the balance of payments, there arose a confusing dispute between Thornton and Ricardo as to the meaning of the term "excess of currency". Thornton, while admitting that a contraction of the currency tended to *cure* an adverse balance, maintained that such a balance could be *caused* by circumstances quite independent of the currency. In that case, he maintained that it was an incorrect use of words to call the currency excessive:

At the time of a very unfavourable balance of trade, it is very possible, I apprehend, that the excess of paper, if such it may be

1 Thornton, *op. cit.* p. 142.

called, is only an excess above that very low and reduced quantity, to which it is necessary that it should be brought down, in order to prevent the existence of an excess of the market above the mint price of gold. I conceive, therefore, that such an excess, if it arises on the occasion of an unfavourable balance of trade, and at a time when there has been no extraordinary emission of notes, may fairly be considered as an excess created by that unfavourable balance, though it is one which a contraction of notes tends to cure.[1]

Ricardo maintained that an unfavourable balance could only exist if *caused* by an excess of currency, and, therefore, that whenever the market price of gold rose above the mint price the currency must be considered excessive. Thornton took the example of an extraordinary importation of corn occasioned by the failure of the domestic harvest, and maintained that this could not be paid for by the immediate export of goods, but must produce an export of gold, and, in an inconvertible paper system, an increase in its price. Ricardo's comment on this was as follows:

Mr Thornton has not explained to us why any unwillingness should exist in the foreign country to receive our goods in exchange for their corn, and it would be necessary for him to show that, if such an unwillingness should exist, we should agree to indulge it so far as to part with our coin....If the sellers of corn in England to the amount, I will suppose, of a million, could import goods which cost a million in England, and would produce when sold abroad more than if the million had been sent in money, goods would be preferred; if otherwise, money would be demanded.[2]

To ensure that the former was the case, the Bank had only to bring about a sufficient contraction in the note issue. Further:

If, which is a much stronger case, we agreed to pay a subsidy to a foreign power, money would not be exported while there were any goods which could more cheaply discharge the payment. The interest of individuals would render the export of money unnecessary.[3]

This is not a valid reply to Thornton's case. Thornton ad-

---

1 Thornton, *op. cit.* p. 151.　2 Ricardo, *op. cit.* p. 14.　3 *Ibid.* p. 16.

mits that a contraction of the currency will cure an unfavourable exchange, but he contends that the unfavourable exchange need not therefore have been caused by an excess of currency, and that contraction is not necessarily the most expedient remedy. Ricardo leaves these two points unanswered, and concentrates only on the one which Thornton admits. One might just as well argue that, since bicarbonate of soda is a cure for indigestion, therefore indigestion cannot be caused by over-eating, but must be entirely due to a lack of bicarbonate of soda.

Viewed from a distance the dispute seems only a quibble, but it is an interesting example of the tyranny of words in economic thought. To say that an unfavourable exchange is caused by an excess of currency implies that the fault and the appropriate remedy lie in the currency. It was largely because of the way in which it was phrased that this very doubtful proposition was accepted with so little question.

The discussion of the foreign exchanges is made somewhat obscure by Blake's attempt to distinguish between monetary and non-monetary causes of depreciation. He says:

The price of bills will depend in the same manner as that of any other commodity, upon two causes, First on the abundance or scarcity in the market compared with the demand for them; and secondly on the value of the currency in which they are to be had, compared with that in which they are to be bought.[1]

These two things are, he insists, independent.

Corresponding to the first is Blake's "real exchange", in the discussion of which he assumes two currencies perfect in weight and fineness, and bearing a constant proportion to the transactions which each has to perform. The exchange rate will then be determined exclusively by the supply and demand for bills in the market. Extraordinary imports of corn or government remittances abroad will cause an unfavourable real exchange, and this will stimulate exports and check imports. It will, however, produce no effect on domestic prices. The limits to the movement of real exchanges will be set by the cost of trans-

[1] W. Blake, *Observations on the Principles which Regulate the Course of Exchange*, 1810, p. 6.

mitting bullion, but so long as there is a law against the melting of coin, there will be a rise in the market price of bullion in the exporting country. Such is Blake's view of the non-monetary causes affecting the exchanges.

He next assumes that "the price of foreign bills is not affected by any variations in their abundance or scarcity",[1] and proceeds to discuss changes in the weight or fineness of the coinage, and the proportion which it bears to the transactions undertaken with it. Any variations in these things will be reflected in a change in domestic prices, and a corresponding change in nominal rates of exchange, for

A foreign bill, or an order for payment of a given sum of foreign money abroad, will not be sold unless for such a sum as will counterbalance the diminution in its value.[2]

Changes in the nominal exchange will have no effect on prices or on imports and exports, and the price of gold will change along with that of all other commodities.

Having thus separately determined the "real" and "nominal" rates of exchange, Blake explains that the "computed" rate, at which transactions are actually undertaken, will be the sum of the two.

The weakness of the theory is in its attempt to separate things which are inextricably interwoven. The monetary forces which Blake discusses in connection with the nominal rate actually produce their effect on the exchanges through changes in imports and exports and so in the volume of bills, and so the distinction between "real" and "nominal" is visionary and misleading. By contrast with the Bullion Committee, however, Blake does admit some circumstances in which exchange rates can be influenced by non-monetary factors.

The Bullion Committee follows a very similar train of thought. The idea of the "real" par of exchange is applied to an inconvertible paper currency as follows:

It is manifest that the exchange between two countries is at its real par when a given quantity of gold or silver in the one country is

---

1 W. Blake, *op. cit.* p. 37.   2 *Ibid.* p. 46.

convertible at the market price into such an amount of the currency of that country, as will purchase a bill of exchange on the other country for such an amount of the currency of that other country as will there be convertible into an equal amount of gold or silver of the same standard fineness.[1]

The Committee assumed that changes in the supply and demand for bills in the market were, in the circumstances which they were considering, unimportant, and hence the depreciation of the exchanges, apart from corrections for changes in the price of the precious metals in other countries and for transport costs, was due entirely to the state of the domestic currency. Hence the nominal rate would be the actual rate subject to these corrections, and the difference between the real and nominal rates would measure the depreciation of the currency.

Another misleading dispute, that as to whether gold had risen or notes fallen in value, arose as the result of an inadequate analysis of the factors determining the value of the precious metals under an inconvertible paper system. The Report is inclined to treat the rise in the price of bullion and the fall in the exchange rates as two separate phenomena each of which is proof of the depreciation of the currency. This is largely due to confusion between a convertible and an inconvertible currency, and confusion between an inconvertible currency and clipped coin.

Under a convertible system with no obstacle to the export of the precious metals, the market price of bullion in new coin or banknotes can never exceed the mint price, and the price in banknotes can never exceed the price in new coin. But unless there is an effective law making light-weight coins legal tender at their face value, then such coins will fall in value both in bullion and notes in proportion as their weight is below standard. Hence prices in clipped coin will rise, while remaining constant in new coin or notes. If we now suppose, as there was in England at this time, a law forbidding the export of coin or of bullion obtained from the melting of coin, when there is a demand for exportable gold, its price may rise both in coin and

1 Bullion Report, ed. Cannan, p. 30.

notes, the limit to the rise being the premium required to induce people to break the law.

Now in an inconvertible system the link between gold and notes is broken, and gold becomes a commodity like any other. As new supplies are small in relation to stock, its price will be determined under the conditions which Marshall calls "market equilibrium". Unless we suppose a sudden increase in industrial demand, the upper limit will be fixed by the state of the exchanges. Since, after the exchanges have been below par for any considerable time, the supply of gold will be small, and since demand will be very elastic at that price, there will be a strong tendency for the market price of gold to approach this upper limit. If there is a law against export, the price of bullion will be higher than that of new coin, both in notes, while clipped coin will be related to new coin in proportion to its weight. The only link between notes and gold of any sort will be through the exchanges; there will be no direct connection as there is between new and clipped coin and bullion. Hence the price of bullion and the state of the exchanges must be considered not separately, but together. The opponents of the Report might very profitably have emphasised this in discussing whether gold had risen or notes fallen in value.

THE BANK OF ENGLAND AND THE COUNTRY BANKS

I hope now to have made clear the various theories of money, prices, international trade and the foreign exchanges. It remains now to discuss the banking questions arising out of them. The dominant questions were, on what principle Bank of England notes should be regulated, and what relation existed between Bank of England notes and those of the country banks.

As regards the former, we have the evidence of the directors before the various committees, and the bitter attacks of the Bullion Committee and its supporters on their policy.

The views of the directors were an attempt to rationalise a system which had arisen through custom and convenience and with very little regard for theory. First and foremost they stressed that it was no business of the Bank to exercise any control over the state of credit or the course of trade. Their job was simply to supply the money required to meet "the legitimate needs of commerce". The accepted proof of legitimate need was the presentation of a good bill, having not more than sixty days to run, for discount at the rate of 5%.

As to what determined this rate of interest, there was some disagreement among the directors. They were inclined to admit, at any rate after the experience of 1817, that an increase in the quantity of money would lead to a reduction in the rate of interest, and Harman says: "The criterion of a superabundant issue is when money will not produce a sufficient interest."[1] On the other hand, Pole is asked:

Do you not conceive that the rate of interest in this country depends more upon the demand for capital in this country, and upon the profits of trade, than upon the issues of the Bank?[2]

He answers unequivocally, "Yes". When Harman is asked what he considers the criterion of a sufficient currency, he replies:

If it is meant to allude to discounts, I should have only the old answer to give: undoubtedly good paper being sent into the Bank for discount, of which we must judge as best we can, that is the criterion; I take it for granted that established houses of good character would not come to the Bank to pay 5 % for money if they did not want it.

The last sentence is the key to the directors' attitude. If established firms of good repute wanted money, they ought to have it, and if they did not want it, they would not be much more likely to pay 4% or even 3% than 5% for it; such was evidently the reasoning of the directors. Whitmore and Pearse denied that the Bank's issues could be excessive so long as it discounted only good bills, whatever the rate of interest, and Dorrien was evidently of the same opinion when he told the Committee of 1819:

1 Commons Committee of 1819, p. 42.   2 *Ibid.* p. 38.

The demand for discounts proceeds from the wants of the public, and if the Bank were to discount at a lower rate than 5 %, in my opinion there would be no greater application than if we were to discount at the present rate.[1]

Here is another instance of that neglect of the connection between price and demand, which we have noticed.

Apparently, then, the real criterion upon which the directors relied was the goodness of the paper and not the rate of interest. That the rate happened to be 5 % was simply due to the fact that the directors were operating in a sellers' market, and their commercial instincts therefore inspired them to charge as much as the law would allow.

When pressed as to the relation between their issues and the exchanges, the directors took refuge in a simple denial that there was any connection at all, and most of those who defended them against the attack of the Bullion Committee took up the heretical form of the price adjustment theory, and maintained that a decrease in issues, so far from producing a rise, would lead to a further fall in the exchanges. The following resolution was passed by the Court in 1819:

That this Court cannot refrain from adverting to an opinion strongly insisted on by some, that the Bank has only to reduce its issues to obtain a favourable turn in the exchanges, and a consequent influx of the precious metals. The Court conceives it to be its duty to declare that it is unable to discover any solid foundation for such a sentiment.

That it is contended by those who recommend the reduction of the paper currency, that it will have the effect of lowering prices, and that foreigners will thereby be induced to take more of the produce and manufacture of the country.

That the Court considers this expectation to be founded on error, inasmuch as a low rate of exchange has always been considered most favourable to exports; but that, even should a temporary effect be produced, it would probably be only a disadvantageous anticipation of the regular consumption, and result in a serious reduction upon the trade of the country.

1 Commons Committee of 1819, p. 42.

Here is yet another example of the belief that demand cannot be permanently increased by a reduction in price. It is admitted that a reduction of issues would bring about a fall in prices, though it is denied that the Bank ought to produce such a fall; but the crux of the argument is the denial that the fall in prices would produce any permanent improvement in the balance of trade or the exchanges. The resolution was rescinded in 1827, on the motion of William Ward, but even in 1819, some of the directors had doubts, and several of them dissented in their evidence from the views to which they had collectively outlined.

The line taken by Ricardo and the Bullion Committee follows naturally from the premises which we have described. The Bullion Committee describes the views of the directors as "a doctrine wholly erroneous in principle, and pregnant with dangerous consequences in practice".[1] So long as notes were convertible, however, the attitude of the directors did not matter, since any excess of notes would be returned in exchange for gold:

The fallacy on which it rests is not distinguishing between the advance of capital to merchants, and an additional supply of currency to the general mass of the circulating medium.

The notes so issued, not being convertible into gold:

Will remain in the channel of circulation until put in again to the Bank itself in discharge of the bills which were originally discounted ...and before they come to be paid in exchange for these bills, they have already been followed by a new issue of notes in a similar process of discounting...this process may be as indefinite as the range of speculation and adventure in a great commercial country.[2]

It had been laid down as an axiom that gold was the standard of value, and that notes were depreciated if they exchanged for gold at more than £3. 17s. 10½d. per oz. It had been said that an unfavourable trade balance and unfavourable exchanges could only exist if caused by the state of the currency. That the high price of bullion and the lowness of the exchanges were one

1 Bullion Report, p. 46.   2 Bullion Report, p. 50.

and the same thing was only imperfectly realised. From all this it followed that the state of the exchanges or the price of bullion, or both, should be the standard by which the issue of notes was to be regulated. Ricardo says:

If they [the directors] had acted up to the principles which they avowed to have regulated their issues when they were obliged to pay their notes in specie, namely to limit their issues to the amount which should prevent the excess of the market above the mint price of gold, we should not have been now exposed to all the evils of a depreciated and perpetually varying currency.[1]

The Bullion Committee expressed its view as follows:

Your Committee beg leave to report to the House as their most clear opinion, that as long as the suspension of cash payments is permitted to subsist, the price of gold bullion and the general course of exchange with foreign countries form the best general criterion from which any inference can be drawn, as to the sufficiency or excess of paper currency in circulation, and that the Bank of England cannot safely regulate the amount of its issues without having reference to the criterion presented by these two circumstances.[2]

It was recommended that the issues of the Bank be gradually reduced, at the discretion of the directors, to such an extent as to permit the resumption of cash payments at the end of two years, at the latest.

The method of regulation of the issues was left to the directors, and Thornton was the only writer who examined the question in any detail. He concluded that the goodness of the bills was not a sufficient safeguard against over-issue and that, while it would be possible to limit discounts by a sufficient rise in the rate of interest, this could not be done at the time he was writing, as the 5% which was the maximum allowed by the usury laws was ineffective. He was thus one of the first to suggest the systematic use of Bank rate as a means of credit regulation. With the law as it was, however, he saw no other way out than simple rationing.

1 Ricardo, *op. cit.* p. 59.　　　　2 Bullion Report, p. 45.

The question of the possible excess of country bank issues received more space than was warranted by the ideas involved, and the discussion was made more difficult by the impossibility of obtaining accurate statistics and the consequent wild guesses which were made at the volume of country notes in circulation. In general, though not without exception, the supporters of the Bullion Report maintained that the country banks could not issue to excess unless the Bank of England was doing so too, and that, therefore, the sole responsibility for the state of the currency rested upon the Bank. The opponents of the Report denied this, and so far as they admitted any excess of issues at all, they minimised the responsibility of the Bank, and threw the blame on the country banks.

The argument in favour of the innocence of the country banks was based on the analogy with the position of the Bank of England before the suspension of cash payments. Just as its notes were then payable in gold, so were their notes payable in Bank of England notes. When its notes were convertible, an excess of issues on the part of the Bank would raise prices in England, and cause the notes to be returned to the Bank in exchange for gold to be exported. So now, an excess of issues by a country bank would raise prices in its neighbourhood relatively to prices in London, that district would have an unfavourable balance of payments with London, and the country notes would be returned for Bank of England notes, with which purchases would be made in London. No adequate reply was found to this, and the controversy lingered on long after the resumption of cash payments. The reason for this was probably that the argument came so very near to the truth. Where it erred was just where the same argument applied to the Bank erred, in ignoring frictions and time lags. There will be some time before people realise the changed position and can make the necessary adjustments, and during that time the excess issues will remain. In fact, they can only be eliminated *after* they have materially raised prices and, if the issuing bank is prepared to reduce its reserve and incur some risk of ultimate suspension, the excess can be maintained for a considerable time. It was only after the resumption that bitter experience showed this to be the case with the Bank of England, and so allowed the earlier controversy to appear in its true light.

To sum up. The war, and the suspension of cash payments, led to a decline in the foreign exchanges, and a rise in the price of bullion, but there were a number of factors contributing to this. One was the increase in the note issue produced by a bad discount policy and inflationary government borrowing, but others were bad harvests, subsidies to allies, and military expenditure abroad, and the restrictions on our exports imposed by the Continental system and the American policy of non-intercourse. To have maintained the exchanges at par in face of all these things, prices and incomes at home would have had to be reduced much below their pre-war level, and this could only have been done by a great contraction of credit, with all its attendant frictions. Now it is by no means certain how many, if any, of these things should be met by a forced reduction of the internal price level. When the Bullion Committee, instead of saying that the fall in the exchanges could not have taken place so long as convertibility had been maintained, said that it was caused by an excess of currency, it at once implied that the currency ought to be reduced, and passed over all the other considerations without discussion. Moreover, it did not examine the mechanism by which a contraction in the quantity of money affects prices, and so greatly underestimated the difficulties involved in the process.

On the other hand, the general principles of the Bullion Committee were perfectly sound, and it was quite right in maintaining that the discount policy of the directors was incompatible with the maintenance of cash payments. Its biggest achievement was not in its theory of money prices or international trade, which was far from original, but in the application of this theory to the working of a central bank. It was its theoretical demonstration of the need for an active policy of credit regulation by reference to the exchanges, combined with the failure of the old policy in the post-war years, which paved the way for future experiments.

Its opponents failed to point out the shortcomings of the Report because they shared the inadequate views on the price mechanism and the rate of interest, and the clumsy phraseology which had produced them. Instead, they launched abortive attacks on the strongest positions of the enemy, or dissipated their energies in a vain search for a new standard of value. Nevertheless, so great were the difficulties which the Report overlooked, that it is perhaps as well for our chances of winning the Napoleonic war, that the less sound arguments, and the stronger prejudices prevailed for so long as they did. The blindness of Vansittart caused less trouble than might have done the shortsightedness of Ricardo.

From the point of view of its permanent contribution to monetary theory, the Restriction Period is, for such an eventful time, surprisingly barren. In the fields of money and prices, and of international trade and the foreign exchanges, it produced only a restatement of theories all of which had been stated before, and many of which were over a century old. Ricardo had the doubtful honour of driving home the theory that interest was determined by the marginal yield of capital, but that too had already been suggested by Hume and Smith. The two most original contributions, though both only in embryo, came from Thornton—his income theory of transfer, and his suggestion that Bank rate might be used for the systematic regulation of discounts.

Chapter Four

THE FIRST YEARS OF RESUMPTION, THE CRISIS OF 1825, AND THE BANK CHARTER ACT, 1833

FALLING PRICES, 1821-4

The price fall, which had begun in 1819, continued with but slight interruption until 1824. The general index, 150 at the end of 1818, fell to 120 at the beginning of 1821, to 112 in the third quarter of 1822 and, after a slight rally in 1823, to 104 in the third quarter of 1824. Wheat prices fell disastrously in 1821 and 1822, but then recovered somewhat.

In the second quarter of 1821, when cash payments were resumed, the average circulation of Bank notes had been £22·9 mn.; a year later the figure was only £17·3 mn., but a large quantity of coin had been issued, so that the combined circulation of notes and coin had almost certainly increased. This decline was balanced chiefly by the decline in government securities, as the government completed the repayment of the promised £10 mn. Commercial discounts remained fairly constant at a very low level, and bullion, in spite of the large issue of coin, fell by less than £2 mn.

Ricardo blamed the Bank for the too rapid contraction of their issues. During the resumption debates he had said:

> The Bank should only reduce their issues cautiously; he only feared that they would do it too rapidly. If he might give them advice, he should recommend them not to buy bullion, but, even though they had only a few millions, if he had the management of their concerns, he should boldly sell. Every sale would improve the exchanges and, until the price of gold fell to £3. 17s. 6d., there was no necessity for the Bank to make any purchases at all.[1]

1 Hansard, vol. XL, p. 742.

In the years that followed, Ricardo often returned to this point, and emphasised that the evils of the time arose from the Bank's not having followed his advice.

Tooke, on the other hand, maintained that the act of 1819 was quite inoperative. In his usual manner he points out discrepancies in time between changes in the note circulation and in prices. He maintains that the fall in prices was general over Europe, and finds ample cause for it in the state of markets. The repayment of the Bank's advances was a natural consequence of the favourable terms on which Exchequer bills could be funded, and would have taken place whether the act had been passed or not. Though the circulation of notes had declined, that of notes and coin together had increased. In fact:

There is not a vestige of ground for supposing that the smallest part of the fall in prices, or of the derangement of credit, in 1819, or from 1819 to 1822, can, according to any evidence of facts or any consistent reasoning, be traced to the operation, direct or indirect, of that measure.[1]

ATTEMPTED REFLATION

But the arguments of the theorists were drowned in a chorus of complaint from practical farmers, faced with low prices and high taxes. There were no less than twelve hundred petitions on agricultural distress presented to Parliament between 1819 and 1821. In the country the movement was led by Cobbett, and in the House by a farmer's party, organised by Western. Those who attacked the Bank, and those who opposed the resumption act, believers in the devaluation of the standard and in bimetallism, advocates of "the equitable adjustment of contracts"[2] and grumblers against taxation, all joined in a furious onslaught upon the government. Any pretext was good enough to air their views, debates on distress petitions, on Western's motions for committees of enquiry, and on their reports, on motions for an enquiry into the effects of resumption. The records drag through

[1] Tooke, *History of Prices*, vol. II, p. 76.
[2] A popular phrase, which Wodehouse, Tory M.P. for Norfolk, claimed the doubtful honour of having coined.

hundreds of weary pages of Hansard, and, in all, the same arguments were bandied, and the same abuse hurled about the House.

The government stood firm in its refusal to modify the act
of 1819, or to grant a committee to enquire into its effects, but
it was willing to make concessions in other ways. Parliament
was informed that negotiations were in progress for the prolongation of the Bank's charter until 1843 in return for the
allowance of joint-stock banks in an area within sixty-five miles
of London. But the Bank was opposed to the idea, and nothing
was done until 1826.[1]

A conversion scheme was announced, whereby £150 mn.
of Navy 5% stock was exchanged for a 4½% stock at the rate
of 105 of the new for 100 of the old. The transaction created a
further £7 mn. of debt, and the Bank caused some indignation
by charging its normal commission for the management of this.

The life of the small note, which should have expired on
1 May 1823, was prolonged until 1833, and £2 mn. of taxation
was remitted on malt and salt.

But the most criticised measure was the Dead Weight scheme.
One of the expenses of the government was pensions to those
who had served in the Napoleonic wars, a charge which would
naturally decrease as time passed and the recipients died. It was
proposed to sell a fixed annuity for forty-four years, in return
for the sum required to make each year's payments, and the
proposal was thus equivalent to raising a loan in the early years
and repaying it in the later ones. There was no eagerness to buy
the annuities, and they were first vested in trustees and then
taken over by the Bank (March 1823). Ricardo, Hume and
others did not fail to point out that the scheme was only trans-
ferring to posterity, on rather disadvantageous terms, a burden
which should have been met out of current income, and Lord
King moved a sarcastic preamble to the bill:

Whereas an impatience of taxation, no less ignorant than irre-
sistible, pervades all His Majesty's subjects, and it is highly expedient to afford some relief, and whereas the minimum of relief

1 Hansard, 9 April 1822.

which will give satisfaction, and the least intelligent plan which can plausibly be stated, is that of extending the burden of military and naval pensions over a longer time than the natural lives of the present annuitants, and defraying the expense of the first sixteen years by a series of annual loans... therefore be it enacted that a series of loans shall be raised in a circuitous manner, and that the Lords Commissioners of the Treasury shall have the power to lend to themselves, and to borrow of themselves, and to conceal the whole transaction from themselves, and other ignorant and well-disposed persons.[1]

This, of course, refers to the time when the annuity was vested in trustees. The Bank's contract was terminated in 1828, but before that time it had paid £13,089,419, for which it received an annuity of £585,740.

As a further measure of relief the government borrowed £4 mn. from the Bank on Exchequer bills. There were various suggestions for the use of this, including loans to parishes for public works, and the buying up and storing of surplus wheat. The loan is often referred to as the "public works" loan, though I have found no record of any works which were financed by it. Liverpool was at pains to point out, however, that the loan was not needed for the year's supply, but "to extend and quicken the general circulation".[2]

Up to this point, there had been a division of opinion between the government and the Bank. In announcing the "public works" loan, Liverpool referred to the "extraordinary and injurious" refusal of the Bank to lower its discount rate from 5%, when the market rate was no more than 4%, and continued:

Finding it impossible to induce the Bank to lower its rate of interest on discounts, conformably with the expectations held out in 1819, His Majesty's government resolved on borrowing four million pounds on Exchequer bills from the Bank, with a view to applying that sum in some manner to the relief of the country.[3]

But in June 1822 the Bank changed its policy. Bank rate was reduced to 4%, £1,200,000 was advanced on securities, some

1 Hansard, vol. VII, p. 1396.　　2 Hansard, vol. VII, p. 915.
3 Quoted by R. G. Hawtrey, *A Century of Bank Rate*, p. 14.

purchases of stock were made, and the Bank even departed from precedent to the extent of making loans on mortgage.

It was generally believed that these measures produced an expansion in the circulation of the Bank of England and of the country banks, and that this led to the boom of 1825 and the subsequent crisis, though Tooke again held a quite opposite view.

So far as the Bank of England is concerned, notes rose only from £17·3 mn. in the second quarter of 1822 to £19·3 mn. in the third quarter of 1823, while gold, for which I have no quarterly figures, increased from £11·1 mn. on 28 February 1822 to £12·7 mn. on 31 August 1823. Comparing the same two dates, public securities show a decline from £12·5 mn. to £11·8 mn., in spite of the "public works" loan. Private securities increased from £3·5 mn. to £5·6 mn.; this includes loans on stock and on mortgage, for commercial discounts fell from £3·4 mn. in the second quarter of 1822 to £3·0 mn. in the third quarter of 1823.

Henry Burgess, secretary to the Country Bankers' Committee, compiled the following scale showing the variations in the issues of 122 country banks, including most of the largest and most powerful ones:

1818	1819	1820	1821	1822	1823	1824	1825
12,200	11,991	11,487	11,352	10,778	10,748	11,640	12,478[1]

These figures suggest that the variation in the country notes was much less than was generally supposed, and that, so far from increasing, they actually declined in the year following the extension of the currency of the small note.

Tooke's view is further borne out by movements of interest rates. Consols, which stood at about 76 at the end of 1821, rose to over 80 in October 1822; they then fell back, however, to only 73 in March 1823, partly owing to fears of war in Spain, and it was not until September 1823 that the level of October 1822 was again reached. It thus appears that the efforts of the authorities failed to produce any sensible decline in long-term rates. The 4% Bank rate was almost certainly ineffective, as is shown by the continued decline in commercial discounts. It

1 Committee of 1832, evidence of Henry Burgess.

seems, therefore, that we cannot accuse the Bank of having unduly depressed interest rates in 1822–3, though it is quite another matter to say that it kept them unduly low in 1824–5. Further, it would appear that the stimulating effect of the relief measures came not through monetary channels, but through the stimulus to demand afforded by a budget deficit.

BOOM AND CRISIS, 1824–6

It is probable that, quite apart from the relief measures, trade would have revived in 1823. Industry recovered more quickly than agriculture, and even in 1822, Londonderry could state that

The manufacturing and commercial interests of the country have undergone so favourable a change that, taking them generally, at no period in the history of the country have they been in a position of more healthful, though temperate, prosperity,

without suffering any of the wrath which was usually visited upon expressions of government complacency.[1] By the beginning of 1824, though prices were still low, the sense of well being was general, and we hear no more of the grumbles of two years previously.

Low interest rates continued during 1824, and a second conversion was carried out, reducing the old 4% (not those which had been created in 1822) to a 3½% stock. This was less successful than the previous one, and the Bank had later to find £5 mn. to pay off dissentient holders.[2]

When there was added to the other expansionist influences the prospect of large new markets in South America following our recognition of the independence of the Spanish colonies, the boom developed apace.

Towards the end of 1824 there were to be seen the three features which were to be characteristic of the boom, a great speculation in stocks and shares, a rise in domestic prices, and an increase in imports creating an adverse balance of payments.

It is said that there existed, before 1824, 156 joint-stock companies, with a paid up capital of £34 mn. During 1824–5 there

1 Hansard, vol. VI, p. 354.   2 Committee of 1832, Q. 1839.

appeared the prospectuses of 624 companies with a nominal capital of £372 mn. Many of these never opened subscription lists, but it is estimated that £17 mn., or half the previously existing paid up capital of such companies, was actually subscribed.[1] Of this a great proportion was lost in operations abroad. In addition, foreign loans to the extent of £32 mn. were raised, and £25 mn. was actually remitted abroad. The boom, and the subsequent crash, were aggravated by the fact that only a very small first payment was demanded on shares, so that people were encouraged to take up far more than they could afford to keep, in the hope of selling out in a rising market before further calls fell due. Prices reached their highest point in Feburary 1825, after which there was a slight fall, followed by a pause, and then a disastrous crash in May and June.

Commodity prices began to rise in the summer of 1824, but the movement did not become rapid until the autumn. Naturally the greatest rises were in commodities in which there was a speculative market, especially cotton. The general index rose from 104 in the last quarter of 1824 to 115 in the first quarter of 1825, and to 122 in the second quarter. There was then a fall to 118 in the third, and 117 in the fourth quarter. But so long as the credit structure on which it rested remained unshaken, the high level of prices was substantially maintained. It was only after the financial crash of December that we have the bankruptcies and distress sales of the spring of 1826 producing a really large fall in prices. The index then fell to 111, 102 and 99 in the first three quarters, and only began to recover at the end of the year.

Tooke quotes the following figures for the import of certain raw materials:

Commodity	Imports, 1822	Imports, 1825
Cotton...	142,837,628 lb.	228,005,291 lb.
Wool	19,058,080 ,,	43,816,966 ,,
Raw silk	2,060,292 ,,	2,855,792 ,,
Flax	610,106 cwt.	1,055,233 cwt.
Tallow...	805,238 ,,	1,164,037 cwt.[2]

1 H. English, *Joint-stock Companies formed during* 1824 *and* 1825, 1827.
2 Tooke, *op. cit.* vol. II, p. 155.

The exports to South America, which might have balanced these imports, were sold, if at all, only on credit, so that payment was not received until later. Further, there was the effect of foreign loans and new English companies operating abroad. Thus it was that the exchanges turned against us in the autumn of 1824, and remained at or near gold export point until the autumn of 1825.

Signs of trouble were sufficiently apparent in the spring of 1825. McCulloch, in an article in *The Edinburgh Review*, and Baring in the House, expressed their fears, and Liverpool condemned speculation and warned the speculators that, in the event of a crisis, they need expect no help from the government in the form of the issue of Exchequer bills.[1]

Until the crisis was well advanced, the Bank continued its policy of *laissez faire*, discounting all approved bills at the published rate. The moderate increase in the circulation continued, from £19·1 mn. at the end of 1823 to £19·7 mn. in the first quarter and £19·9 mn. in the second quarter of 1824. But there could be little criticism of this, for the amount of bullion was still very high, £14·2 mn. in January and £13·8 mn. in April 1824. But in the summer of 1824 the exchanges were falling, yet the circulation rose to £20·6 mn., and by October the bullion had fallen to £11·6 mn. In the first quarter of 1825 the circulation further rose to £21·1 mn., while the bullion in February was no more than £8·8 mn. This is the part of the Bank's policy which, deservedly, met with severe criticism. The directors explained that they were only meeting commitments previously formed in the shape of paying off the dissentient holders of the 4%, and meeting the instalment of the Dead Weight, but their critics pointed out that they could easily have done this by reducing their commitments in other directions. The fact was that the men who had most influence in the Court were those who had passed the resolution of 1819 that "A restriction of the circulation of Bank notes will not, in the directors' opinion, result in a favourable turn of the exchanges".[2] The Bank had once again run into difficulties

1 Feavearyear, *The Pound Sterling*, p. 221.
2 Quoted, W. Marston Acres, *The Bank of England from Within*, p. 303.

through refusing to regulate its credit policy by reference to the exchanges.

The effect of this increase in issues was to keep down interest rates, to enable speculation to proceed and the unsound firm to maintain itself for longer than would otherwise have been possible. Market rate remained at 3·5 % throughout 1824, and it was not until the autumn of 1825 that it rose to 4%.

During the summer the Bank kept the securities fairly constant and allowed the withdrawal of gold to produce a gradual decline in the circulation. This policy was maintained until the autumn, by which time the exchanges had become favourable again and the external demand for gold had been replaced by an internal one.

The first failures among the speculators placed some of the country banks in difficulties; many of them were actually insolvent, and others were in a dangerously illiquid position. It was generally believed that their danger was increased by the existence of the small notes, since these were held by poor and ignorant people, who were especially liable to panic.[1]

It was in this position, with its reserve reduced in August to only £3·6 mn., that the Bank tried to contract its issues by more than the decline in its bullion. But market rate had now risen above Bank rate, and the volume of the Bank's commercial discounts was rising. In November there were complaints from the City that the Bank was returning good bills, a most unusual procedure.[2]

The crisis spread to London on 7 December, when the house of Thornton, Pole & Co. asked the Bank for assistance; a loan of £300,000 was given, but in spite of this the firm stopped payment on 12 December. They were followed by other London banks, and in December some seventy banks, in town and country, failed. It became almost impossible to discount bills, for the true rate of interest had risen far above the 5 % permitted by the usury laws. There were, however, ways of getting round the law for those who had the right

1 Cf. Palmer, Committee of 1832, QQ. 271 seq.
2 Feavearyear, op. cit. p. 221.

securities. For instance, Consols were at one time sold for $75\frac{1}{2}$ spot, and $80\frac{1}{8}$ for the account only twenty-five days ahead.[1]

On 13 December the Bank raised its rate to 5 %, no longer in the least deterrent, and decided to discount freely all good bills brought to them. They even relaxed their normal rules, and were "not over nice" as to the security they accepted.[2] Discounts rose at one time to £15 mn., and the quarterly average was £7·9 mn. for the last quarter of 1825 and £10·9 mn. for the first quarter of 1826. At the request of the government £500,000 of Exchequer bills were purchased.[3] The reserve was now very low, and the Bank consulted the government on its policy. The government endorsed the policy of free lending and approved the issue of small notes, provided that it was only temporary, and that the Bank took advantage of the favourable turn in the exchanges to improve its reserve. They categorically refused, however, to consider a suspension, and advised the Bank, if its reserve should be exhausted, to pin a notice on its doors, saying that it had no more gold, but would resume payment shortly. The printing of a limited amount of government legal tender money was considered, but rejected.[4]

The Bank therefore resolved "to pay to the last guinea", a million of small notes were issued, and some relief was produced. By the 17th the worst was over. The Rothschilds bought several millions of gold for the Bank, at a cost of £100,000 above the market price, and "what was more important, whether from fatigue, or whether from being satisfied, the public mind had yielded to circumstances, and the tide turned at that moment, on that Saturday night" (17 December). The reserve touched its lowest level of £1,027,000 on 24 December, but by that time "confidence had become as nearly as possible perfect" again.[5] The acute phase of the crisis was thus short-lived, and Liverpool and Robinson were accurate if injudicious, when they began a letter to the directors of January 1826 with

1 Hawtrey, op. cit. p. 15.
2 Committee of 1832, evidence of Jeremiah Harman, p. 154.
3 Ibid. App. 4.
4 Ibid., evidence of G. Baker Richards.   5 Ibid.

the words: "The panic in the money market having subsided, and the pecuinary transactions of the country having reverted to their accostomed course...."[1]

But though the panic had subsided, conditions were still far from normal. The note circulation had risen to £25·7 mn. at the end of December,[2] and the quarterly average was £24·5 mn. for the first quarter of 1826 and £23 mn. in the second quarter. Market rate of discount was 5 % for the first quarter of 1826, and between 4 and 5 % for the whole year, and it was only at the end of the summer that the Bank's discounts fell to about their normal level.

It is after the passing of the second phase of the crisis that we come to the period of bankruptcies and sharply falling prices. Many firms had only been able to conceal their insolvency because of the ease with which they could obtain discounts, and now their forced sales still further depressed an already falling market. The commissions in bankruptcy recorded in the *London Gazette* for each quarter of 1824–6 are as follows:

1824 ...	264	270	184	281
1825 ...	245	254	180	462
1826 ...	824	824	368	574

The general price index touched a low level of 99 in the third quarter, and the fall in speculative commodities was even greater than this.

The opposition, confusing commercial distress with "the panic in the money market", taunted the government with their letter to the Bank, and there was a strong demand for the issue of Exchequer bills, "the wise remedy of Mr Pitt", as one speaker called it. Liverpool had long since announced that no issue of Exchequer bills would be made, and he stuck firmly to that resolve. The government did, however, use its influence with the Bank. On 14 February, at the government's request, another £2 mn. of Exchequer bills were purchased, and on the 28th the directors considered the following memorandum, signed by Liverpool and Robinson:

1 *Parliamentary Papers*, 1826, vol. XIX.
2 Tooke, *op. cit.* vol. II, p. 187.

1. In the event of the Bank consenting to advance money on the security of goods in the present circumstances of the country, it is understood that these advances should not exceed the sum of three millions in the whole.

2. That, assimilating the principle of these advances to advances made in the ordinary course of discount upon bills of exchange, they shall be subject to repayment in three months.

3. The government to propose to Parliament that the provisions of the act respecting Merchant and Factor, which will be in force in October next, shall be brought into immediate operation in respect of any goods which may be pledged to the Bank under the proposed arrangement.

4. If the Bank should think proper to make advances in conformity to these suggestions, the government agree to submit to Parliament the necessary measures for enabling them to reduce the present amount of the advances of the Bank to the government, by a repayment of six millions, such repayment to be made as soon as may be practicable, and at all events, before the close of the present session of Parliament.

On consideration of this, the following resolution was passed:

That this Court, having distinctly understood the determination of His Majesty's Government not to make any advances for the relief of commercial distress, now prevailing, reluctantly consent to undertake the measure proposed to an extent not exceeding three millions, upon the terms and conditions expressed in the communication of the First Lord of the Treasury, and the Chancellor of the Exchequer.[1]

Boards were set up to make the advances in eight important towns, but less than £400,000 was taken.

The advances on goods were the last outstanding event of the crisis. From that point, the third phase moved smoothly to its conclusion, a few months of painful liquidation followed by slow and steady recovery. By the end of 1826 prices were again rising, monetary conditions had returned to normal, the crisis was no more than a memory.

1 Committee of 1832, App. 4.

THE LEGISLATION OF 1826

The crisis over, the government applied itself to preventing a similar situation in the future. Much of the trouble had been due to the weakness of the country banks, so something must be done to strengthen them. It was decided to suppress the small notes, to allow the formation of joint-stock banks beyond a radius of sixty-five miles of London, and to encourage the Bank to set up branches in the provinces.

The government prohibited the stamping of small notes by order in council, and brought in a bill to prevent the stamping of any such notes after 5 February and to terminate the currency of existing ones in April 1829.[1]

The debates on the Promissory Notes bill, which were long, confused and acrimonious, can best be described in the words of Smart:

Where one set of speakers thought the small notes indefensible, and another thought them right in theory but liable to great abuse in practice, and a third, considering them wrong either one way or the other, argued that "this was not the time to abolish them", while bimetallists, paper money advocates, free traders, protectionists, all saw a chance of ventilating their views, it might be expected that anything like a short abstract would be impossible.[2]

Liverpool, introducing the bill in the Lords, argued that the abolition of the small note would add to the Bank of England's control over the machinery of credit:

The country banks might go on increasing their circulation while the Bank of England, aware of the state of the exchanges, were taking measures to reduce their issues. Now if the circulation of the £1 and £2 notes were replaced by a metallic currency, this could not be the case.[3]

Baring launched a vigorous attack on the Bank for having unduly contracted its issues in November, and for tying up too

1 7 Geo. IV, c. 6.   2 *Economic Annals*, vol. II, p. 347.
3 Hansard, 17 Feb. 1826.

much of its resources in advances to the government; he advocated bimetallism and joint-stock banks giving security for their issues, and tersely summed up the general opinion on the small notes when he described them as "a perfect nuisance".[1]

On the other side it was argued that the small notes ought not to be suppressed until there was gold to take their place, that gold could only be obtained by deflation, and so that the change would lead to a renewal of the troubles of 1821–2.

The country bankers, possibly as Tierney suggested[2] by way of a strike to coerce the government, withdrew the notes much more quickly than had been intended; to meet the lack of small currency caused by this, the government introduced an amendment allowing the stamping of Bank of England small notes up to 10 October. For this they were attacked for capitulating to the country bankers on the one hand, and for discriminating in favour of the Bank on the other, but the bill eventually passed into law in its amended form.

A proposal to extend the suppression of the small note to Scotland was dropped in face of a storm of protest, to which Sir Walter Scott contributed under the name of Malachi Malagrowther.

The second measure proposed by the government involved the alteration of the Bank's charter, and for this its consent was required. On 13 January 1826 Liverpool wrote to the Governor:

The failures which have occurred in England, unaccompanied as they have been by the same occurrences in Scotland, tend to prove that there must have been an unsound and delusive system of banking in one part of Great Britain, and a solid and substantial one in the other.

He continued:

The effect of the law at present is to permit every system of banking *except* that which is *solid* and *secure*.

He hoped that the Bank would establish branches, and would forgo its exclusive right of joint-stock note issue, and he warned

1 Hansard, 10 and 20 Feb.   2 *Ibid.* 20 Feb.

the Bank that it was useless to ask for the prolongation of the charter beyond 1833:

With respect to the continuation of their exclusive privileges in the metropolis and its neighbourhood, it is obvious, from what passed before, that Parliament will never agree to it. Such privileges are out of fashion, and what expectation can the Bank, under present circumstances, entertain that theirs will be renewed.[1]

The directors at first refused, but there must have been some suggestion that they might modify their attitude in return for some compensating advantage, for a second letter from Liverpool, on the 23rd, contains the passage:

Against any proposition for such compensation, the First Lord of the Treasury and the Chancellor of the Exchequer formally protest; but if the Bank should be of the opinion that the concession should be accompanied by other conditions, and that it ought not to be made without them, it is for the Bank to bring forward such conditions.

Seeing that the government was firm, the directors, on the advice of the Committee of Treasury, gave a grudging assent, and the way was cleared for the introduction of the bill.[2]

The Bank Charter Act, 1826,[3] as it finally passed into law, allowed joint-stock banks outside a radius of sixty-five miles from London, permitted them to sue and be sued in the names of their officers, and contained a clause encouraging the Bank to open branches.

The debates on this bill were a good deal less controversial than those on the abolition of the small notes. Both joint-stock banks and Bank of England branches met with some opposition from country banking interests, but most speakers were in general agreement with the bill, though some criticised it for not going far enough.

The debate also revealed a good deal of hostility towards the Bank, apart from criticisms of its policy at any particular moment, a hostility which was also shown in Grenfell's annual motion for an account of the public balances in the hands of the

1 *Parliamentary Papers*, 1826, vol. XIX.   2 *Ibid.*   3 7 Geo. IV, c. 46.

Bank. There was a good deal of jealousy of the Bank's monopoly, a feeling that its profits were too large, and that the profit
on the note issue should go to the state; and there was a widespread objection to the arbitrary power which the Bank was
supposed to possess of manipulating the level of prices and the
value of property. We have seen that Liverpool, himself, was
hostile to the continuance of the Bank's monopoly and, in
introducing the Promissory Notes bill, he hinted at further
changes in the future:

The measure which he had to propose on this subject, he admitted, was but a half measure. And why was it so? Because their
Lordships would recollect that they had the chartered rights of the
Bank to contend with; this was an obstacle to their going further
at present; they ought to go further whenever they could.[1]

We have seen that the two points on which the Bank was
most generally criticised were for having increased its issues
in the autumn of 1824 and the spring of 1825, in spite of the
unfavourable exchanges, and the loss of gold, and for having
unduly contracted them in November. The decision to discount
freely in December was generally approved, though some
people pointed out that it would be dangerous if applied in
different circumstances, and objected to the precedent of the
Bank coming to the aid of commerce.

The Committee of 1832 provided an opportunity to review
judgements after a period of reflection, and first impressions
were not very much modified. Palmer attributed the crisis to
the reduction of interest on government securities, which had
driven people to seek a more profitable and more risky outlet
for their money.[2] The Committee sought an admission that the
reduction in notes from the spring to the autumn of 1825 was
the immediate cause of the crisis, but Palmer and Ward evaded
the issue by suggesting that the reduction was due to the action
of the public rather than of the Bank, an explanation which is
tenable for the summer, but not at all for the autumn, when the
Bank was known to be returning good bills.

1 Hansard, 17 Feb. 1826, p. 462.   2 Committee of 1832, Q. 606.

THE CRISIS AND BANK OF ENGLAND POLICY

The crisis marks the last gasp of one theory of Bank policy and the conception of another. The "legitimate needs of commerce" policy, though discredited in the post-war restriction years, was still held by the senior directors in 1819, and was followed from 1819 to 1822. The directors clamoured for the repayment of their advances to the government, and as they were repaid, the Bank's issues declined, for the legitimate needs of commerce were satisfying themselves without paying anything like 5%.

It was this which brought about the first departure from the old principle, the reduction of the rate of discount in 1822. This was at least a rediscovery of something which the eighteenth century knew well, that the legitimate needs of commerce might vary. From 1822 to 1824 the Bank took up government securities again and tried other means of increasing its issues. William Ward reads into this that the Bank had overstocked itself with gold in preparation for the resumption and was trying to work the reserve back to the one-third ratio which he thought desirable. But we may doubt whether any such idea entered the heads of most of the directors. We have seen how grudgingly the Dead Weight was taken up and the "public works" loan was made, and we can imagine the Court still clinging to its old ideas, but reluctantly giving ground before the concerted pressure of the government and the profit motive.

But when the demand for discounts increased in 1825 it was another matter. "The legitimate demands of commerce" must be met, and if this involved an increase in issues when the exchanges were adverse and the reserve fast ebbing away, that could not be helped.

But from the early summer of 1825 there are signs of a rather different attitude. Perhaps the older directors were alarmed at the shrinkage of the reserve and paid more attention to their younger colleagues. One would give a lot for a full report of the discussions which took place in the Court that year, but in the complete absence of such reports one can only conjecture from the very scanty evidence. According to the evidence of Palmer and Ward, and the opinion of Tooke, the Bank tried to keep its securities constant, and thus allow the drain of bullion to produce an equal diminution in either the circulation or the deposits. Accounts were not frequent enough for us to say for how long and with what effect this policy was pursued, but the mere fact that the Bank was believed to be acting in this way is important, for it is a complete break with the old tradition. Here is a policy, if only a rudimentary one, of regulation by reference to the exchanges; the policy, in fact, which Palmer was to explain in detail in 1832.

It may have been partly this desire to keep the securities even which led to the return of bills in November, though the general impression seems then to have been that the Bank was actually trying to contract its securities. This return of bills, too, seems to have been a complete break with the tradition which had grown up since 1795.

Nor is there any inconsistency between the new policy and the free discounting of December, for then the exchanges were favourable, and it was recognised by the Palmer school, that while contraction was the remedy for an external drain, it only aggravated an internal one, due to lack of confidence in the country banks.

These were the two important lessons which the Bank learned from the crisis, that it must take account of the exchanges in framing its credit policy, and that it must distinguish between an internal and an external drain. A change of policy is usually the result of a process of thought going on gradually in the minds of men, and it is hard to name the day, or even the year, of the change. So far as one can ever do such things, however, we may say that the crisis of 1825 saw the change from the Harman policy to the Palmer policy, from "meeting the legitimate needs of trade" to "keeping the securities even".

THE YEARS OF QUIET, 1826–32

The later part of 1826 saw the slow recovery from the crisis, with confidence gradually reviving and interest rates falling. Market rate fell to 4% at the end of 1826 and 3% in the summer of 1827, and Bank rate was reduced in July 1827 to 4%, where it remained until 1836. But this was not nearly low enough to allow the Bank to compete in the discount market, and in the third quarter of 1827 commercial discounts had fallen to less than £1 mn. The directors, as witness the evidence of Palmer, quoted elsewhere, had quite reconciled themselves to the change.

Trade showed a steady recovery, though by no means to boom levels, but acute distress persisted in agricultural districts. The general price index continued to fall, to 96 at the end of 1827, and from then until the close of 1832 it fluctuated between 91 and 96.

The fall in prices brought an influx of bullion to the Bank; in February 1827 the treasure was over £10 mn., and it remained so, as far as we can tell, until August 1828. There was then a slight drain, important only because it produced another outburst from the bimetallists, and an enquiry by a Committee of the Privy Council into the desirability of a double standard.

The efflux of gold, which began in 1831, threatened to be much more serious. To a demand from France and Belgium, consequent on the political troubles in those countries and an abnormal import of corn, there was added an organised run for gold as part of the Reform Bill agitation. The treasure was reduced to little over £5 mn. before the turning-point was reached at the beginning of 1832.

It is the survival of this drain which is the main point of interest in the period, as the Bank's policy then was taken by some later writers as the model of the sound working of the principles laid down in 1832 and from which, they claimed, the directors subsequently departed. We can follow the position of the Bank at the beginning of each month in the returns furnished to the Committee of 1832. In order to eliminate fluctuations caused by the quarterly advances, I compare corresponding months from May 1830 to April 1832, in the following table (Table IX). The general trend is clear enough. The efflux of bullion led to a diminution of notes of approximately half that magnitude, and the balance was rather more than made up by a decline in the deposits, so that the securities actually de-

Table IX

COMPARISON OF BANK OF ENGLAND RETURNS FOR CORRESPONDING MONTHS, MAY 1830—APRIL 1832

£ millions

Month		Circulation	Deposits	Securities	Bullion
May	1830	22·2	10·7	24·6	10·9
	1831	19·5	9·9	24·5	7·2
June	1830	21·3	11·5	23·6	11·5
	1831	17·8	10·0	22·7	7·4
July	1830	19·6	18·7	28·9	12·2
	1831	17·3	11·3	23·6	7·4
August	1830	22·7	13·2	26·6	11·6
	1831	19·7	10·0	25·9	6·5
September	1830	20·7	11·2	23·6	10·7
	1831	18·5	8·3	22·9	6·3
October	1830	20·2	10·4	22·4	10·6
	1831	18·3	7·2	20·8	6·2
November	1830	20·7	10·9	22·2	9·5
	1831	18·6	8·6	24·5	5·1
December	1830	18·9	11·4	22·9	9·5
	1831	17·4	7·6	22·3	5·3
January	1831	17·9	12·9	23·4	9·5
	1832	17·0	8·9	22·5	5·6
February	1831	20·4	11·7	25·9	8·6
	1832	19·1	9·1	25·6	5·1
March	1831	19·7	10·8	24·5	8·2
	1832	18·0	8·0	23·1	5·3
April	1831	18·8	9·4	22·6	7·8
	1832	17·9	7·4	21·9	5·7

clined slightly. The securities were, however, much the most stable of the four items, so that we may say that the Palmer principle was being genuinely applied. The effect on the market was to cause the rate of discount to rise to 4% at the end of 1831, but it was not found necessary to raise Bank rate, and there is no sign of panic or crisis conditions.

Acting on the advice of the government, the Bank opened

a number of branches during these years. The first was at Gloucester in July 1826, and others followed at Manchester and Swansea (1826), Birmingham, Liverpool, Bristol, Leeds and Exeter (1827), Newcastle (1828) and Hull and Norwich (1829). The services performed by these branches, and the feeling of the country bankers towards them, we have already described.

During the six years from 1826 to 1832 the operation of the Bank had been smooth and singularly frictionless, and by the time the Select Committee on the Renewal of the Bank Charter was appointed its conduct, and the mere lapse of time, had done a great deal to allay the suspicion and hostility with which the Bank was regarded immediately after the crisis.

THE COMMITTEE OF 1832, AND THE BANK CHARTER ACT, 1833

The Committee took enough evidence to fill a large volume, yet its Report occupied only two pages, and consisted merely of a statement of the terms of reference and of the following conclusion:

> On all these, and some collateral points, more or less information will be found in the minutes of evidence; but in none is it so complete as to justify the Committee in giving a decided opinion.

The evidence showed, however, that the most weighty opinion was now sympathetic towards the Bank and in favour of a renewal of the charter. George Carr Glynn expressed his appreciation of the quarterly advances, and thought that the rate of interest had been kept extraordinarily steady during the past six years and that the Bank had exercised "a very wise and liberal discretion" with regard to discounts; he was in favour of renewing the charter, and making Bank notes legal tender.[1] Samuel Jones Lloyd, Sir Coutts Trotter and Samuel Gurney all expressed their satisfaction both with the system and the general conduct of the Bank, and Tooke "believes that the circulation has been exceedingly well conducted during the past three or

1 Committee of 1832, evidence of G. C. Glynn.

four years".[1] Palmer's full exposition of the principles by which the directors were guided was further calculated to allay suspicion. Some of the country bankers complained of the Bank's competition through the branches, but the only general complaint came from Messrs Smith, Dyer and Hart of the Bank of Manchester, who later revealed that they had a particular grievance in that the Bank had refused them a discount account.

In spite of the Committee's view that there was not sufficient evidence, the government decided to bring in a bill, and Althorp submitted a series of proposals to the Bank in August 1833. The charter was to be renewed for twenty-five years, with the option to the government of terminating it after twelve years; bank notes were to be made legal tender, except from the Bank itself, for sums of £5 and more; the usury laws were to be repealed so far as they concerned bills of not more than three months to run; there were to be no joint-stock banks of issue within twenty-five miles of London; all banks of more than six partners were to be considered as joint-stock banks, and no new ones were to be formed except by royal charter; note-issuing joint-stock banks were to be required to hold half their capital in government securities and to publish accounts; Bank of England accounts were to be published weekly for a date three months previously; half of the government debt to the Bank was to be repaid, and the charge for management of the National Debt was to be abolished; the Bank was to accumulate a "rest" of £3 mn. and, after this had been done, any surplus profit after the payment of a dividend of 10% was to go to the state.

The directors submitted criticisms and counter-proposals. They opposed the reduction of the radius of their monopoly and suggested the retention of the sixty-five mile limit; they suggested that accounts should be sent weekly to the Chancellor of the Exchequer, but that only the monthly average should be published; they desired that only a quarter of the government debt should be repaid, and that the charge for managing the National Debt should not be abolished, but only

[1] Committee of 1832, Q. 3884.

reduced by £100,000; they recognised the right of the state to participate in the profits of the note issue, but proposed either a deduction from the charge on the National Debt of £1 for every £100 of notes and deposits above £24 mn., or else that the state should take half of any profit remaining after the accumulation of a "rest" of £3 mn., and the payment of a dividend of 9%.

The government accepted the proposals of the directors, including the second alternative for dealing with profits, except that they insisted on a reduction of £120,000 instead of £100,000 in the charge for managing the Debt. In this form, accordingly, the measure was introduced into the House.[1]

Before these proposals were made, the rumour that it was intended to make Bank notes a legal tender called forth an indignant protest from the country Bankers' Committee, in which they asserted that this would give the Bank an arbitrary power, and

Would expose the pursuits of agriculture, manufactures and commerce to the control of a set of men who have no intercourse with the country, no sympathy with the people, no knowledge of their wants and circumstances—who are not identified with their prosperity, and could suffer nothing from their adversity—who from their habits, cannot have the information required to guide them aright, and have no personal risk or public responsibility to guard them from doing wrong.[2]

The bill was modified in several important respects before its passage. Althorp very reluctantly abandoned the clauses concerning the country banks, save for a declaratory clause making it clear that non-issuing joint-stock banks were legal within the sixty-five mile limit, and a revision of the law with regard to stamps, so as to give more exact information as to the volume of country notes. The latter was introduced as a separate act.

The government considered this as a breach of its agreement with the Bank, and therefore abandoned its claim to a share in the profits. But even so the directors felt that they

1 Select Committee on Joint Stock Banks, 1836, Appendix.   2 *Ibid.*

had a grievance, and the Court of Proprietors adopted a tone of injured righteousness, and passed a strongly worded resolution.

The legal tender clause was slightly modified, as it was suggested that, if £5 notes were made legal tender, it might be impossible to obtain gold from the country banks for wages and other small payments. Hence the wording of this clause was changed from "£5 and over" to "over £5"; with this exception, the main provisions passed unimpaired into law.[1]

The debates on the bill showed a general agreement on the desirability of renewing the charter, but a good deal of difference on particular points, especially the financial bargain with the Bank, the legal tender clause, and the method of publication of the accounts.

Torrens, however, attacked the Horsley Palmer principles, asserting that "the new mode of management was as vicious in theory as it was pernicious in practice", and that

The Bank directors had created a new element of fluctuation, and according to their new system of management, the circulation must vibrate with every vibration of those public and private deposits, over which the directors could have no control.

He foreshadowed the principles of the Currency School in suggesting that the Bank should issue £29 mn. of inconvertible paper, and make issues in excess of that amount only in exchange for gold.[2]

Peel showed how far his views differed from what they became before he introduced the act of 1844. He was opposed to making Bank notes legal tender, "thought that there was great advantage in permitting the issue of notes by solvent country banks", and believed that the chief cause of crises had disappeared with the abolition of the small note: "Since 1825 there had been no instance of a commercial panic because precautions were then taken to prevent the main source of it, by abolishing the £1 and £2 notes."[3]

1 3 & 4 Wm. IV, c. 98.   2 Hansard, 31 May and 28 June 1833.
3 *Ibid*. 28 June.

Thus was passed an act which was of immense importance in nineteenth-century banking history. The making of Bank notes legal tender gave them an advantage over the notes of other banks, which paved the way for the complete unification of the note issue; the modification of the usury laws made Bank rate an effective instrument for regulating credit in time of market stringency; and the declaratory clause with regard to joint-stock banks made possible their great development in the capital.

Chapter Five

THE HORSLEY PALMER EXPERIMENT, AND THE BANK CHARTER ACT, 1844

THE NATURE OF THE EXPERIMENT

Between the end of the Restriction Period and the beginning of the "Currency" and "Banking" controversy there occurred, almost without notice, a great change in the attitude of the Bank directors towards the regulation of their issues. In 1819 the senior directors still thought that the function of the Bank was to supply "the legitimate demands of commerce", and that the only criterion by which to judge of the sufficiency of the circulation was the demand for the discount of first-class commercial bills at what might be deemed a reasonable rate of interest. The Bank formally denied that the note issue could have any effect on the foreign exchanges. In 1827, however, William Ward secured the rescinding of this resolution, and during the next few years there was developed the new rationale of the matter, which was explained to the Committee of 1832 by Palmer.

The connection between Bank of England issues and those of the country banks, between banknotes and prices, and between prices and exchange rates, is now freely admitted, and over-issue is defined in relation to the foreign exchanges:

Over-issue means excess of prices having regard to the prices of other countries. It is quite clear that a bank can only issue legitimately on a demand, and that demand arises upon the prices of the country, but these prices may, by excitement or speculation, be above their relative value with respect to foreign countries; in such case, I maintain an over-issue to exist; and I say this without meaning in the slightest degree to infer a charge against the Banking Interest for that action.[1]

1 Committee of 1832, Q. 371.

Such an over-issue would show itself in an unfavourable exchange and a demand for gold from the Bank, and the corrective would be a reduction of issues.

Asked "What is the process by which the Bank would calculate upon rectifying the exchanges by means of a reduction of its issues?" Palmer replies:

The first operation is to increase the value of money; with the increased value of money there is less facility obtained by the commercial public in the discount of their paper; that naturally tends to limit transactions, and to the reduction of prices; the reduction of prices will so far alter our situation with respect to foreign countries, that it will be no longer an object to import, but the advantages will be rather upon the export; the gold and silver will then come back into the country and rectify the contraction which previously existed.[1]

The only problem, then, was to regulate the issue of banknotes in such a way that this mechanism could work as smoothly as possible, and here it was that Palmer described the rule, which is generally associated with his name:

The principle, with reference to the period of a full currency, and consequently of a par of exchange, by which the Bank is guided in the regulation of their issues (excepting under special circumstances) is to invest and retain in securities bearing interest a given proportion of the deposits and the value received for the notes in circulation, the remainder being held in coin and bullion; the proportion which seems to be desirable, under existing circumstances, may be stated at about two thirds in securities and one third in bullion, the circulation of the country, as far as that may depend upon the bank, being subsequently regulated by the action of the foreign exchanges.[2]

A "full currency" was said to exist when the exchanges were on the point of becoming unfavourable, and when, consequently, the Bank's bullion was at its maximum. Starting from this position, the securities should be kept at a constant amount, so that a reduction in the Bank's gold stock would lead to a corresponding reduction either in the notes or the deposits.

1 Committee of 1832, Q. 678. 2 *Ibid.* Q. 72.

Just as at earlier times, the directors were very anxious to disclaim any active power over the volume of circulation and the level of prices; Palmer emphasises the fact that "the Bank are very desirous not to exercise any power, but to leave the public to use the power which they possess, of returning Bank paper for bullion".[1] The Bank would add to its securities when bullion was coming in, or contract them when it was going out, only in exceptional circumstances. Furthermore, it would not, in general, anticipate expected variations in the exchanges, and, on this ground, Palmer defends the late action of the Bank in the crisis of 1825.

It was an historical accident that, in the late 1820's, the exchanges did turn against us when the Bank held about a third of its liabilities in bullion. But, if the securities are always kept even, there is obviously no reason why this should always be so. Hence the dilemma in which the directors subsequently found themselves. The one-third ratio was exceeded, and still bullion came in. The only way in which the ratio could be maintained was by adding to the securities, and so violating the second of Palmer's principles. The Bank had the power either to keep the securities even, or to keep a proportion of gold to liabilities of one-third at a time of "full currency", but it was only in the special circumstances which existed just before 1832 that the two things were consistent with one another. Before the Committee, Palmer had emphasised the keeping of the securities even, and had stated that securities would be bought as gold came in only in special circumstances. But, as practical men, the directors were very averse to keeping more than a third of their assets in a form which yielded no return, and so all occasions on which the ratio was exceeded came to be regarded as special. In fact, securities were often bought when the bullion was considerably less than one-third of the liabilities, as we shall see. Hence it was that the "rule of 1832" came to be so riddled with exceptions that Palmer was accused of merely rationalising the chance happenings of the past and not propounding a new policy at all.

1 Committee of 1832, Q. 11.

THE BOOM AND CRISIS OF 1836

The first two years after the renewal of the charter were quiet and fairly prosperous. The complaints of the agricultural interest were still loud, and a Select Committee of 1833 found that they had some justification. But a similar Committee on the state of manufactures found, not distress, but considerable prosperity. Industrial activity increased steadily to the end of 1835, when Tooke thus describes the situation:

The extraordinary activity which prevailed in the manufacturing and mining districts was necessarily accompanied by a very extensive employment of the working population at full wages. At the same time, the extensive work upon the lines of the great railways, which was in progress, served to employ considerable numbers of agricultural labourers, and the earnings, even in money, by the operative classes, were, in some cases, greater than in the periods of the highest prices of provisions.[1]

The general price index, which stood at 94 at the end of 1832, rose to 100 at the end of 1833, fell back to 95 in the third quarter of 1834, but then rose steadily to 103 at the end of 1835, and jumped to 116 in the second quarter of 1836. The price of corn, however, was affected by a series of very abundant harvests, and dropped steadily down to the end of 1835. Three per cent Consols rose from 83 to 90 during 1833, and continued at about that price. The market rate of discount, which had risen to 4% at the end of 1931, fell to $2\frac{1}{2}$% in 1833, but rose again to 3·8% at the end of 1835. Then, in 1836, when prices were rising sharply, and speculation was rife, the rate was actually lower at 3·6% in the first quarter, and 3·5% in the second. This shows how little the Bank was, as yet, concerned with checking fluctuations by means of the rate of interest and lends some support to those who criticised its policy.

The act of 1833 provided for the repayment to the Bank of a quarter of its capital, and the payment was made in 3% annuities at the rate of £100 for each £90 of debt, an operation for which the government was much criticised.

1 *History of Prices*, vol. II, p. 255.

In studying the Bank's operations from 1832 to 1844 we have a series of weekly statements,[1] which I have combined into monthly averages, and which appear in Chart II. The rhythmical fluctuations are, of course, due to the payment of the dividends and the quarterly advances made by the Bank at that time.

The efflux of bullion in 1831–2 is reversed after the spring of that year and, by October 1833, there existed what Palmer would describe as a "full currency". The position then was:

Circulation	...	£18·9 mn.	Securities	...	£23·9 mn.
Deposits	...	£12·8 mn.	Bullion	...	£10·9 mn.

the bullion just over a third of the notes and deposits combined. From then, until March 1835, there was a drain, attributed by Palmer to loans to Portugal, and in the latter month the figures read thus:

Circulation	...	£18·1 mn.	Securities	...	£24·5 mn.
Deposits	...	£10·0 mn.	Bullion	...	£6·3 mn.

Total liabilities had fallen by £3·6 mn., but of this only 0·8 mn. was in the circulation, against a loss of gold of 4·6 mn. The ratio of gold to liabilities had shrunk to little over a quarter. Moreover, March 1835 is exceptional for the low level of the deposits, and any of the months immediately preceding or following would have shown a more adverse picture. That the ratio should fall during a drain was, of course, a normal part of the Palmer system, but it is notable that the reduction in the amount of the liabilities was not quite as large as that in the bullion, and that such reduction as there was operated almost entirely upon the deposits.

From March 1835 to March 1836 there was again an influx of bullion, and, according to Palmer's principle, the Bank ought to have remained passive, allowing its liabilities to increase only by the amount of the gold which it received, so that the desired ratio might have been restored. The position in March 1836 was as follows:

Circulation	...	£17·8 mn.	Securities	...	£26·1 mn.
Deposits	...	£13·3 mn.	Bullion	...	£8·0 mn.

1 Appendices to Reports of Select Committees on Banks of Issue, 1840 and 1841, and Committee of Secrecy on Commercial Distress, 1848.

The circulation was a trifle smaller than in the previous year, but both the deposits and the securities had considerably increased, and the ratio remained little more than a quarter.

This deviation from the rule of 1832 was justified by Palmer on a plea of special circumstances. There was an accumulation of savings-bank money in the Bank during 1834. Then there were the balances of the East India Company arising from the termination of its charter and the liquidation of its trading assets. These balances began to accumulate in 1834, and reached a maximum of £4·7 mn. in January 1837. The Bank paid interest on this money, contrary to the usual rule, and re-lent it to the bill market. The Bank's case was that, otherwise, the Company would have lent the money directly, and that it was, therefore, acting only as an agent in the matter, performing a service for the Company and, at the same time, preserving for itself a greater measure of control over the currency than it would otherwise have had. Lastly, there was the loan raised in August 1835 to compensate the West Indian slaveowners. The government offered a discount of $3\frac{1}{2}\%$ for the prompt payment of the loan, and the Bank offered advances on stock at 3%, so that there was a profit on borrowing from the Bank to pay up the loan. The money thus subscribed before it was needed was simply left on deposit with the Bank. Palmer explained that it was usual for the Bank to assist the subscription of a loan by advancing subscriptions subsequent to the second on the security of the first two, and that the present strange transaction was simply an alternative to this. Anyway, these deposits, as they lay idle in the Bank, can have had no inflationary effect, and the only loser seems to have been the government.

The directors claimed that these deposits were "special", that the Bank knew when they would be required and, meanwhile, was entitled to lend the whole of them at interest, and that they should be left out of account in applying the rule laid down by Palmer. Palmer, himself, constructed a revised table leaving out these transactions, and this naturally showed a much greater uniformity in the securities and a decline in total liabilities much nearer the decline in bullion.

It is important to note the effect of these transactions on the rate of interest. Bank rate remained, during all this time, at 4%, but this was not the only way by which the Bank exerted its influence. There were also the quarterly advances. These advances were usually made for about six weeks only and at the market rate of interest, and from September 1832 to May 1835 this principle was followed. In August 1835, however, there was a great departure from principle. Market rate remained at 3·8%, yet the advances were offered at $3\frac{1}{2}$%, and the offer was made on 5 August, more than three weeks earlier than usual, and for the unprecedentedly long period of 76 days. The favourableness of the terms is shown by the fact that the amount borrowed rose from £2·5 to £5 mn. In November 1835 and February 1836 the advances were offered again, at $3\frac{1}{2}$%, for periods of 56 and 63 days respectively, and £5 mn. was taken each time. As we have seen, this led to a fall in the market rate of discount at a time when the prices both of stocks and commodities were rising fast. In the third quarter, market rate was rising, averaging 4·5%, yet advances from 2 June to 12 August were made at only 4% and it was not until September that the charge was raised to 5%. On 25 August 1835 came the offer of advances on stock at $3\frac{1}{2}$%, a further break with tradition.[1] Furthermore, there were the East India deposits, which the Bank was re-lending at such rates as it could get from the brokers. It seems, then, that we can hardly acquit the Bank of the charge of having forced down market rate at the very time when it should have been rising, in the first and second quarters of 1836, and of having delayed its rise during the autumn of that year.

Meanwhile credit facilities were being further increased by the formation of new joint-stock banks (not that this implies any censure on their conduct), and dangerous symptoms were beginning to appear. There was a burst of new flotations on the stock exchange similar to, though smaller than, that of 1825, and there was great speculation in a number of commodities, notably tea and cotton. The high range of prices would prob-

1 Speech of J. Hume, Hansard, 8 July 1839.

ably have turned the exchanges against us in any case, but the process was accelerated by the reduction of the gold content of the American dollar, leading to the absorption of gold in place of silver by that country.

At its peak, in March 1836, the Bank's reserve was only £8 mn., and from that point it was reduced to only £4 mn. in January 1837. Palmer stated that the Bank's policy was to keep the securities even "as near as circumstances would permit". Bank rate was raised to 4½% in July and to 5% in September; quarterly advances had been made from 2 June to 12 August at 4% and £3·6 mn. had been taken. But the next advance was made on 1 September, rather later than usual, at 5% and for only 49 days, and the amount taken dropped to £1·3 mn. For the moment Bank rate was above market rate, but this did not last, as market rate averaged 5·3% for the last quarter of 1836 and 5·5% for the first quarter of 1837.

Quarterly and seasonal fluctuations make a month-to-month comparison of Bank statements misleading, so we will test the working of Palmer's rule by comparing corresponding months in the periods March 1835 to February 1836, when gold was coming in, and March 1836 to February 1837, the period of the drain (Table X). It will be noticed that the circulation for corresponding months remained very uniform, the variations falling almost entirely on the deposits on the one hand, and the securities and bullion on the other. The one exception is the increase of rather over £1 mn. in the circulation in January 1837, consequent upon the failure of the Northern and Central Bank. The security figures illustrate the inflationary policy which we have mentioned. The May, June, July and August figures reveal a considerable excess in 1836 over 1835, for the expansion which was continuing during the summer of 1836 had not begun in the corresponding period a year before. The September figures are approximately equal, and in October and November it is the 1835 figures which are the larger. In 1835, at this time, the Bank was lending at less than market rate, while in 1836 Bank rate was temporarily above market rate, and the Bank was trying to reduce its commitments. The remaining months show an approximate equality, for the expansion of credit in the beginning of 1836 is offset by assistance to the Northern and Central Bank, and the American houses in the following year, when Bank rate was again below market rate. Thus we see that "special circumstances" had caused very considerable deviations from the rule.

Table X

COMPARISON OF BANK OF ENGLAND RETURNS FOR CORRESPONDING MONTHS: MARCH 1835–FEBRUARY 1837

£ millions

Month		Circulation	Deposits	Securities	Bullion
March	1835	18·1	10·0	24·5	6·3
	1836	17·8	13·3	26·1	8·0
April	1835	18·8	11·8	27·3	6·1
	1836	18·5	14·0	27·6	7·6
May	1835	18·6	10·1	25·2	6·0
	1836	18·0	12·8	26·2	8·4
June	1835	17·8	11·0	24·8	6·5
	1836	17·2	14·9	27·8	7·1
July	1835	18·9	13·8	29·2	6·3
	1836	18·6	16·2	31·4	6·2
August	1835	18·5	12·5	27·5	6·2
	1836	18·4	13·4	29·2	5·5
September	1835	17·5	13·8	27·7	6·3
	1836	17·4	12·2	27·3	5·2
October	1835	17·6	18·3	32·4	6·1
	1836	17·6	13·7	29·2	4·8
November	1835	17·5	18·2	31·5	6·4
	1836	17·4	12·6	28·3	4·3
December	1835	16·7	19·6	31·4	7·5
	1836	16·9	15·8	31·6	4·2
January	1836	18·0	18·5	31·4	7·6
	1837	19·1	16·0	32·5	4·0
February	1836	18·2	14·5	28·0	7·7
	1837	18·5	10·3	28·2	4·0

The further course of the crisis may be briefly summarised. From September the foreign drain of gold ceased, to be replaced by an internal one. Prices, which had reached a peak in the second quarter of 1836, at first fell gradually, the general index standing at 113 for the end of the year. Thenceforward, there was a sharper fall to 96 in the third quarter of 1837, a fall which Tooke states was confined to the speculative commodity markets. In November the Northern and Central Bank applied to the Bank of England for assistance and, in spite of generous support, it stopped payment in January. This, however, was the only major banking failure. The rapid fall in prices at the beginning of 1837 found a number of commercial firms in distress, especially those in the American trade. In February some of these applied for, and received, assistance from the Bank, but in June they stopped payment. But commercial failures, like banking ones, were fewer in 1836 than in 1825, and one has the impression that the resulting difficulties were less widespread.

A comparison of this account with that of the crisis of 1825–6 will show how very similar was the course and timing of events. In each case there was an expansion of the Bank's liabilities and a reduction in the market rate of interest at a time when trade would naturally have been reviving. In each case there followed a period of intense activity, rising prices, and speculation on the stock exchange and in commodity markets. This turned the exchanges against us, and led to a drain of gold. Then, before the drain had produced great monetary stringency, the boom broke, and prices fell, though not yet at all rapidly. The foreign drain was checked, but there had occurred some failures and loss of confidence, and this produced an internal demand. Too late, the Bank raised interest rates and tried to contract its liabilities. Falling prices and monetary policy thus combined to produce embarrassment, failures and loss of confidence, and, when these reached crisis proportion, the Bank was again induced to change its policy, and to offer liberal assistance to firms in distress. This banking crisis produced a more rapid fall in prices, through the forced sales of firms which were in difficulties, and this continued for some months.

The crisis died down in the summer of 1838, leaving behind a trail of argument and recrimination. Palmer, in his *Causes and Consequences of the Recent Pressure on the Money Market*, tried to throw the whole blame on the joint-stock banks. Samuel Jones Lloyd, Thomas Tooke, and others pointed out that the increased facilities created by the joint-stock banks had been largely offset by a decline in the number of private banks; they cited the fact that only one of the joint-stock banks had failed as proof of their good conduct, and charged the Bank with having caused the crisis by its undue depression of the rate of interest and delay in taking any precautionary measures.

Select Committees of the House of Commons enquired in 1836 and 1837 into the conduct of the joint-stock banks, but they were concerned more with legal details than with the general effect of the new institutions on currency and credit. Within their limits, however, the enquiries vindicated the banks, which, with the notable exception of the Northern and Central, were generally shown to be managed by men of long experience in private banking, and run on cautious and rational principles.

THE LAST YEARS OF THE HORSLEY PALMER EXPERIMENT, 1837–44

The return to normal conditions produced its effect on the Bank and, by February 1838, the bullion was again just over a third of the liabilities:

Circulation	...	£19·3 mn.	Securities ...	£22·9 mn.
Deposits	...	£11·1 mn.	Bullion ...	£10·3 mn.

Bank rate was reduced to 4% in February, market rate for the quarter averaging only 3·2%, and at about the same time £1 mn. of gold was shipped to the United States. Of this transaction Macleod says: "Of all the acts of mismanagement in the whole history of the Bank, this is perhaps the most outstanding."[1] As the bullion was, even after this, more than a third of the liabilities, and as there was no reason to fear trouble in the immediate future, it is difficult to concur in this censure. It does, however, illustrate the eagerness of the directors to get rid of any bullion in excess of one-third of the liabilities. Palmer stated that the purpose of the shipment was to enable the American banking system to put its house in order and so

1 Macleod, *Theory and Practice of Banking*, p. 1016.

facilitate trade with the United Kingdom, and "to prevent the derangement of the English currency".[1]

The year 1838 was uneventful, but the beginning of 1839 brought a marked turn for the worse. The domestic price level was rising, the Silberling index moving from 102 at the beginning of 1838 to 108 in the last quarter, and 112 in the first two quarters of 1839. The harvest of 1838 was so bad as to make necessary an abnormal import of corn to the value of £10 mn.[2] American securities were being sold in large quantities on the London market. The return of Russia to a silver standard from one of inconvertible paper produced, indirectly, a demand for gold. Finally, there was, towards the end of 1838, financial pressure on the Continent, culminating in the failure of the Bank of Belgium and of Lafitte's Bank in Paris.

The reserve was falling rapidly during the spring. Market rate of discount rose to 4·3 % for the second quarter, and Palmer mentions a demand for discounts, beginning in April, which was met by the sale of Exchequer bills.[3] But it was not until 16 May that Bank rate was raised to 5 %, and the reserve for May averaged no more than £4·1 mn. A credit of £500,000 was opened in Paris, and the Dead Weight Annuity was put up for sale. But no satisfactory offers were received, so in July it was pledged to a group of Paris bankers as security for a further credit of £2·5 mn. The treasure reached only 2·5 mn. in August, and remained at that point for three months, while the credit in Paris was being gradually used up. Market rate rose to 6% in the third and 6½% in the last quarter of 1839. Bank rate was raised, on 1 August, to 6%, the first time that the formerly conventional level of 5% had been exceeded. By the turn of the year the pressure was abating, and Bank rate was reduced to 5% in January, though use continued to be made of the credit in Paris until April.

The crisis of 1839 was unlike the two preceding ones in that it was not followed by any extraordinary commercial or bank-

1 Palmer's evidence before Committee of 1840.
2 Tooke, *op. cit.* vol. III, p. 71.
3 Palmer's evidence before Committee of·1840.

ing failures, and that the fall in prices was very gradual. The
Silberling index stood at 110 for the second half of 1839 and the
first quarter of 1840, and then remained for a whole year at 108.
It was not until the summer of 1841, long after the crisis had
passed, that there was a sharp fall.

There is no sign in 1839 of the artificial reduction of the rate
of interest which had preceded the two former crises. During
1838 Bank rate was 4%, while market rate fluctuated between
3·2 and 2·7%. During the successive rises of 1839 Bank rate
still remained above market rate, and it was only during the last
months of 1839, when the pressure was at its height, that the
relationship was reversed. Nor was there the abuse of the
quarterly advances which we noticed in 1835–6. Except for the
last advance of 1838 and the first of 1839, all advances were
made on bills of exchange only; all were for the normal time;
and only the advance of February 1839 appears to have been at
all below market rate. Even then, however, only £1·8 mn. was
demanded.

This first use of Bank rate as a means of credit regulation
provoked the following statement of theory from Palmer:

> The principle, as I understand it, of 1832, was, in the event of any
> pressure on the Bank, the directors should have the power to advance
> the rate of interest, at their discretion, without limit, for bills not
> exceeding three months to run, with a view to so far enhancing the
> value of money as to drive down the prices of commodities.[1]

This, Palmer claimed, had been done, though the evidence of
the Silberling index hardly supports the claim.

It was widely held by critics of the Bank, and admitted by
Palmer, that Bank rate should have been raised sooner. Tooke
also criticised the directors for asking too high a price for the
Dead Weight, and entering into a humiliating agreement with
foreign bankers rather than part with this profitable asset. But
the sale of the annuity within this country would not of itself
have produced an effect similar to the credit in Paris, for the
sale would have created a shortage of money and a still further

1 Committee of 1840, Q. 1419.

Table XI

COMPARISON OF BANK OF ENGLAND RETURNS FOR CORRESPONDING MONTHS, 1838–9

£ millions

Month		Circulation	Deposits	Securities	Bullion
January	1838	19·0	12·7	24·2	9·9
	1839	18·6	12·5	24·3	8·3
February	1838	19·3	11·1	22·9	10·3
	1839	18·5	8·1	22·2	7·0
March	1838	18·4	10·4	21·2	10·3
	1839	17·8	7·8	21·9	6·4
April	1838	19·5	11·5	23·9	9·7
	1839	18·6	8·3	24·6	4·9
May	1838	19·2	10·5	22·8	9·6
	1839	18·1	7·3	23·9	4·1
June	1838	18·4	9·2	20·3	10·0
	1839	17·5	7·0	23·2	3·9
July	1838	20·3	11·3	24·6	9·7
	1839	18·4	9·7	27·7	3·1
August	1838	19·8	10·3	22·0	9·5
	1839	18·0	7·2	25·9	2·5
September	1838	18·7	8·3	20·1	9·5
	1839	17·2	5·8	23·6	2·5
October	1838	18·8	9·6	21·4	9·2
	1839	17·3	6·2	24·1	2·5
November	1838	18·4	9·1	20·6	9·4
	1839	16·4	5·7	21·9	3·1
December	1838	17·7	10·3	20·9	9·5
	1839	15·8	6·9	21·4	4·1

demand for discounts, which could only have been checked by a rise in the rate of interest, probably to the point which would have produced many commercial failures and a catastrophic fall in prices. The Bank would have claimed, we think justly, that as the chief causes of the difficulty were external and would probably be temporary, it had the right and the duty to spare the country the pain of extreme contraction of credit.

Again the Bank was criticised for not adhering to the rule of keeping the securities even. Comparing the corresponding months of 1838 and 1839 (Table XI) we find that the 1839 figures are greater from April to November, the difference reaching £3·9 mn. in August; but even so, the securities increased by very much less than the bullion declined. Of the balance, some fell on the circulation, but considerably more on the deposits. This led to the argument as to how far deposits were the same as money, and gave those who believed that there was an essential difference a powerful argument in favour of the separation of the departments.

Besides the crisis, the year 1839 was notable for a very violent attack on the Bank in the Commons by Joseph Hume. Hume moved for a committee to consider the conduct of the Bank, and submitted four resolutions, accusing it of having violated the principles of 1819 and the rules laid down by its directors, of bringing about arbitrary variations in the rate of interest to its own profit and the confusion of honest traders, and of having occasioned by its conduct the crises of 1825 and 1836, and the difficulties of 1839. He went into details of Bank policy, and his speech is an excellent summary of the main criticisms which were current. The motion was rejected, but the speech is significant of the violent antagonism which the Bank had provoked in some quarters.[1]

The years 1840–4 were uneventful, and again the Bank was fortunate in having a few quiet years for the wrath which had fallen on it to die down, before the time came for the renewal of its charter.

Select Committees of the House of Commons enquired into the question of the note issue in 1840 and 1841, examining many witnesses and asking some thousands of questions without reaching any conclusion. The account of the Bank's actions given by Palmer and Norman has formed the basis of much of the preceding pages, and we shall have to deal with the various theoretical arguments in the next chapter.

As we have seen, prices at first fell only slightly after 1839, but, from 108 in the first quarter of 1841, the index began to fall sharply to only 84 in the third quarter of 1843. 1838 was the beginning of a run of bad harvests, and it was not until 1841 that the corn crop was again above the average. These two facts are enough to explain the continuance of a low gold reserve and high rates of interest. Bank rate fell to 5 % in January 1940, and

1 Hansard, 8 July 1839.

remained there for two years, market rate meanwhile never
going below 4%, and rising to 5½% at the end of 1840. Instead
of again raising Bank rate, the directors limited the usance of
bills to 65 days. In spite of these high rates, and of very general
depression of industry in 1841, the return of gold was only
hesitating, and the reserve in October 1841 was only £4·1 mn.

Then falling prices and good harvests produced their effect,
and there was a great influx of gold. Bank rate was reduced to
4% in April 1842, and market rate fell very much lower, being
little more than 2% for the greater part of 1843 and 1844. At
the same time, trade and industry were reviving. By February
1844 the position of the Bank was as follows:

| Circulation | ... | £21·6 mn. | Securities | ... | £22·4 mn. |
| Deposits | ... | £13·4 mn. | Bullion | ... | £15·9 mn. |

The bullion was thus unprecedented in amount, and much more
than a third of the liabilities. During the influx the Bank had
adhered very closely to the rule of keeping the securities even
and had not fallen into the temptation of expanding credit in
order to rid itself of the excess gold. It was, therefore, in conditions of reviving trade and expanding credit, on which the
action of the Bank was restraining rather than otherwise, that
the Bank charter came up for reconsideration.

THE BANK CHARTER ACT, 1844

As a result of the crises of the 1830's Peel had profoundly
modified the views which he held in 1833, and his new bill embodied to the full the principles of the Currency School. The
main provisions, as they eventually passed into law, were as
follows:

No new banks of issue were to be allowed, and existing ones,
other than the Bank of England, were to be limited to a monthly
average not greater than the average of the three months preceding the introduction of the bill.

Any issuing bank which suspended payment, ceased issuing
for any reason, or entered into an amalgamation as a result of

which the new form had more than six partners, was to forfeit its right of issue.

The Bank of England was to be divided into two departments. The issue department was to issue notes against securities to the value of £14 mn., and against any bullion which it might hold, provided that the amount of silver should never be more than one-fifth of the total bullion. The issue department was obliged to buy gold bullion at £3. 17s. 9d. per oz. of standard fineness, and to pay its notes on demand in sovereigns (equivalent to selling gold at £3. 17s. 10½d. per oz.).

The banking department was left free to conduct its business in the same way as any other joint stock bank.

The fiduciary issue could be raised by order in Council to the extent of two-thirds of the issue of any bank which forfeited its rights, the profits of such extra issues to go to the state.

The accounts of the Bank were to be published weekly.

The charge for the management of the national debt was to be reduced by £120,000, and the Bank was to pay £60,000 a year in lieu of stamp duty on its notes, leaving a net payment from the government to the Bank of £68,000.

On these terms, the charter was to be renewed for twenty-five years, with the option to the government of terminating it any time after ten years.[1]

The debate on the bill was dull. Peel and Charles Wood gave sound expositions of the views of the Currency School, but there was no good protagonist of the Banking School.

Peel indulged in the common sport of making gibes at those who favoured any other monetary standard than gold at £3. 17s. 10½d. per oz. "There is no more reason", he said, "for making the sovereign pass for twenty-five shillings than for making the foot consist of sixteen inches instead of twelve."[2] He insisted on the distinction between banknotes and other instruments of credit:

I think experience shows that the paper currency, that is promissory notes payable to the bearer on demand, stand in a certain

1 7 & 8 Vict. c. 32.   2 Hansard, 6 May 1844.

relation to the gold coin and the foreign exchanges, in which other forms of paper credit do not stand.

Once the note issue were regulated according to sound principles he believed that other forms of credit could safely be left to adjust themselves. Defending the monopoly of note issue, he pointed out that the virtue of competition was to produce the largest possible supply at the lowest possible price, and that "we do not want an abundant supply of cheap promissory paper". The separation of the departments would ensure the automatic regulation of the note issue, and the conduct of the rest of its affairs could then be left entirely to the Bank:

With regard to the banking business of the Bank, I propose that it should be governed by exactly the same principles as would govern that of any other body dealing with banknotes.

Charles Wood stressed the virtues of the separation of the departments:

The essential point is that, in all its fluctuations, the currency should so vary as to preserve its value in the same manner as would occur in a metallic circulation...the variations should correspond in time and amount with those which would occur in a circulation consisting of the precious metals.

The precious metals can only be obtained by the sacrifice of capital, and

The increase of notes, therefore, ought to be subject to the same check as would operate on the increase of a metallic circulation, that is a previous sacrifice of capital in the deposit of bullion to the extent of the increase in paper.[1]

The reasoned objections of Tooke and Fullarton are not represented in the debate, and the opposition was led by Hawes, who denied that banknotes could ever have any influence over prices, and that any over-issue had taken place either during or since the Restriction Period. The opposition

1 Hansard, 6 May 1844.

was as feeble in numbers as in argument, and the bill was passed by the Commons by 135 votes to 30, and by the Lords without a division.

Thus was passed the act which regulated the working of the Bank up to 1914, and of which substantial traces still remain. It remains briefly to consider its effects.

Peel believed, and with good reason, that the passage of the bill had secured for all time the convertibility of the banknote. The gold in the issue department could be exhausted only if the notes in circulation were reduced to £14 mn. The notes actually held by the public had never been so few as this since the resumption of cash payments, and this £14 mn. would now have to include not only notes held by the public, but the reserve of the banking department as well. It was inconceivable that a drain of gold could persist in the face of such a drastic contraction.

A number of opponents of the act pointed out that a much more likely contingency than the exhaustion of the gold reserve was that the reserve of the banking department might be exhausted while the issue department still had a considerable quantity of gold. This contingency seems to have been envisaged by Peel, for when the London bankers submitted a memorandum urging that some provision be embodied in the bill for its relaxation in time of crisis, he replied:

His Majesty's servants do not consider it to be consistent with their duty to apply to parliament for a discretionary authority to be vested in any public department... to sanction an increase of issues by the Bank upon securities, excepting under the circumstances provided for in the bill.[1]

But on 4 June 1844 he wrote to the Bank directors concerning this possibility:

It may occur in spite of our precautions, and if it does, and *if it is necessary* to assume a grave responsibility for the purpose of meeting it, I daresay men will be found willing to assume such responsibility ... I would rather trust to this than impair the efficiency and possible

1 Parker's *Peel*, vol. III, p. 142.

success of those measures by which one hopes to control evil tendencies in the beginning, and to diminish the risk that extraordinary measures may be necessary.[1]

So far as the sponsors of the act imagined that they had reduced the art of central banking to a rule of thumb they were quite mistaken.

The effect of a drain of gold fell first on the banking department, for notes were taken from it in order to be exchanged for gold. A suspension of the banking department would have been almost, if not quite, as serious as the suspension of convertibility. The directors had now to guard against the one by just the same means and in just the same circumstances as they formerly had against the other. The Bank could not directly control the total volume of notes, but it could control the amount in the hands of the public, by varying the reserve of the banking department. It still had just the same instruments for controlling the public demand for notes—changes in the terms for discounts and advances, and the buying and selling of securities—as it had before the passage of the act. Furthermore, the reserve of the banking department was subject to just the same influences as had formerly affected the gold reserve, and for the efficient protection of the one, as of the other, the Bank was bound to watch the foreign exchanges, and all the complex factors affecting the balance of payments. It still had the same unwritten obligation as lender of last resort, and it still had to weigh in the balance its duty to commerce and its duty to its creditors, and to make the same delicate and difficult decisions.

In fact, though the act, by a device of accountancy, transferred the seeming point of danger, it left both the powers and responsibilities of the Bank very much as they had been before. The subject of our later chapters will therefore be not something quite new, but the continuation of the story of how the Bank gained experience and power in the performance of the same general functions.

1 *Ibid.* p. 140.

Chapter Six

THE CURRENCY AND BANKING CONTROVERSY

As we have seen, the toil and trouble of the Bank Restriction Period gave rise to very few new developments in economic theory. It did, however, canvass and secure general acceptance for views previously held only by the authors of little read works on technical economics. Progress in the social sciences has often been made up of periods when thought made rapid advances, followed by times of intellectual quiet in which the time lag between the thought of the few and the beliefs of the many was made up. The Restriction Period was of the latter sort. The result of this work of consolidation was the emergence of a body of orthodox economic doctrine such as had not previously existed. First and foremost, so far as our present subject is concerned, it was agreed that the standard of value was and ought to be gold. The advocates of an issue of government inconvertible paper, of a silver standard, or of bimetallism, still raise their voices in time of trouble, but they are voices crying in the wilderness. Secondly, the broad outlines of the quantity theory were generally accepted. The changes in prices of the post-war years had induced a more careful consideration of the mechanism which connects the volume of money with the price level. If money be taken to include all instruments of payment, then the dispute was not whether the volume of money really did influence prices, but as to the relation between different sorts of money, and their varying degrees of potency. In fact, however, the word was not used in this comprehensive sense, and the problem resolved itself, like so many others, into a matter of definition. What is money? Thirdly, there was accepted the theory of international price adjustments advocated by Ricardo and the Bullion Report, which had effectively displaced both its converse, the view that high domestic prices promote a favourable balance of trade, and Thornton's income theory of transfer.

In fact, during the quarter of a century following the resumption, monetary theory slides down to a lower plane. We are concerned less with general principles and more with administrative details. How was the Bank to regulate its issues so as to ensure the maintenance of convertibility? What was the effect of the growth of deposit banking and the cheque system? and so on.

I shall, however, start as before with fundamental theory, and then try to show how its implications were worked out in practical details.

MONEY, INTEREST AND PRICES

The events which followed the resumption had brought about a more careful study of the connection between money and prices; neither side regarded it in the facile way which we have noticed in the Restriction Period, and neither denied it altogether. Between Overstone and Tooke, the most moderate members of their respective schools, there is a large measure of agreement. Overstone says:

Probably after the most laborious investigation of it, we can only come to the conclusion that, the immediate effect of any variation in the amount of the circulating medium may be overestimated, whilst there undoubtedly exists a very intimate connection between them. Indeed, unless this is admitted, the whole doctrine of regulating the circulation by reference to the exchanges falls to the ground, and we are left without any principle on which the management of the circulation can rest.[1]

And again:

Fluctuations in the currency are seldom if ever the original and exciting cause of fluctuations in prices and in the state of trade. The buoyant and sanguine character of the human mind; miscalculations as to the relative extent of supply and demand; changes of taste and

1 *Remarks on the Management of the Circulation in* 1839, p. 120.

fashion; legislative enactments and political events; excitement or depression in the condition of other countries connected with us by active trading intercourse; an endless variety of casualties acting upon those sympathies by which masses of men are often urged into a state of excitement or depression; all or some of them are generally the original exciting causes of those variations in the state of prices. ... The management of the currency is a subsidiary agent; it seldom originates, but it may and often does exert an influence in restraining or augmenting the volume of commercial oscillations.[1]

The way in which changes in the quantity of money work their way through to prices is thus described by Overstone:

Contraction of the circulation acts first upon the rate of interest—then upon the price of securities—then upon the market for shares etc.—then upon the negotiation of foreign securities—at a later period upon the tendency to enter into speculation in commodities—and lastly upon prices generally.[2]

The whole of Tooke's *History of Prices* is aimed at the statistical refutation of the rigid form of the quantity theory, yet he is at great pains to combat the accusation that he denies any connection between the quantity of money and prices:

In no instance have I advanced any general proposition so extreme as that "No mismanagement of the currency could create, intensify or prolong the evils of commercial oscillations". I have merely endeavoured to show that, managed as the currency has been, although an undue amount of issue may have aggravated the evil when it existed, yet prices and the state of trade have been, "So long as the paper has been convertible, and the issuers of it solvent, only indirectly and distantly connected with variations in the amount of the currency, whilst other causes have affected them more immediately and powerfully". It is distinctly stated in the account which I have given of the great disturbances of the state of the markets for commodities in 1825, that, although originating in other causes which would have operated to a great extent under a purely metallic varia-

1 *A Letter to J. B. Smith*, p. 167.
2 "Thoughts on the Separation of the Departments", *Collected Tracts*, p. 253.

tion, the management of the paper circulation at that time, more especially as being attended with the insolvency of so many of the issuers, and thus deranging commercial credit, was calculated to aggravate the operation of those causes; while, on the other hand, reasons have been adduced for the inference that the tendency to commercial oscillations between 1827 and 1832 was mitigated by the management which then prevailed, compared with what it would have been under a circulation varying strictly with the variations in the amount of bullion.[1]

Here there would seem to be but little difference. Tooke holds, however, another view of the matter, which he never entirely reconciled with the one we have quoted. He thus describes it:

And here we come to the ultimate regulating principle of money prices.

It is that the quantity of money constituting the revenues of the different orders of the state, under the head of rents, profits, salaries and wages, destined for current expenditure, according to the wants and habits of the several classes, that alone forms the limiting principle of the *aggregate of money prices*—the only prices which can properly come under the designation of *general prices*. As the cost of production is the only limiting principle of supply, so the aggregate of money incomes devoted to expenditure for consumption is the limiting principle of demand for commodities.[2]

The deficiency of this, as it stands, is that it leaves us with no determinant of the total level of money income. Tooke might have made this consistent with his previous admission of the influence of the quantity of money on prices, if he had shown any connection between the quantity of money and the level of incomes, for example through the rate of interest. But Tooke never made such a step, and so he never comes as near to the modern view on this point as does Overstone in the passage last quoted.

The reason for this was probably that his distinction between money and capital, and insistence that the rate of interest was determined by the supply and demand for capital, formed a very inconvenient starting-point for an analysis of how changes in the quantity of money affect money incomes.

The rate of interest had been debarred, by the developments which we noticed in the Restriction Period, from any active part in the theory of prices, and though it occupied a good deal of space in the writings of the 1830's, it did not play any important part in the controversy. Norman states definitely that interest represents the profit on capital, and so cannot afford any indication of the sufficiency or excess of money,[1] and this seems to have been accepted by both sides. On the other hand, it was plain that the Bank could, and on several occasions since the resumption had, influenced the rates quoted in the discount market. So one had the uneasy dualism which was conspicuous later in Marshall's evidence before the Gold and Silver Commission, and which survives in some writers to this day, the rate being regarded as fixed in the long period by the marginal yield of capital, though influenced, in the short period, by the supply and demand for money.

The logical foundation of this dualism is in Tooke's distinction between currency and capital.[2] Banknotes perform two functions, payment from consumers to dealers, and payment from one dealer to another. In the former transactions, notes perform the function of currency; in the latter, they make transfers of capital. Now reserves of banknotes, and bank deposits, are stores of loanable capital. It is, therefore, for command over capital that interest is paid, and it is by increasing the supply of loanable capital that an increase in notes or bank deposits reduces the rate of interest. Speaking of the expansion of deposits by the Bank of England in an attempt to increase the circulation, Tooke says:

The deposits so accumulated would, by the operation of a greatly reduced rate of interest, gradually find employment as capital at home and abroad.[3]

He denies, however, that such a reduction in the rate of interest will necessarily produce any increase in commercial transactions:

1 *A Letter to Charles Wood*, p. 70.   2 *History of Prices*, vol. III, p. 227.
3 *An Enquiry into the Currency Principle*, p. 64.

The truth is that the power of purchase by persons having capital and credit is much beyond anything which those who are un- acquainted practically with speculative markets have any idea of. The error lies in supposing the *disposition* or *will* to be co-extensive with the power.[1]

Tooke attacks the Currency School for not distinguishing between currency and capital, but the distinction is implicit in their writings. There is, however, the difference that the Cur- rency School insist that an abundance of capital does lead, in a way not clearly defined, to a rise in prices. By the side of the passage from Overstone already quoted (p. 122) we may set the following from Norman:

The state of the money market at any given time depends on the supply and demand of loanable accommodation, money and its equivalents.... While the supply is increasing, the demand remain- ing constant, the rate of interest will fall. But this effect of variations in the circulation is only temporary; its ultimate effect is to be found in the prices of commodities.[2]

It is when we come to the subject of credit that we encounter the first major difference between the two schools. The Banking School attached great importance to credit, and held that the volume of credit which could be raised on a given cash base was very variable. They pointed to the great volume of country notes, bills of exchange, deposits and cheque payments, and to the machinery of the bankers' clearing house, whereby im- mense payments were made without the passage of a negotiable instrument at all. Was it reasonable, they asked, to suppose that this enormous volume of purchasing power was sensitive to small changes in a Bank of England note issue amounting to only about £20 mn. in all?

Provided it could be shown that this edifice of credit expanded and contracted in response to expansions and contractions in banknotes, then it would be true to say that prices depended on the volume of notes in circulation. But this the Banking School denied. However great the actual volume of credit might

1 *Ibid.* p. 79.   2 *A Letter to Charles Wood*, p. 49.

be, Tooke and Fullarton maintained that there was always, in normal times, a great untapped reserve. The man of proved credit would never lack accommodation when he needed it:

But the point above all others which claims our attention is this—that, notwithstanding the prodigious scale on which currency thus derives aid from credit, the fund always exceeds the demand upon it, and there is unquestionably at all times afloat a superfluity of forms of credit applicable to the purposes of circulation, which are never called into use simply because they are not wanted, but which might at any time, and would be called into use were the public to be deprived for any considerable period of those resources on which they more habitually depend.[1]

This preoccupation with the wonders of credit led the Banking School on occasions not only to deny that the credit structure was sensitive to fluctuations in the note issue, but even to assert that the two varied inversely, a contraction of notes being offset by an expansion of credit.

The Currency School accepted the obvious fact that only a small fraction of payments were made in coin or notes, but they denied that the volume of other forms of credit could increase for any long time in face of a steady contraction in the note issue, and maintained that the whole structure of credit must quickly conform even to small changes in the base. Beneath the somewhat confused terminology one gets the impression that the real difference was over a point of fact. Were cash ratios in fact subject to a wide degree of variation? This is a fact which, at this distance of time, it is almost impossible to check. That there was a good deal of variability is certain, but, on the other hand, history seems to show that the banks were not prepared to go on expanding their accommodation for more than a limited time in face of contraction by the central bank. This view would appear also to be supported by the fact, admitted by both sides, that the Bank could cause at any rate temporary fluctuations in the market rate of interest. This difference of opinion, as we shall see later, lies at the very root of the controversy over the principles involved in the Bank Charter Act.

[1] Fullarton, *On the Regulation of the Currency*, pp. 46–7.

INTERNATIONAL TRADE—PRICES AND EXCHANGES

We have seen that many writers of the Restriction Period inherited from the Mercantilists and Hume the idea of an optimum distribution of the precious metals, but that they give us no very clear idea of how the initial equilibrium, and the relative price levels corresponding to it, were attained. A solution to this problem was provided by Senior, who suggested that the natural level of prices in a mining country was determined by the cost of producing the precious metals and, in a country which had no mines, by the cost of acquiring them from a mining country. This view, imperfect as it seems to-day, was accepted by both sides in the Currency and Banking controversy.

There was fundamental agreement on the mechanism by which domestic prices affected the exchanges, though the Banking School laid more emphasis than did their opponents on frictions and time lags. As to the nature of an adverse balance, and hence the appropriate remedy, there was, however, an important difference.

The Currency School followed the tradition of Ricardo and the Bullion Committee in supposing that an unfavourable balance was *caused* by unduly high domestic prices, and therefore must necessarily require correction through a contraction of the currency. The Banking School, on the other hand, believed that a balance which would otherwise have been favourable might be upset by special and entirely non-monetary circumstances—in most cases, if not in all, when these circumstances had ceased to operate, the exchange would again become favourable, and the gold which had flowed out would return. This is the foundation of the theory of the terminability of drains, developed in particular by Fullarton. He carefully analyses the various causes of an outflow of gold. Among those having no connection with domestic currency and prices, he mentions changes in the standard of a foreign currency, a failure of credit in a foreign country, and an abnormal importation of corn owing to the failure of the domestic harvest.

A drain caused by any of these, he contends, will cease as soon as the disturbance which gave rise to it has passed, and meanwhile it is unnecessary and undesirable that trade and industry should be subjected to the inconvenience of monetary pressure.

The Banking School were confirmed in their opposition to contraction by the fact that they realised much more acutely than their opponents the difficulties involved. In this they were heirs of the opposition to the Bullion Report, while the Currency School were the heirs of Ricardo. Though they never took quite the facile view that he did, they were inclined to make light of the evils of contraction provided that it was undertaken steadily and in the early stages of a drain.

The Currency School admitted that some drains would work themselves out without any contraction of the currency, but they maintained that this was not the general rule. Furthermore, it was, they said, impossible to tell, in the early stages of a drain, what its real causes were. At the beginning, a slight measure of contraction would suffice and, even if it turned out to have been unnecessary, it would do little harm. The consequences of a mistake in the opposite direction were more serious; if a drain should turn out, after all, to require contraction, by the time this became apparent it would have gone very far, and contraction would have to be sudden and violent if the Bank were to avoid suspension; this sudden and violent contraction would probably bring panic and ruin in its wake. Hence the moral that

The only safe course is to consider a continuous drain of gold from the Bank as conclusive evidence, without reference to vague and uncertain speculations as to the cause of the drain, of the necessity of effecting a corresponding reduction in the circulation.[1]

The Banking School were sometimes inclined to carry their theory too far, but in emphasising the distinction between various causes of a demand for gold they were, nevertheless, making a most important contribution to the theory of central banking.

1 *Reflections Suggested by the Perusal of J. H. Palmer's Pamphlet*, p. 26.

"MONEY" AND "EXCESS OF ISSUES"

Such is the tyranny of words in economic thought that those theories of money prices and exchange rates which we have described were often discussed not in themselves, but as part of an argument over two definitions, that of "money" itself and that of "excess of issues".

The definition of money plays a large part in the writings of the period, and formed the subject of almost endless waste of time by the Committee on Banks of Issue of 1840. The Currency School took the view that only coin and banknotes were money, since only they were accepted in final discharge of an obligation. The definition would have been more watertight if confined to coin and Bank of England notes, as they were the only notes which were legal tender. They admitted that bills of exchange had some of the properties of money, though not all. But when it came to the question of bank deposits, their opponents quite outmanœuvred them. They said:

Suppose I keep fifty pounds in my safe; that, you admit, is money; if I now place that fifty pounds in the Bank of England, and obtain the right to draw a cheque for it at any time, my purchasing power will be just the same, yet you maintain that the quantity of money will have diminished.

This led to the attempt to distinguish between deposits created by the paying in of money, and deposits created by advances, and so on to endless confusion. Overstone met the same charge in a different way by asserting that, under the scheme for the separation of the departments, the reserve of the banking department would be money. One of the improprieties of the existing state of affairs, he asserted, was that it left this reserve indefinite in amount.

The Banking School sought to emphasise their differences from the Currency School by taking a different definition of money. Pennington defines it so as to include bank deposits, but Tooke and Fullarton apply the term only to coined metal, and insist that notes, bills and deposits alike are all forms of credit, though forms differing in their efficiency. This seems to be the most logical standpoint.

Obviously the real point at issue was whether there was any close and quickly operating connection between the volume of legal tender currency and that of the various money substitutes; if there was, then the control of the former, as advocated by the Currency School, must produce its effect on activity and prices (though whether that effect would be desirable, might still be ground for argument). If there was no such close connection, however, then the policy of the Currency School could have no effect on prices within any reasonable time and, whatever else it might do, it could not serve the purpose for which it was intended. From some passages in the literature of the controversy the real issue stands out clearly enough, but often it is overgrown and obscured by the verbal quibble.

By implication, the Currency School accepted Palmer's definition of "over-issue", which stated that issues were in excess whenever English prices were so high relative to those of foreign countries as to cause an unfavourable balance of payments. But the rule which they actually applied was that the circulation ought to vary, "exactly as it would have done were it wholly metallic"; that is to say that, for every five pounds' worth of gold withdrawn from the Bank, a five-pound note ought to be withdrawn from circulation, and only issued again in return for five pounds' worth of gold brought in. They maintained that, whenever a drain of gold was not met by an equivalent contraction in notes, a state of over-issue existed.

The Banking School took a quite different view. So long as notes were convertible, they said, the value of the currency could not diverge from its legal value in terms of gold, and, so long as this stability of value was guaranteed, the measure of the correct amount of currency was simply the needs of the public. They made the quite sound distinction between notes issued to meet commercial needs, and notes, such as the Assignats, issued by governments in payment of their expenses. The latter, once issued, remained always in circulation, and each new issue added to the volume of the currency, so that eventual depreciation was almost inevitable. The notes issued by the English banks, however, could remain in circulation only so long as they were needed. If they were issued as an advance, that advance would be repaid as soon as the need for it ceased to be felt; if they were issued in discounts, the demand for discounts would continue only so long as money was required; even if they were issued in the purchase of government securities, unwanted notes would soon find their way back to the issuer in the form of increased deposits and a reduced demand for loans. So the Banking School concluded that a convertible currency, issued by private banks and not by the government, could never be subject to over-issue. It was this idea to which Fullarton gave the name of "the principle of the reflux". Here is his description of the principle:

Perfect convertibility is, no doubt, one essential of any sound and efficient system of currency. It is the only effectual prevention against internal discredit, and the best preventative against any violent aberrations of the exchange with foreign countries. But it is not so much by the convertibility into gold, as by the regularity of the reflux, that any redundancy of the banknote issue is rendered impossible. When a greater number of notes fall into the hands of the individual than he is likely to have any immediate call for, he does not, unless he wants to send specie abroad, present them to the Bank for gold. He merely lodges them with his own banker, who probably either places the sum to the credit of his own deposit account with the Bank of England, or throws them into the discount market, where they help to supply the vacancy left by the continual tide of notes setting back to the Bank. It is the *reflux*, that is the great regulating principle of the internal currency; and it was by the preservation of the reflux, throughout all the perils and temptations of the period of the restriction, that the monetary system of these kingdoms was saved from the utter wreck and degradation which overwhelmed every paper-issuing state on the Continent....[1]

This is almost exactly the view of Whitmore, Pearse and Harman revived under a new and high-sounding name, and it has the same fatal defect, that it ignores the effect of the rate of

[1] *On the Regulation of the Currency*, p. 67.

interest both on the willingness to hold money and on the level of activity and prices. Moreover, this was not a valid reply to the case of the Currency School. Over-issue as they defined it had manifestly taken place on several occasions, and the Currency School maintained that this state of affairs *endangered the convertibility of the note.* Instead of showing that this was not so, the Banking School simply asserted that, *so long as notes were convertible,* over-issue was impossible.

CENTRAL BANKING FUNCTIONS

Neither side attached any great importance to the Bank's power of "regulating the currency" by means of the rate of interest. The Banking School pointed out that Bank rate was only effective when the market was "in the Bank", in other words, when there was a demand for Bank discounts. But market rate was normally below Bank rate, and lately it had risen to that level only after the exchanges had been unfavourable for some time and a crisis was imminent. The Currency School found it neither necessary nor desirable that the Bank should have any great influence over interest rates, and Overstone remarks:

So long as the issues are not allowed to fluctuate in an arbitrary manner, the power of the Bank to influence or determine the rate of interest is very slight. Under such circumstances, the regular proportion between supply and demand will fix the price of money as of all other things; and if the Bank makes its advances below the market rate, the loss falls on itself, while the benefit goes to those who deal with it.[1]

It is interesting to note, in passing, that Gilbart objected to the raising of Bank rate to meet an efflux of gold, and believed that the Bank should never charge more than 5%: "A bank which has a monopoly of the circulation should not take advantage of the law to charge an extortionate rate of interest."[2]

1 *A Letter to J. B. Smith,* p. 173.
2 *An Enquiry into the causes of the Pressure on the Money Market during the year* 1839, p. 41.

Both the Currency and Banking Schools objected to the growing habit of looking to the Bank for assistance in time of crisis. Torrens argues that

If they (the directors) could be prevailed upon to attend with strictness to their essential duty of regulating their issues by the course of the foreign exchanges, they would never be called upon to perform the superfluous duty of watching over and supporting commercial credit. When they cease to inflict disease, they will be no longer required to administer remedies.[1]

Overstone maintains that such support is not really necessary, as the resources of the financial system are so great that, even in times of the utmost stringency, large loans are to be had by those offering a sufficient rate of interest. He quotes the example of the United States Bank which, after receiving limited assistance from the Bank of England, raised a much larger sum in the London market. Of this he says:

Whilst it proves the limited power of the Bank to discharge its assumed duty of supporting credit, it offers most satisfactory evidence of the unlimited means for this purpose which exist in the country, and which may be called forth according to the extent of the emergency.[2]

With this we may compare one of Tooke's many passages on the subject:

There is, indeed, no point connected with the regulation of the currency upon which I have a stronger conviction—a conviction in which I am supported by the concurrence of several of my mercantile friends who unite a knowledge of principle with great experience in business—than that the directors of an establishment, which is entrusted with the administration of a sound paper circulation, ought not to be allowed to consider themselves at liberty to depart from the strict rules laid down for regulating it in consequence of any view they may entertain, of the claims of the mercantile interest for accommodation, or the inconvenience to trade from not regarding them.[3]

1 *A Letter to Lord Melbourne*, p. 44.   2 *Remarks etc.*, p. 85.
3 *History of Prices*, vol. III, p. 112.

There was also a large measure of agreement among the principal writers as to the desirability of a single bank of issue, or at least of maintaining the existing monopoly of the Bank in London. It has been said of the Banking School that they stood for "free trade in banking". There were those who believed in free trade in banking—Joseph Hume was one of them—but so also were there believers in a silver standard, in depreciation and in government inconvertible notes. But if we think of the Banking School as those people who followed the general opinions of Tooke and Fullarton, nothing could be more un-true. They deny both that country notes have any influence on the exchanges and that they are sensitive to fluctuations in Bank of England issues, but Tooke is definitely in favour of a single bank of issue. In describing his plan for a larger reserve, he says:

Accordingly, if it should be deemed desirable by the legislature to enforce upon the Bank of England the necessity of habitually maintaining a larger amount of bullion than it has hitherto main-tained, the Bank of England would be entitled to require, in the view both of compensation for the expense, and of being the better able to regulate the circulation, to be the sole source of the issue of paper money.[1]

Fullarton regarded it as an open question whether complete unification would be preferable to the system as it existed, but he never suggested that the Bank's privileges in the capital should be revoked.

With regard to the relation between Bank of England and country issues, the Currency School were, in general, the heirs of the Bullion Report. Torrens, in 1837, is maintaining that it is impossible for country notes to expand and fill the gap caused by a contraction of Bank of England notes,[2] and his plan of 1840, of which more later, was based on multiple issues. The conversion from this view is most marked in Overstone; in 1837, he writes of the events of the preceding year:

1 *History of Prices*, vol. III, p. 196.
2 *A Letter to Lord Melbourne*, p. 46 seq.

We are not warranted in coming to the conclusion that the action of the joint-stock banks is utterly beyond the control of the central issuer; the Bank must first prove that it has really tried the effect of a steady and uninterrupted course of contraction, and that in the face of this, the issues of the country banks have as steadily increased. Such may be the case, but Mr Palmer's pamphlet has not furnished us with any evidence of it, and the information, imperfect and unsatisfactory as it is, which he does give us, directly tends to the opposite conclusion.[1]

But the events of the year 1839 appear to have convinced him of the heavy responsibility of the country banks. He describes the course of their issues in that year, and concludes that they increased during the early stages of the contraction by the Bank of England and that, when forced to reverse their policy, they did so suddenly and violently. With these facts before us, he concludes:

Can we doubt that the experience amply confirms what general considerations would lead us to expect, viz. that a multiplicity of issuers, subject to no general rule for their guidance, must tend to disturb the due regulation of the currency.[2]

Henceforward, Overstone was wholly in favour of unitary issues, and in his later writings he re-interprets the events of 1836 in a light much less favourable to the country banks.

There was also general agreement in condemning the way in which the Bank had applied the rule of 1832, especially during the two crises, when the directors' departure from the rules which they had prescribed was too flagrant to be overlooked. Palmer's argument about "special deposits" provoked the devastating comment from Overstone that

This method of getting rid of a certain part of the deposits and securities with a view to obtaining a table which shall exhibit a desired result, is not satisfactory because it does not rest upon any distinctive principle.[3]

1 *Reflections etc.* p. 17. 2 *Remarks etc.* p. 94.
3 *Reflections etc.* p. 8.

But Tooke regards the actions of the Bank with no more favour than his opponents. It is hardly consistent with his contention that over-issue is impossible, but he nevertheless reproaches the Bank with having issued to excess in the spring of 1836, and for having unduly delayed contraction both in 1836 and 1839. He pours ridicule upon the unwillingness of the directors to part with the Dead Weight, and deplores their desire to expand the circulation as soon as the bullion approached one-third of the liabilities:

It is quite clear that no system at all has been followed, and what is more, no system existed. The principle which was supposed to have been propounded by the directors in 1832, and which has been reasoned upon in the controversies to which the partial disturbance of the circulation gave rise in 1836–7, will be found on examination of the terms in which it was announced and explained, to be nothing like an intelligible principle. The exceptions and reservations overlay the rule, and leave the management, such as it has been, free from the charge of inconsistency, simply because no consistent principle has been laid down for its guidance.[1]

PROPOSALS FOR REMEDIES

It was by no means a foregone conclusion that a remedy for the evils of the 1830's would be sought within the existing framework, for there was a strong body of opinion in favour of a refusal to renew the Bank's charter, and the setting up of some form of national bank instead. The most distinguished exponent of a national bank had been David Ricardo, and in 1837 Samson Ricardo reprinted the *Plan for a National Bank*, together with comments and suggestions of his own. He contends that the interest of the public and the proprietors must necessarily be opposed, as was shown by the conduct of the Bank in 1835 and 1836. Whenever the reserve approached one-third of the liabilities, the Bank, for its own profit, adds to the securities and stimulates speculation. When this speculation has

1 *History of Prices*, vol. III, p. 92.

proceeded to a great length, the Bank raises its discount rate, which is again profitable to itself, but tends to cause general alarm. There follows a period of distress, when the Bank is asked for additional accommodation, and this again brings it profit, as is shown by the increase in the "rest" in times of pressure.

Torrens, with whose name the plan for the separation of the departments is most generally associated, was not entirely faithful to it. In 1840 he published an alternative *Plan for maintaining the paper currency of the kingdom in the same state as it would exist were it entirely metallic*. There was to be a licensing stamp for all issues; all banks of issue were to be entitled to receive stamps up to the average of their past year's circulation on the deposit of a quarter of that amount in gold at the mint; further stamps were to be issued only on the deposit of gold to the full value of the notes; any bank might withdraw gold on the presentation of notes to the same value, and all banks were to be obliged to buy gold at the mint price. The scheme, however, found little favour. Overstone, too, seems to have toyed with the idea of a national bank, but he never reached the point of formulating a plan.

If the Currency School had these occasional leanings towards a national bank, the Banking School wholeheartedly and consistently opposed it. Tooke points out that the action of such a bank must produce

a much more rigid principle of limitation to the credit part of the circulation, and a consequent occasional greater rise in the rate of interest upon the more sudden collapse, which must, under such a regulation, follow the reaction from any casual undue expansion of credit, than under the present system.

Tooke and Fullarton also feared that a national bank might be used for inflationary purposes by an insolvent government, and that it would impair the efficiency of the reflux.

We must now turn to the more serious proposal of the Currency School. In the debate on the Bank Charter Act of 1833, Torrens had suggested the formation of a government bank, issuing £29 mn. of inconvertible paper, and then exchanging gold for notes and notes for gold at the mint price. Later he developed Overstone's idea of dividing the Bank into two departments, of which one was to issue notes against a fixed amount of government securities, and then exchange notes for gold and vice versa, while the other was to carry on normal banking business.

The chief virtue claimed for the plan was, of course, that it would make the circulation behave exactly as if it were purely metallic. The reason why Palmer's rule failed to achieve this was clearly pointed out. Overstone says:

The rule ought to be that variations in the amount of the circulation shall correspond to variations in the amount of bullion, and the adherence of the Bank to this rule ought to be obvious upon the face of the published accounts. By this means, and by this means only, can we obtain a paper currency varying in amount exactly as it would have varied had it been wholly metallic.

Had Palmer's rule been applied to the circulation alone, it would have amounted exactly to this:

But when this rule is further applied to the regulation of conduct of a banking concern, it is necessarily found to be wholly impracticable. It is in the nature of a banking business that the amount of the deposits should vary with a variety of circumstances; and as its amount of deposits varies, the amount of that in which these deposits are invested (viz. the securities) must vary also. It is, therefore, quite absurd to talk of the Bank, in its character of a banking concern, keeping its securities even. The reverse must necessarily be the case.[1]

Another argument urged in favour of the separation was that it would set apart the issuing of notes and the granting of accommodation to commerce, and so preserve the issuing body from all temptation to partake of the changing moods of the speculator. Some writers seem to have hoped that the separation would thus eliminate all fluctuations of trade, but the dis-

1 *Reflections etc.* p. 31.

tinguished protagonists of the scheme never suggested any such thing. All they said was that it would remove the specifically monetary causes of fluctuations, and we have seen that Overstone, at least, realised that there were many other causes, some of them more important than money.

If we agree that money, as defined by the Currency School, ought to vary as if it were wholly metallic, then the wisdom of the separation of the departments is self-evident. The whole question is whether such variation is desirable.

The opposition of the Banking School took five main lines. First, the separation would not produce the desired effect on the volume of money; secondly, even if it did, the desired effect on the exchanges would not necessarily follow; thirdly, even if both these things did happen, the result might be neither necessary nor desirable; fourthly, the plan would cause an unnecessary contraction of the circulation; and fifthly, it would place the banking department in an impossible position.

It was argued that an efflux of gold would not produce a corresponding diminution in the amount of notes in circulation, because firms having large foreign exchange dealings kept accounts with the Bank, and would obtain gold not by presenting notes, but by drawing on their deposit. Also it was contended that there were large hoards of gold which were subject to considerable variations, and which would act as a cushion between the effects of the exchanges and the note issue.[1] This latter point is admitted by Torrens, who turns it to his own advantage by claiming that it gives the scheme that very elasticity which its opponents declared that it lacked.[2]

Even if a contraction in banknotes resulted from an efflux of gold, that would not necessarily produce any immediate and sensible effect on prices. We have already dealt with the opposing views on this point, and seen that the Banking School believed the connection between legal tender money and prices to be very indirect.

1 *An Enquiry into the Currency Principle*, p. 9.
2 *An Enquiry into the Practical Working of the Proposed Arrangement for the Renewal of the Charter of the Bank of England*, 1844, p. 34.

Thirdly, if a reduction of prices was brought about, it would be only at great cost. We have seen that the Banking School were much more sensitive to the evils of contraction than were their opponents. These evils were emphasised by Gilbart with reference to 1839:

The fall in prices has driven hundreds of traders into the *Gazette*, the decline in trade has thrown thousands of people out of employment, property of every kind has become less saleable, money cannot be obtained even for the most useful and necessary purposes, a general want of confidence prevails, and our only consolation is that, nevertheless, the Bank of England still retains a few sovereigns in her vaults.[1]

All this, the Banking School argue, is in many cases at least, unnecessary. For the causes of drains are often ephemeral and quite unconnected with the general structure of currency and prices; in such cases the Bank has only to see that it has an adequate reserve at the beginning, and then passively await the end of the drain and the return of what it has lost.

Fourthly, the argument of the Currency School that the contraction necessary to meet a drain would begin earlier, and therefore be more gradual, was categorically denied. Instead, it was claimed that the principle of metallic variation must necessarily produce fluctuations, and especially contractions in the circulation, even more violent than those which occurred under the existing system. It was attempted to illustrate this from the statistics of 1838–9, but any such arguments laid themselves open to the crushing reply that, had the plan been in operation, the drain of bullion would not have been nearly so great as it was. It was even argued that the act of 1844, as passed into law, would involve immediate contraction, but this, as we shall see, proved a complete miscalculation.

Lastly, it was argued that the banking department having to bear, as it would, the initial brunt of the withdrawal of gold, might be forced to suspend payment while the issue department still held a considerable quantity of gold. Pennington first put forward this prophetic suggestion, and it was then taken up by

1 Gilbart, *op. cit.* p. 37.

Tooke. The Currency School were not inclined to take it very seriously, but replied, better that than a complete suspension of convertibility.

The Currency School were the innovators, the Banking School the critics and the defenders of the *status quo*. Their own remedies were mild and non-controversial. Tooke was simply in favour of a considerably larger reserve, together with a monopoly of issue for the Bank. He suggested that a reserve of £15 mn. should be accumulated before any measures were taken to expand the circulation, and that this should be allowed to fall to £5 mn. before any measures were taken to contract it. Thus the average reserve would be about £10 mn., a figure which had been reached only very occasionally before 1840.[1] The criticisms of this were that the Bank would be unwilling to keep so large a portion of its resources in an unproductive form, and that, if the cause of a drain were deep rooted in the structure of domestic prices, a reserve of any magnitude would eventually be exhausted in the absence of contraction.

Fullarton's remedies were rather more drastic and lay beyond the scope of the general controversy. They included a seignorage on the coinage of gold, the use of silver and foreign securities in making foreign remittances, and the re-issue of £1 notes.

To sum up: The Currency School maintained that there was a close connection between the volume of coin and notes in circulation and the level of general prices. Hence it followed that an unfavourable balance of payments could easily be rectified by the contraction of the note issue. Provided that this were not done with excessive suddenness, they thought lightly of the evil consequences involved. In all this they were the heirs of the Bullion Report. They believed in a single bank of issue, and attacked the way in which the Bank had managed the circulation during the 1830's. Their premises with regard to "money" and "over-issue" contained elements of arbitrariness, but once they were accepted, the separation of the departments was a logical enough deduction from them.

1 *History of Prices*, vol. III, p. 185 seq

The Banking School were in many ways the heirs to the opposition to the Bullion Report, but the opposition as it might have been rather than as it was. They accepted their opponents' theory of the relation between prices and the exchanges, and recognised some connection between the quantity of money and prices. But they believed this connection to be remote, and emphasised—sometimes over-emphasised—the time lags and difficulties involved in bringing about a reduction of prices through the contraction of the quantity of money. In insisting that not all drains called for the remedy of contraction they were doing what the opponents of the Bullion Report should have done, but again they were inclined to over-state their case. Like their opponents they believed in unitary issues, but attacked the conduct of the Bank. In the heat of the controversy they were led to maintain a doctrine of over-issue which was that of the least enlightened opinion in the Restriction Period, and which was inconsistent with their other views. The rest of their differences with the Currency School follow quite logically from the different premises which we have noticed.

It has been said that heresy is the insistence on one-half of the truth. The difference between the Currency and Banking Schools was not so much that they believed in a different truth, but that they insisted upon different halves. It is not surprising, therefore, that the legislation in which the triumph of the Currency School was embodied should have realised neither the hopes of its sponsors nor the fears of its opponents.

Chapter Seven

THE TRIAL OF THE BANK CHARTER ACT
1844–58

CHANGES IN BANK POLICY

Before describing the circumstances which led up to the commercial crisis of 1847 we must consider the changes of policy imputed to the Bank in the years after the passage of the Bank Charter Act. The statement of Peel, which we have already quoted, clearly implies that the Bank should abandon the special duties and responsibilities of a central bank and enter into active competition with the private and joint-stock banks of London. The Bank never adopted such a policy, but it did make a number of changes which were hailed as steps in that direction.

The first change was in the discount policy of the Bank. Palmer had explained that Bank rate should normally be above market rate, and that the Bank should normally invest little of its funds in bills. The great influx of gold almost compelled the directors to add to their earning assets in some way, and they now chose to try to increase their discounts, rather than to buy securities. Morris explained their motives to the Select Committee of 1848, saying:

The practice of buying securities when money was abundant, and the price high, and of selling securities when money was scarce and the price low, caused a loss to the Bank, and inconvenience to the money market, which it was desirable to avoid; it was also considered advantageous that a portion of the Bank's resources should be constantly employed in the discount of bills, and so under control.

This marks a reversal of the policy of the previous fifteen years and a return to the views of Harman, Dorrien and Pole.

In accordance with this decision, Bank rate was reduced in August 1844 to 2½%, at a time when Gurneys were charging 2% for first-class bills.

Up to 1844 the Bank had been in the habit of making all discounts at the published rate, though it sometimes altered the usance of bills which it would take. But in October 1844 rates above the published one were charged, and in March 1845 the form of notice was changed and the published rate was announced as a minimum. In quiet times business was generally done at about the published rate, but in times of stringency there might be a considerable difference. In October 1845, 5% was charged when the published rate was 2½%, and in October 1847 business was done at 9% before the published rate rose above 5%.[1] The Bank thus acquired a means of regulating the total volume of discounts and discriminating against undesirable paper, without the disturbance to confidence which might be caused by a change in the published rate.

Advances on Exchequer bills, East India bonds, etc., which had previously been offered only for a limited time around the end of the quarter, were now made available all the year round. There was also a widening in the range of securities held by the Bank, due to the decline in the marketability of the Exchequer bill.[2] Between 1842 and 1846 nearly £2½ mn. of railway debentures were bought, but the directors seem to have revised their view of these securities, for there were no more purchases between August 1846 and the end of 1847.[3]

These changes imply a change in the Bank's method of increasing and diminishing its liabilities. Buying and selling of securities in the market was virtually discontinued. There were sales of rather over £1 mn. in February 1847, and of £200,000 in October of that year, but, otherwise, transactions were negligible.[4] Greater reliance was placed in alterations, published or not, in Bank rate, and in April 1847 there occurred an instance of the "borrowing on Consols"—selling for cash and

1 Select Committee on Commercial Distress, 1848, App. 12.
2 *Ibid.* QQ. 3943-5.   3 *Ibid.* App. 35.
4 *Ibid.* App. 34.

buying back for the account—which was to become common later in the century.[1]

It has been said that these changes produced a reduction in discount rates, but I do not think this thesis will stand examination. If we assume that the amount of money required for other purposes, and also the amount of public deposits and deposits at the branches, to remain constant, then changes in the funds available for the discount market will be measured by changes in the total of the circulation and of the London private deposits of the Bank. If the Bank increases its own discounts, it can do so only by adding to these deposits or to the circulation. If it increases the circulation or deposits by any other means the money will soon find its way into the discount market. There was evidence of this in the enquiries both of 1819 and of 1832.

Now were the Bank quite passive, the funds available for the discount market would, on our other assumptions, increase or decrease by the amount of the increase or decrease of bullion. With the fixed fiduciary issue, and the system of accounting of 1844, the difference between the changes in the circulation and in the bullion is measured by changes in the reserve. If, therefore, the Bank allows the London private deposits to increase by more or fall by less than the reserve, it is exercising a depressing effect on the rate of discount, and vice versa.

From the appendix to the Report of the 1848 Committee I have compiled a table showing the reserve of the banking department in one column, and in the other the London private deposits, being the total of the bankers' balances and "other deposits" (Table XII). Until the end of 1842, while the bullion in the Bank was at a low ebb, the deposits figure was in excess of the reserve. But with the rapid influx of bullion during 1843 and 1844 the position is reversed, the largest excess of the reserve being in the second quarter of 1844. During all this time the Bank was exercising a deflationary influence at great loss to itself, and it was only natural that when the bullion reached such an unprecedented level steps should be taken to expand the

1 Select Committee on Commercial Distress, 1848, Q. 2641.

Table XII

A. BANKERS' DEPOSITS AND "OTHER DEPOSITS"
B. BANK OF ENGLAND RESERVE

Quarterly averages, £ millions

Year		A	B	Year		A	B
1841	2nd quarter	3·0	2·4	1845	1st quarter	6·4	8·6
	3rd ,,	3·0	1·2		2nd ,,	5·9	8·8
	4th ,,	2·9	2·0		3rd ,,	6·3	8·1
					4th ,,	6·6	6·1
1842	1st ,,	3·2	3·2	1846	1st ,,	7·8	6·7
	2nd ,,	4·1	3·5		2nd ,,	6·3	7·6
	3rd ,,	5·1	3·5		3rd ,,	6·8	9·1
	4th ,,	4·6	5·0		4th ,,	6·1	8·1
1843	1st ,,	6·3	4·7	1847	1st ,,	6·3	6·0
	2nd ,,	5·0	6·1		2nd ,,	6·1	4·0
	3rd ,,	5·6	6·5		3rd ,,	5·7	4·3
	4th ,,	4·9	7·8		4th ,,	6·7	4·1
1844	1st ,,	5·6	8·7				
	2nd ,,	5·3	8·6				
	3rd ,,	6·4	7·7				
	4th ,,	6·1	7·6				

liabilities. We can see this happening in the third quarter of 1844, before the coming into force of the Bank Charter Act, and the reserve is substantially less in this quarter than during any in the next year. At the end of 1845 and the beginning of 1846 the Bank was only taking legitimate steps to ease the pressure resulting from the payment of railway deposits, and for the rest of 1846 the position reverted approximately to that of the previous year. Only during 1847 did the Bank consistently act so as to make the contraction of funds in the discount market less than the contraction of its reserve. It appears, therefore, that the fall in interest rates was a result of the influx of bullion, and that the policy of the Bank did not play any important part in it.

THE CRISIS OF 1847

The passage of the Bank Charter Act was preceded by nearly two years of low interest rates and reviving trade. On 5 September 1844 Bank rate was reduced to 2½%, at which it remained for over a year. It was during this year that there occurred the great boom in railway shares on the stock exchange, prices reaching their peak in October 1845 and then falling rapidly. The continued prosperity was reflected in the rise of the Silberling index from 86 to 91 in the year ending with the third quarter of 1845.

Towards the end of 1845 great uneasiness was caused by the standing order of Parliament requiring railway companies to pay a deposit of 10% of their capital into the account of the Accountant-General at the Bank before any bill concerning them could be considered. It was estimated that this would entail the payment of £25 mn. before February 1846.[1] There was a slight drain of bullion and a great increase in the demand for discounts at the Bank, and Bank rate was raised to 3% on 16 October and to 3½% on 6 November. Discounts rose to over £13 mn. in February 1846, but there was no further rise in the rate.

The difficulties in the country were much more acute than those in London, and there was a pronounced check to activity lasting from the autumn of 1845 to the summer of 1846. *The Bankers' Magazine* refers to "the extraordinary spectacle of a superabundance of money offering itself in the discount of first-class paper, and a degree of pressure and discredit in every other part of the mercantile body".[2] The Silberling index fell back five points, to its level in the autumn of 1844.

The Bank's discounts, along with the railway deposits, shrank steadily during the summer of 1846, and the bullion rapidly increased. On 27 August 1846 Bank rate was reduced to 3%, and the account of the 29th shows nearly £16 mn. of bullion in the issue department, and a reserve in the banking department of nearly £10 mn. This reduction was later much

1 *The Economist*, 4 Oct. 1845.   2 *The Bankers' Magazine*, Oct. 1846.

criticised, but by the former standards of the Bank, and the principles laid down by Peel, it was fully justified.

The upward trend of activity and prices was resumed at the end of 1846, the index reaching 97 in the second quarter of 1847, but several difficulties then appeared. The failure of the Irish potato crop in 1845 and 1846 led to large abnormal imports of food. Government relief in Ireland was financed by a loan of £8 mn., payable in instalments beginning in April 1847. The rise in raw cotton prices owing to the failure of the American crop of 1846 administered a check to our greatest export industry. Finally, the Bank of France found itself in serious difficulties, and borrowed £1 mn. from the Bank of England in January 1847.

At the end of 1846 the exchanges were rapidly falling towards gold point, and Bank rate was raised to $3\frac{1}{2}$% on 14 January 1847 and to 4% a week later. On the 23rd the bullion had fallen to just over £13 mn. and the reserve to just over £6 mn. During the next two months the exchanges were very adverse, and market rate was $\frac{1}{2}$% above Bank rate. There was a great increase in discounts and a considerable loss of bullion; for the first time since the passage of the Bank Charter Act the Bank was operating so as to keep down interest rates at the cost of a dangerous depletion of the reserve. *The Economist* voiced a very general opinion in describing the policy of the directors as "entirely beyond our comprehension".[1]

Rather more than £1 mn. of securities were sold in January and February, and some discounts were charged at rates above the minimum, but otherwise there was no serious contraction until April. Then the pressure was all the worse for having been so long delayed. On 8 April Bank rate was raised to 5%, but D. M. Evans says that:

Very little paper, whatever its character, was done at 5%. First-class bills falling due in May or June were negotiated at $5\frac{1}{2}$%, and similar bills falling due in the early part of July were charged at 6%. Subsequently rates were altogether regulated in this manner, just as it suited the interest of the Court to deal with its customers.[2]

1 *The Economist*, 3 April 1847.
2 D. M. Evans, *The Commercial Crisis of* 1847, pp. 62–3.

The Bank issued what Evans calls "a peremptory demand" for the repayment of the quarterly advances, and the branches were instructed to curtail their discounts for other banks to a half.[1] Further, between 6 and 23 April £1,275,000 of Consols were sold for cash and bought back for the account.[2]

These measures checked the demand for discounts and the diminution of the reserve, but only at the cost of very great inconvenience to commerce, and many of the witnesses before the Committees of 1848 describe the pressure of April as worse than that of October. It was the Bank's handling of the situation in the spring of 1847 which was the focal point of the attacks upon it, and we may fairly say that the directors showed as little sound judgement or regard for any intelligible principle of banking as at any time during the previous half century.

The reserve reached its lowest point, of £2·5 mn., on 17 April, and then recovered fairly quickly to about £5 mn. The exchanges remained low during the summer, but became markedly more favourable in the autumn, and, meanwhile, the reserve remained low and there was a heavy demand for discounts.

The circumstance which precipitated the October crisis was the great fall in wheat prices following an abundant harvest. Firms which had been speculating in corn went bankrupt, among them W. B. Robinson & Co., of which the Governor of the Bank was a partner.[3] Messrs Sanderson & Co., second only to Gurneys in the discount market, were so heavily involved with these firms that they had to stop payment on 20 September, and the shock thus given to the discount market had its repercussions on the East India and Mauritius trades, in which the abuse of accommodation bills had long been notorious. Among those who failed was the great house of Reid, Irving & Co. The final stage of the crisis was brought about by the failure of provincial banks, which had made advances to these firms, including the Royal Bank of Liverpool, the Liverpool Banking Co., the Newcastle Union Bank, Knapp & Co. of Abingdon, Scoles & Co. of Manchester, the North and South Wales Bank, and the Oldham Banking Co.[4] The

1 Select Committee of 1848, Q. 7.   2 *Ibid.* Q. 2641.
3 Evans, *op. cit.* p. 70.   4 *The Bankers' Magazine*, Nov. 1847.

bank failures produced an additional demand for cash from the public, and this, at a time when the reserve of the banking department was already low, made necessary the Treasury Letter of 25 October.

The situation which now confronted the directors was very different from that of April. The commercial boom was now broken, the exchanges were favourable, and the demand for cash was only to satisfy the increased liquidity preference of the public. Many precedents had shown that, in such circumstances, the Bank should make advances liberally, though with discretion, and this was the policy adopted. Bank rate was raised to $5\frac{1}{2}\%$ on 5 August, and there it remained until 25 October, though a considerable amount of business was done at higher rates. On 10 September advances on government securities were offered at only 5%, but on 1 October the market was startled by the absolute refusal of such advances. But this seems to have been a change in the form rather than a restriction of the amount of accommodation, for discounts rose rapidly, and £2,300,000 of "extraordinary advances" were made to firms in distress, a large part of them before the issue of the Treasury Letter.

This letter, signed by Lord John Russell and Charles Wood, was issued on 25 October, the reserve of the banking department having been reduced on the 23rd to only £1,547,000. It suggested that the Bank should make advances at 8% "on bills of exchange, on stock, and on other approved securities", and promised a bill of indemnity should a breach of the law result.

The Governor and Deputy-Governor staunchly maintained that the letter was quite unsolicited and that they were fully prepared to carry on without it, but Samuel Gurney said that, had the letter not been sent, "my firm persuasion is that it would have ended in an infringement of the law, or a stoppage of the Bank".[1]

Such speculation was, however, academic. Events proved that, no sooner had the letter been issued, than the need for it passed away. Gurney says:

1 Select Committee of 1848, Q. 1603.

The effect was immediate. Those who had sent notice for their money in the morning now sent us word that they did not want it—they had only ordered payment by way of precaution....From that day we had a market of comparative ease.[1]

The Bank's position rapidly improved, and on 22 November, with a reserve of £4¾ mn., the Bank released the government from its promise by reducing the rate to 7%. Further reduction soon followed, until 4% was reached on 27 January 1848, with a reserve of over £8 mn.

The usual commercial stagnation which followed the crisis was aggravated by political conditions in Europe, but substantially mitigated by the great volume of railway construction still in hand. The Silberling index shows price movements to have been markedly less than in previous crises. There was a rise of 18 points from the third quarter of 1822 to the second quarter of 1825, followed by a fall of 23 points to the third quarter of 1826. There is again a rise of 18 points from the second quarter of 1835 to the second quarter of 1836, followed by a fall of 20 points to the third quarter of 1847. But from the third quarter of 1846 to the second quarter of 1847 there is a rise of only 10 points, though this is followed by a fall of 15 points to the third quarter of 1848.

This comparative stability of prices is one of several points of interest about the crisis. Another is the check to activity in 1845-6. During this time commodity markets remained comparatively firm, and the prices of public securities were well maintained in spite of the disastrous fall in railway shares. Finally, there was great difference of opinion among the witnesses of 1848 as to the importance of railways. Those who were connected only with the City thought that this was little, while those directly engaged in industry and commerce ascribed to the railways a major role in the events of these four years. All these things I believe to be explained by the peculiar method of railway finance and the timing of railway construction, and these will, therefore, form the subject of a short digression.

1 *Ibid.*

RAILWAY INVESTMENT AND ITS EFFECTS

It has been estimated that 1428 railway companies were proposed between 1844 and 1847, with a capital of over £700 mn., but only a fraction of these ever came into active life.[1] The following table shows the amount of actual railway calls:

Table XIII

SHARE AND LOAN CAPITAL RAISED BY RAILWAYS

£

During	1844	...	...	5,729.138
„	1845	...	...	16,457,094
„	1846	...	...	38,678,680
„	1847	...	...	42,557,974*

* Lords Committee of 1848, App. D.

Table XIV

MONTHLY INCIDENCE OF RAILWAY CALLS

£ thousands

	Date	British	Foreign	Total
1847	January	4,546	1,612	6,158
	February	1,393	—	1,393
	March	3,042	466	3,508
	April	4,215	100	4,315
	May	3,038	402	3,440
	June	2,463	750	3,213
	July	4,334	1,032	5,366
	August	2,225	62	2,287
	September	3,361	800	4,161
	October	3,342	420	3,762
	November	1,896	147	2,043
	December	2,423	—	2,423
1848	January	4,639	222	4,861
	February	2,141	132	2,273
	March	1,849	1,287	3,136
	April	2,210	550	2,760
	May	3,208	39	3,247
	June	2,159	118	2,278
	July	3,900	177	4,077
	August	3,023	99	3,122
	September	2,521	66	2,587*

* From *The Bankers' Magazine*, Oct. 1848. The total is very slightly less than that given in the House of Lords' Report, presumably because the date of the remaining calls was not known. The difference, however, is less than half a million for the year, so it is unlikely to be important for any one month.

1 Evans, *op. cit.* p. 23.

For 1847 and the first nine months of 1848 I give monthly figures of railway calls (Table XIV) and, to show how little effect these had on the discount market, I also quote the rates charged on first-class bills by Gurneys (Table XV). It will be noticed that there were considerable calls for foreign companies which, in so far as they were not offset by exports of constructional material,

Table XV

PERCENTAGE RATE OF DISCOUNT CHARGED BY GURNEYS ON FIRST CLASS BILLS

	Months											
Year	1	2	3	4	5	6	7	8	9	10	11	12
1844	$2\frac{1}{4}$	2	2	2	$1\frac{3}{4}$	2	2	$1\frac{3}{4}$	2	$2\frac{1}{4}$	$2\frac{3}{4}$	$2\frac{3}{4}$
1845	$2\frac{1}{2}$	$2\frac{1}{2}$	$2\frac{3}{4}$	$2\frac{3}{4}$	$2\frac{3}{4}$	$2\frac{3}{4}$	$2\frac{3}{4}$	3	$2\frac{3}{4}$	3	$3\frac{1}{2}$	$4\frac{1}{2}$
1846	4	5	$4\frac{1}{2}$	4	4	4	$3\frac{3}{4}$	$3\frac{3}{4}$	3	3	$3\frac{1}{4}$	$3\frac{1}{4}$
1847	$3\frac{1}{4}$	$4\frac{1}{2}$	$4\frac{1}{2}$	$4\frac{1}{2}$	7	6	$5\frac{1}{2}$	6	6	7	10	6
1848	$4\frac{1}{4}$	$3\frac{1}{2}$	$3\frac{1}{2}$	$3\frac{1}{2}$	$3\frac{1}{4}$	$3\frac{1}{4}$	3	3	3	3	$2\frac{3}{4}$	$2\frac{1}{2}$

Table XVI

RAILWAY CONSTRUCTION

	Miles opened during				
Lines begun	1844	1845	1846	1847	1848
Before end of 1843	196	129	8	—	—
During 1844	—	158	365	140	121
,, 1845	—	6	222	556	618
,, 1846	—	—	84	398	482
,, 1847	—	—	—	54	54
	196	293	595	780	1,191

would be a factor in the adverse balance of payments of 1847.

The figures of calls do not give an exact idea of actual construction, as early calls were for deposits and preliminary expenses. An approximate idea of the time lag can be gained from Table XVI, compiled by Lardner. The average period of construction seems to have been about two years, and the work in hand must have increased greatly about the end of 1846 and the beginning of 1847.

The system by which shares were only in small part paid up,

leaving the holder with a large liability in the more or less remote future, but offering the chance of immediate profit should
the market price of the shares go up, was such as greatly to
tempt the small investor to take up more commitments than he
could afford. Such people would then be driven to sell some
of their holdings, either to avoid further calls, or to meet calls
on other shares which they retained. This was recognised as the
cause of the continued weakness of the railway share market
after the collapse of October 1845. If we make the reasonable
assumption that this new and hazardous adventure attracted a
different type of subscriber from that which supported the
market for public securities, we have an adequate explanation
of the comparative strength of this market at the same time.

Losses on railway shares would probably induce those who
suffered them to make some reduction both in consumption and
in business activities, but the effect of this would probably be
small.

Of far more importance was the financial effect. Trade was
still largely financed by bills of exchange, but of these only a
small fraction—mostly originating in overseas trade and in the
great commodity markets—would be discounted in Lombard
Street. The rest, the internal bills drawn on small merchants and
manufacturers, could be discounted in the London market only
if they bore the signature of one of the well-known country
banks. Besides the business of discounting and accepting bills,
the banks were making advances to industrialists on an increasing scale. There was evidence of this in 1832, and it must
have grown considerably since then.

The pressure of railway calls fell not on the London market,
but on the country banks. Money paid in calls would be withdrawn largely from country banks and paid into the London
bank of the company, or into the Bank of England, as statutory
deposit. These deposits the Bank re-lent to the London market,
which thus escaped any great stringency, but it would be much
less easy for the funds to find their way back to the provinces in
this manner. The whole transaction thus represented an abstraction of cash from the provinces and its transfer to London.

We have no figures for the deposits of country banks as a whole, but S. J. Lloyd submitted the following scale to describe those of his own bank:

1844	1845	1846	1847
343	325	299	225

The official returns show a slackening of savings-bank deposits, and from the autumn of 1846 there was actually a balance of withdrawals. If the country banks were generally facing a withdrawal of deposits, and a transfer of cash to London, common caution would dictate that they should contract their facilities, by way of either discounts, acceptances or advances, to industry. Further, it must be remembered that the financial press had been prophesying disaster ever since the Bank reduced its rate of discount.

I suggest that this loss of cash, and consequent restriction of facilities by the country banks, as a result of the railway boom, affords an explanation of all those peculiarities about the boom and crisis of 1847 which we have noticed.

THE NEW GOLD SUPPLIES

The most important single factor in monetary history in the third quarter of the nineteenth century is the great increase in gold output, following the discovery of the mines of California and Australia.

The total value of gold in existence had been estimated at £354 mn. in 1803 and £560 mn. in 1848.[1] The estimated output of California and Australia during 1848–56 was as follows:

				£
1848–9	...	...	...	1,773,000
1850	...	...	...	5,500,000
1851	...	...	...	10,074,000
1852	...	...	...	23,578,000
1853	...	...	...	25,239,000
1854	...	...	...	25,440,000
1855	...	...	...	27,404,000
1858	...	...	...	29,417,000

1 Except where otherwise stated, the figures in this section are taken from Tooke and Newmarch, *A History of Prices*, vol. VI, section VII.

Adding the output of old mines, Newmarch estimates total production in 1848–56 at £174 mn., or 27% of the total stock of 1848.

One effect of the influx of gold was to cause the displacement of silver in those countries, notably France and the United States, which had a bimetallic standard. The premium on gold in Paris disappeared, while in England the price of silver rose from 4s. 11d. to 5s. 2d. per oz.

Great Britain was already, in large measure, the financial centre of the world, and it was through Great Britain that most of the movements of the precious metals took place. It is not possible to trace these movements in detail, as import and export figures take account only of bullion shipped as "freight". The real figures are believed to have been more than double the official ones.[1]

But the general course of events is clear. In the very beginning of the exploitation of the Australian mines there was actually an export of gold from England, to supply the new community with a currency. This was soon reversed, and thereafter both Australia and America exported gold in return for commodities, most of which were supplied by England. The result was a very favourable trade balance, an influx of bullion, and very low interest rates. The Bank's bullion stock rose to the unprecedented level of £22 mn. in 1852. Bank rate was 3% or less all the time from November 1848 to June 1853, and Consols rose above par.

The increased demand for exports, and the long period of cheap money, led to an increase in employment and to demands for higher wages, and Newmarch estimates the rise in wages between 1851 and 1856 at between 15 and 20%.[2] The Jevons price index rose from 65 in 1852 to 74 in 1853 and 83 in 1854. This rise in incomes and prices turned the balance of payments against us in the autumn of 1853, and the drain of bullion was only checked by a rise in interest rates. Thenceforward, until after the crisis of 1857, we have a high level of activity, gold disappears as fast as it arrives, and the Bank only prevents

1 *The Economist*, 30 Sept. 1854.   2 Newmarch, *op. cit.* vol. VI, p. 176.

its reserves from serious depletion by the maintenance of high rates.

Figures for imports and re-exports are still given only in unreal "official values", but I quote the declared value of exports of British produce and manufactures. Before 1848 the figure rarely exceeded £60 mn., but from 1852 to 1857 it is as follows:

				£
1852	...	...	...	78,176,000
1853	...	...	...	98,933,000
1854	...	...	...	97,184,000
1855	...	...	...	95,688,000
1856	...	...	...	115,826,000
1857	...	...	...	122,155,000[1]

One curious feature was that imports were generally bought for cash and exports sold on credit, so that an expansion in both imports and exports of the same amount would cause a temporarily unfavourable balance of payments.[2]

It was estimated that the net result of specie movements was to produce a 30% increase in the metallic currency, and gold began to displace notes as small currency.[3]

The manufacturers have stated to our agents that the practice is now to pay wages in gold, whereas formerly it was very much the practice to pay a note to half a dozen men, which, again, was exchanged at a retail shop.[4]

So Weguelin told the 1857 Committee. The result was a decrease of Bank of England notes of £5 and £10, partially offset by an increase in those of larger denomination.

Concurrently with this increase in currency there was a great increase in joint-stock banking in London. New banks were formed, and the old ones increased their business, with the result that the deposits of the London joint-stock banks were £43,107,724 in 1857, compared with only £8,750,774 in 1848.

1 Report of Select Committee on the Bank Acts, 1847–8, p. 11.
2 *The Economist*, 3 Sept. 1853.
3 Committee of 1857–8, Q. 19.   4 *Ibid.* Q. 51.

1848–57

The depression of 1848 was less severe than might have been expected, though recovery was delayed by the uncertainty of the European political situation. The usual post-crisis accumulation of bullion was hastened by the increase of world supplies. Bank rate was reduced to 4% in January 1848, $3\frac{1}{2}$% in June, and 3% in November, yet by the end of the year the bullion was £15 mn. and the reserve over £11 mn. In November 1849 Bank rate fell to $2\frac{1}{2}$%, and for over a year the Bank held over £15 mn. of bullion. A fall in the French exchange caused a rise to 3%, but in the autmun of 1851 there came a great increase in the flow of gold from the new mines. Bank rate fell again to $2\frac{1}{2}$% in January 1852, and to the unprecedentedly low level of 2% in April. The rates charged by Gurneys were always from $\frac{1}{4}$ to $\frac{1}{2}$% below Bank rate, and only for a few brief periods during 1851 was the market "in the Bank".

From 1849 to 1853 there was a steady increase in general activity, though not without setbacks in particular industries, especially in 1851. But it was not until 1853 that the Jevons index, which refers to March of each year, showed a marked rise in prices, jumping from 65 to 74. The year 1853 was a critical one, marking the end of a long spell of cheap money and the beginning of a long period of high interest rates and recurrent prices. The Australian market became glutted, and there was a marked decline in exports to that country; the end of the year showed the harvest to have been very poor; the cotton industry was disorganised by the great Preston strike; and to all these disturbing factors there was added the dispute with Russia, which, by the end of the year, seemed certain to lead to war.

In face of a drain of bullion, and a growing demand for discounts, Bank rate was raised from 2 to $2\frac{1}{2}$% and then to 3% in January, to $3\frac{1}{2}$% in June, and in September by stages of $\frac{1}{2}$ to 5%. On 1 October bullion had fallen to £15·6 mn., the reserve to £6·3 mn., and discounts had risen to £8·7 mn.

The Crimean war, by comparison with other European conflicts of the past century and a half, was not a great strain on our resources. In particular, there was not the large-scale government borrowing which occurred during some phases of the wars of 1793–1815. The total addition to the National Debt was as follows:

				£
1854–	...	...	...	6,556,495
1855–6	...	...	...	28,857,413
1856–7	...	...	...	7,446,574
			Total	42,860,484[1]

With this compare the net borrowing of £37·4 mn. out of the much smaller national income of 1813, a scale which was continued for several years.

It is not surprising, therefore that the war should have had no very marked effect on general economic life. It did, however, affect the Bank by causing a considerable drain of bullion to the East. Stores bought from Greek merchants in Constantinople were paid for in English and French Treasury bills. These were then sent to Marseilles, and sold to French bankers, who sent them to the Bank of France or the Bank of England for discount.[2]

So far from causing an inflationary boom, the first year of the war brought a definite check to commerce. Tooke remarks on the poor trade of 1854;[3] the Jevons index fell from 83 in March 1854 to 80 in March 1855, and there was a slight decline in the value of exports.

The position of the Bank improved at the end of 1853, but there was a renewed drain at the beginning of 1854, and in May Bank rate was raised to $5\frac{1}{2}$% with little over £5$\frac{1}{2}$ mn. in the reserve. Then, for a year, there was a steady improvement; Bank rate fell to $3\frac{1}{2}$% in January 1855, the bullion rose to £18 mn., and the reserve to nearly £12 mn.

But this happy position soon gave place to the first of three autumnal crises. Bullion fell to just over £11 mn., and the reserve to £4·3 mn., and discounts rose to over 9 mn. Bank rate was raised by stages of $\frac{1}{2}$%, beginning in September, and

1 *Parliamentary Papers*, 1875, vol. XLII, p. 95.
2 *The Economist*, 5 Jan. 1856.   3 Tooke, *op. cit.* vol. v, p. 306.

on 26 October it was 6% for bills of less than 60 days and 7% for those of 65 to 95 days. The peculiar feature of this crisis is that it was preceded not by an increase but by a decline in imports.[1] It was explained by *The Economist* that the Bank of France was reluctant to raise its discount rate and, instead, sent bills to the Bank of England for discount, and bought gold with the proceeds, even though the London-Paris exchange was well above normal gold export point.[2]

The crisis did not lead to any commercial depression but, on the contrary, the year 1856 brought a spectacular increase in trade and also in foreign investment. Prominent among the latter were Indian railways, which absorbed some £11 mn. of British capital between 1850 and 1856.[3]

The Bank was stronger again in the early part of 1856, in spite of a loan to Turkey.[4] Bank rate was reduced to 5% on 29 May, and to 4½% a month later; bullion rose to over £13 mn., and the reserve to over £7 mn., while discounts shrank to about £4 mn. A poor position compared with the palmy days of 1852, but it would have been regarded as quite satisfactory a decade previously.

At the beginning of October 1856 there were crises over most of Europe following intense activity in railway building and other enterprises. The effect in London was again to cause a sudden increase in the demand for discounts from the Bank, and the reserve fell to only £3·5 mn. Bank rate rose to 7% on 13 November.

Again the crisis was followed by a slight improvement, but the Bank remained weak. The Continent had suffered far more severely than England from the pressure; English prices were now out of equilibrium, and they still continued to rise during the spring of 1857. That a restriction of credit sufficient to bring down prices was so long delayed was due only to the influx of new gold from the mines. In spite of this, the Bank's bullion hovered between £10 and £12 mn., and the reserve was generally below £6 mn., while the demand for discounts re-

1 *The Economist*, 15 Nov. 1855.   2 *Ibid.*, 29 Sept. 1855.
3 *Ibid.* 4 May, 1856.   4 Tooke, *op. cit.* vol. VI, p. 199.

mained large. Except for twelve weeks at $5\frac{1}{2}$% from July to October 1857, Bank rate remained at 6% or more.

The crisis was eventually precipitated, as had been others before, by events in America. The first failures there received little attention; "speculation is known to be one of the permanent maladies of the transatlantic republic; occasional embarrassments are merely regarded as the result of this peculiarity".[1] But during October news came through of the failure of the Ohio Life and Trust Co., of bank suspensions in New York and other cities and of a disastrous fall in American stock-exchange prices. Repercussions in England were first felt in the two cities most closely connected with the American trade, Liverpool and Glasgow.

Bank rate was raised to 6% on 8 October, to 7% on the 12th, and to 8% on the 19th, by which time the reserve had fallen to £$3\frac{1}{2}$ mn., and discounts had risen to £$9\frac{1}{2}$ mn. On 27 October the Liverpool Borough Bank stopped payment. On the previous day the Western Union Bank of Scotland had applied to the Bank for assistance, but this was refused, partly from doubts as to the Bank's solvency, and partly because the rendering of aid would involve "the abstraction (of gold) altogether from London".[2]

Nevertheless, the Bank was liberal with its assistance in other directions, more so than it would have been had it not remembered the precedent of 1847. The Governor and Deputy-Governor denied that they had any previous knowledge of the Treasury Letter, but stated that

The Bank could not have risked what she did, had she been certain that by no possibility would government give any relief; but feeling that she was bound, as a public institution, to make common cause with commerce, she certainly gave greater assistance.[3]

It was the trouble in Scotland that eventually brought about the infringement of the Bank Charter Act. The struggling Western Union Bank stopped payment on 9 November, following the failure of the great firm of Dennistoun, Cross & Co.

1 Evans, *op. cit.* p. 34.   2 Select Committee of 1857–8, Q. 24.
3 *Ibid.* Q. 86.

Two days later came the suspension of the City of Glasgow Bank and the failure of the bill-broking firm of Sanderson & Co., which had been reconstructed after the crisis of 1847. This was Scotland's first experience of a joint-stock bank failure for many years, and it created a panic demand for gold, over £1 mn. being taken in two days.

Bank rate was raised to 9% on 5 November, and to 10% on the 9th; on the 11th the discounts were over £13 mn. and the reserve less than £1 mn., and on the following day, with the reserve at only £581,000, there was issued a Treasury Letter similar to that of 1847, except that the specified rate of interest was now 10% instead of 8%. This time the fiduciary issue was actually exceeded. The issue department transferred £2 mn. of notes to the banking department in exchange for securities, and they were not repaid until 24 December, though the excess in the hands of the public lasted for only eighteen days.

The letter did not produce the immediate relief that it did in 1847. It was followed by further bank failures in the provinces, notably those of the Northumberland and Durham District Bank and the Wolverhampton and Staffordshire Bank. Bank of England discounts rose to a peak of £17·2 mn. on 22 December, and bullion was reduced to £6·3 mn. But by the end of the year, discounts were down by £2 mn., bullion had risen to £11½ mn., and the reserve in the banking department was over £6 mn. after repaying the £2 mn. which had been borrowed from the issue department. Bank rate was reduced to 8% on 24 December, and by 11 February 1858 it had fallen to 3%. The adjustment of commercial difficulties continued, however, into the spring, and in March 1858 the Jevons index stood at 76, a drop of nine points on the year.

THE BANK AND THE MARKET

It was becoming established that the first instrument for the Bank's control of the market was Bank rate, and between the passage of the Bank Charter Act and the crisis of 1857 there were no less than fifty changes in the rate, of which twenty-four occurred in the last three years. The directors' decisions as to the rate were influenced by many things, and one cannot deduce any clear rule from the accounts. The balance of payments, the rate of interest in foreign countries, the state of trade, were doubtless always considered in a general way; there is a close, though by no means inseparable, connection between changes in the reserve of the banking department and in Bank rate; but the most immediate determinant appears to have been simply the public demand for discounts.

The Economist congratulates the Bank on

Laying aside all those antiquated and vague notions about regulating and conserving the currency, the exact meaning of which no one ever yet succeeded in defining, but by which the Directors of the Bank in former times professed to be governed,[1]

and following the simple rule of varying the rate according to the state of the reserve, and the public demand for discounts.

In spite of the more active discount policy after 1844, Bank rate was normally above market rate, and the volume of the Bank's discounts was not large. In times of pressure, however, the position was reversed; the Bank raised its rate by less than the market, and the directors did not hesitate to discount liberally. Their recognition of an obligation in this respect is shown by the evidence of Weguelin, already quoted.

After 1847, changes in the published rate were preferred to the charging of rates above the minimum. During the week ending 1 October 1853 a third of the discounts were made at 5% when the published rate was 4½%. In the autumn of 1856 there were considerable dealings at 7%, when Bank rate was only 6%, and at the extreme end of the year the greater part of business was done at 6½%. During the crisis of 1857 rates above the minimum were charged on a large scale only during the week ending 14 October. Apart from these occasions, published rates were closely adhered to.[2]

Open market operations were unimportant between 1848 and 1854, but considerable in the three following years. Between April and July 1855, when the reserve was increasing rapidly, £650,000 of securities, chiefly Exchequer bills, were

---

1 *The Economist*, 9 Aug. 1855.   2 Select Committee of 1857–8, Q. 397.

bought; the autumn pressure was accompanied by large sales, £1,125,000 between the end of July and 22 September, just over £2 mn. between that date and 27 October, and a further £280,000 before the end of the year. During 1856, net transactions were smaller, but some £500,000 of new securities were acquired during the summer. During 1857 there were sales of £680,000 between 18 May and 14 November, and of £1,866,000 between 16 November and 31 December. Once the crisis was passed, this policy was naturally reversed, and there were purchases of over £2¼ mn. before the end of February 1858. These amounts were not, however, large in relation to changes in discounts, and it seems that open-market operations were used rather as a quick method of adjustment to sudden changes than as an instrument of long-term policy.

I know of no instance of "borrowing on Consols" other than that of 1847, already mentioned.

The crisis produced one step which now seems rather retrograde. The Bank considered that the discount houses were taking advantage of their re-discount facilities, and financing an undue extension of accommodation paper. Weguelin thus described the change which was made:

Hitherto the discount houses have had access to the Bank at all times for discounts; the change made is to decline giving them discounts any longer, but to make their transactions with the Bank confined entirely to advances. These advances will be the usual quarterly advances, and if they apply at any other time, they will be considered special, and dealt with accordingly.[1]

This looks like an attempt on the part of the Bank to repudiate its responsibility as lender of last resort. In fact, however, accommodation in some form was never refused in time of serious pressure, and the measure was probably no more than an attempt to dragoon the brokers into more cautious habits. It gave rise to much controversy, however, and was the cause of a famous dispute between the Bank and Gurneys, which we shall have to describe in the next chapter.

1 Select Committee of 1857–8, Q. 397.

Chapter Eight

THE GREAT BOOM
1858–73

GENERAL CHARACTERISTICS

The general characteristics of the period 1858–73 are too familiar to need detailed description. Prices and wages were rising, in spite of occasional checks, unemployment was low and industry and trade, especially foreign trade, were rapidly expanding. Foreign investment, both in railway building and in government loans, was increasing, and we had a large favourable balance of payments on income account. The world stock of gold was growing fast, but the metal was being drawn into circulation as soon as it was coined, and central bank reserves remained low, and rates of interest high.

The various price indices show discrepancies in detail, but give the same general impression. The Sauerbeck food index fell from 98 in 1860 to 88 in 1864, but rose to 107 in 1873. The Sauerbeck raw material index rose from 100 in 1860 to 119 in 1864, fell to 99 in 1868, rose again to 115 in 1872, and fell to 114 in the next year. *The Economist* index rose from 123 in 1860 to 172 in 1864, fell to 117 in 1868, and rose to 134 in 1873. The years 1860–8 reveal the pattern with which we are familiar—rapidly rising prices, followed by credit stringency, a slight fall in prices, monetary crisis, and then a sharp fall in prices as traders make distress sales. In 1873 both the rise and the fall in prices was less marked and the crisis less severe, as disturbances on the Continent checked the inflationary forces before they had time fully to develop.

The Trade Union unemployment figure averaged just under 4·7%. Unemployment was high in 1858, as a result of the crisis of 1857, in 1861–3, owing to the dislocation caused by the American Civil War, and in 1867–9, following the crisis of

1866. In all other years it was below 4%, and in 1873 it fell as low as 0·9%. Mr G. H. Wood's wage index shows an almost continuous rise from 110 in 1858 to 155 in 1873: the rise was the sharpest during the two periods of expanding trade but there is practically no decline in the intervening depression.

Imports and exports more than doubled during the period, imports rising from £164 mn. in 1858 to 371 mn. in 1873, and exports from £139 mn. in 1858 to £314 mn. in 1872. The expansion was fairly continuous, and there was only a slight check following the crisis of 1866. These figures exaggerate the unfavourable visible balance of trade, as imports are entered c.i.f. and exports f.o.b., though, in both cases, the greater part of the payments for transport and insurance would accrue to Englishmen. It is hard to obtain a reliable estimate of invisible exports, but certainly they more than bridged the gap.

The world production of gold, which averaged only 3·24 tons a year during the first half of the nineteenth century, rose as a result of the discoveries in California and Australia to an average of 24·54 tons a year between 1851 and 1885.[1] Between 1858 and 1871 net imports of gold were £74·5 mn., of which £64 mn. represented "interior demand", i.e. either industrial use or addition to the stock of circulating money.[2] Estimates of the gold coin in circulation varied widely, but it may be taken as round about £80 mn. at the end of the period. The Bank of England reserve of £10 to £15 mn. was thus only a small proportion of the whole amount of monetary gold in the country, a matter of some importance for the Bank's operations.

THE LONDON MONEY MARKET

During these years there took place two notable changes in the international position of the London money market. The first in time was the growth of the international acceptance business. This seems to have had its origin in the American trade in the 1830's, when bills drawn by a British on an American firm

1 Layton and Crowther, *Introduction to the Study of Prices.*
2 Hawtrey, *A Century of Bank Rate*, p. 47.

would be accepted by the London agent of the latter. In the 1850's the system was extended so that bills drawn by a foreign house on a firm in a third country were accepted by a London firm and so rendered available for discount in the London market. In this way a large part of the trade of the world came to be financed, and London became a sort of clearing house for international payments.

It was this fact which was largely responsible for the second change, the development of London as an international banking centre. Accepting houses might require a deposit to be kept with them as security, and foreign houses found that a deposit in London afforded them the means of making payments in any part of the world with the minimum of trouble. A further incentive to the holding of money in London was the freedom of England from the civil and political disturbances which troubled the rest of the world. In this connection it is interesting to note that the American Civil War was the first occasion on which "hot money" came to London in sufficient quantity to excite the notice of the press. Bagehot mentions the growth of foreign deposits after the Franco-Prussian war,[1] but there are numerous references to their existence in considerable quantity in the 1860's.

The effect of both these changes was, of course, to make the London money market much more sensitive to conditions in foreign centres. It was easier for foreigners to draw money from London and, as such money must in the last resort come from the gold reserve of the Bank of England, the Bank was subject to demands more frequent and potentially more serious than before. The position was aggravated by the fact that there was absolutely no deterrent to the free export of gold from England, whereas in most Continental centres the central bank was able to exert varying degrees of pressure to prevent export. The nature of these changes was frequently pointed out by Bagehot and others, who urged the Bank to meet its new responsibilities by keeping a larger reserve.

At the same time as changes in the international relations of

1 *Lombard Street*, p. 17.

the market were making the Bank's position more delicate, changes in its internal structure were making the Bank's control more precarious. The deposits of the joint-stock banks were growing rapidly. In 1858 the deposits of the five largest London joint-stock banks were £39,194,892; in 1873 they had grown to £82,539,171. The same sort of growth probably took place in the country as a whole, though we have no figures to check it. Competition between the banks led to a high rate of interest being offered for deposits—1 % below Bank rate was the normal for London—and this meant that deposits had to be employed as closely as possible and the reserve of unearning cash reduced to a minimum. Hence the growing desire for a very small cash ratio and a strong "second line of defence", money at call and discounts. The means of gratifying these desires were furnished by the growing volume of bills of exchange and by the new joint-stock discount companies founded in the 1860's. There was thus a double influence at work. On the one hand, the deposits of the banking system as a whole were increasing much faster than those of the Bank of England, and a greater amount of credit was being built up on a given cash basis. On the other, a greater proportion of banking resources was seeking employment in the discount market. Thus the funds employed in that market, directly or indirectly, by the Bank were coming to bear a smaller and smaller proportion to the resources of the market as a whole.

The Bank's position was further complicated in 1869 by the action of the government. In Mr Lowe's finance bill of that year the assessed taxes, which had formerly been spread out over the year, all fell due in January. This meant that, during the first two months of the year, government deposits in the Bank were usually large, the resources of the outside market were correspondingly smaller, and the control of the Bank therefore at its strongest. In the autumn, however, precisely the opposite result occurred, and as the normal course of trade was much more likely to produce a drain of gold in the autumn than in the spring the change materially weakened the Bank.

Another evil of the increased competition in banking was that less attention was paid to the nature of the bills discounted, and hence there arose some of the worst possible abuses of accommodation paper. To these abuses the Bank's own action contributed. Formerly, discounts were made only to customers having a discount account, and this required the deposit of a fairly substantial sum. Now, however, the discount account became a mere formality; a deposit of as little as £5 was accepted, and it could be paid in immediately before a transaction and withdrawn immediately after it. Further, the Bank looked only to the name on the bill and not to the transaction underlying it, and it was thus made possible for a house of established reputation to raise money on accommodation paper to an almost unlimited extent.[1]

FOREIGN INVESTMENT AND THE BANKING SYSTEM

The years immediately following the Californian and Australian gold discoveries saw a big increase in British foreign lending, not only to the gold-producing countries themselves, but also to India and the Continent of Europe. This flow of lending continued until 1873. Until 1866 the loans were preponderantly for industrial purposes—railways, mines, telegraph systems and steamship companies. The crisis of 1866, revealing as it did the rottenness of many of the railway companies, put a damper on this sort of lending, and its place was taken by a new crop of foreign government issues.

It is possible, theoretically, to distinguish three different effects which, according to circumstances, foreign lending might produce on the internal economy of the lending country.

First, the foreign loan may be indirectly the result of a favourable trade balance in the lending country. The existing system of prices, incomes and consumers' preferences may dictate that a certain country has a favourable trade balance; that country will then absorb gold, and interest rates will fall there and rise in the countries which are losing gold; and hence

1 W. T. C. King, *History of the London Discount Market*, p. 189.

those countries may find it profitable to borrow abroad. In this case the foreign lending is a purely permissive element; it is necessary, because in its absence the states with a debit balance must lose gold until interest rates, incomes and prices are so readjusted that the inequality in balances of payments is removed. But the favourable balance of the lending country cannot be called a consequence of its foreign lending; rather is it a consequence of the state of incomes, prices and consumers' preferences existing before the lending took place. Furthermore, and this is important from the point of view of the banking system, foreign lending in this case will be preceded by an influx of gold and followed by an efflux.

Secondly, foreign lending may actually be the cause of a favourable trade balance, either directly, because a large part of the loan is actually spent on the exports of the lending country, or indirectly through movements in interest rates and prices. If the former is the case, then any part of the loan which is not spent on the exports of the lending country must either be left on deposit there or withdrawn in gold; if the latter, then there must, of necessity, be some loss of gold before interest rates rise. Foreign lending of this type will, therefore, be more embarrassing to the central bank than will lending arising out of a favourable trade balance.

Thirdly, a long-term foreign loan may simply be offset by short-term lending in the other direction thus producing no effect at all either on gold movements or on the international balance of trade. This is likely in the initial stages of a loan—funds subscribed would naturally be left on deposit at a bank in the lending country until they could be disposed of. But this would probably be only a short time, and, otherwise, foreign short-term funds would have to be attracted by higher short-term interest rates in the lending country. We may note in passing that England at this time was estimated to have a net short-term debt of some £50 mn. and that though long-term rates were lower in England than on the Continent, short-term rates were generally higher.

In practice any particular loan would probably show all these characteristics, but different types of lending would exhibit them in different proportions. There were three main types of lending, new government issues, new industrial issues and the buying of existing foreign assets by Englishmen. New government issues would be raised solely because of favourable market conditions and would generally produce little consequential increase in the exports of the lending country. In an extreme case, such as the Franco-Prussian indemnity loan, the sole object would be the absorption of gold by a foreign power. New industrial issues would be governed by the market conditions and partly by the fact that much of the money would be spent in England, and here there would be a large and direct consequential increase in exports. The buying of foreign assets by an Englishman would not be likely to produce any direct increase in exports; but there is a high probability that the foreigner would leave his money on deposit or invested in short-term assets in England.

The loan of which some of the proceeds are withdrawn in gold, and the rest left on deposit, affords special difficulties to the central bank, as its reserve will be depleted on the one hand, while, on the other, its control over the market would be impaired. This was a feature especially marked in the Franco-Prussian indemnity loan.

The effect of foreign lending received very little theoretical discussion in the nineteenth century and, so far as we know, very little consideration from the Bank directors. Unlike most Continental markets, the London capital market was entirely free, and I know of no instance of the Bank having used any moral suasion against a loan. Neither do I know of any instance of a rise in Bank rate in order to check lending, as distinct from the efflux of gold which might follow. The issuing houses apparently assumed that this would be so, for there are instances of their bringing gold to London in order to depress interest rates and facilitate an issue. This was done by Barings and the Russian government in 1899. Such an operation would only be undertaken if the people concerned were confident that the Bank would not take any counter-measures.

THE POLICY OF THE BANK

The primary object of the Bank directors, working under the conditions laid down by the act of 1844, was, of necessity, to maintain an adequate reserve in the banking department, and their chief instrument of policy was Bank rate. The working of a rise in Bank rate was now well understood. First, it attracted money from country bank reserves to London and induced foreigners to send more funds and to refrain from removing existing ones. Secondly, it reduced British prices and gave Britain a more favourable balance of payments. And thirdly, if a rise in Bank rate was followed, as it often was, by other central banks, prices were reduced the world over, and so a part of the world's money stock was released from active circulation and passed into central bank reserves.

There is a general correlation between changes in Bank rate and changes in the reserve, but it is only very rough. By this time telegraphic information was available as to gold in transit, and the knowledge that a large quantity of gold was due in London shortly might induce the directors to fix a lower rate than they would otherwise have done. But other far more general considerations were taken into account. It is an accepted principle of banking, which is as valid for central as for ordinary banks, that a reserve which is adequate for one time may be very far from adequate for another. There were changes in the reserve associated with the making and receiving of government payments, changes due to seasonal fluctuations in the domestic circulation and to the half-yearly demand for Scotland, and changes resulting from seasonal changes in foreign trade. All these things were allowed for, and they would cause a rise in Bank rate only if the reserve was or had been subject to other adverse influences as well. On the other hand, there were factors which, though they might not show in a present depletion of the reserve, might be expected to affect it in the more or less distant future. Such factors were the state of domestic and foreign prices, the probability of abnormal imports of corn, the rate of interest in foreign centres, and foreign wars and crises. It was generally supposed that such things as these were taken into consideration by the directors, and that action might be taken in anticipation of the effect which they were expected to produce on the reserve.

For Bank rate to accomplish its purpose, it was, of course, necessary that it should be effective, i.e. that a rise in Bank rate should be followed by market rate. The difficulty in making Bank rate effective was inherent in the changes which we have described and was clearly perceived by many, including Bagehot, but it did not become acute until the 1870's. The reason for this was probably that the Bank still employed a large amount of money in the market, even though this was not a great proportion of the market's whole resources. Bagehot points out that the resources of the market were normally very closely used up and so a change in the discount policy of the Bank might make the difference between ease and stringency.

Immediately after the passage of the act of 1844, opinion leaned to the view that the Bank had little influence over the rate of interest and must simply accommodate its charges to the "supply and demand for capital". But during the 1850's the tone changed, and for most of the present period the financial press is full of admiring comment on the power of the Bank and the ease with which changes in Bank rate achieve their purpose. For instance, *The Economist* of 2 January 1864 refers to a prospective drain of bullion, and states:

We need not be alarmed at it after the recent and most wonderful proofs of the effective nature of the remedy in our hands; the Bank of England has only to raise its rate of discount, and supplies flow into it from all quarters.

This is but one of many examples.

Bank rate can most easily be made effective in proportion as the Bank itself makes a large proportion of discounts, or as the discount houses are dependent on the Bank for re-discounts or advances. This dependence need not be continuous, but it must always be imminent, if a rise in Bank rate is to carry the market with it. Regarded from the point of view of making Bank rate

effective alone, the policy of the directors was often inconsistent. On the one hand, they endeavoured to maintain a considerable volume of their own resources in the market, as is
shown, among other things, by the relaxation of their rules
about discount accounts. The main motive for this was probably the desire for profit, combined with a reluctance to invest
too large a proportion of assets in long-dated securities. On the
other hand, the refusal of discount facilities to the brokers in
1858 tended to make the market more independent and so to
diminish the Bank's control. The motives here would seem to
be mixed. Neave's explanation of the rule refers to the power
of the discount houses to make large withdrawals from the
Bank, and states that "the immense drain upon the Bank in the
last panic has shown that this power is an inconvenient one".
Here is a lingering trace of the old shirking of the responsibilities of lender of last resort, which we have so often noticed.
Then, too, there was, no doubt, a dislike of assisting those
whom the Bank regarded as its rivals. Finally, it was generally
believed that the bill brokers were encouraging accommodation
paper. The Bank had an indirect interest in repressing bad bills,
as they eventually led to failures, and failures to demands on the
Bank, and the directors may have hoped to raise the quality of
the paper by restricting the facilities of the market.

CHEAP MONEY, 1859–60

The crisis of 1857 brought the usual aftermath of cheap money,
and from February 1858 to January 1860 Bank rate was 3% or
less, save only for a few weeks when it rose to $4\frac{1}{2}$% as a consequence of the stock-exchange panic of April 1859. For the rest
of 1860, however, money was dearer, owing to the rise in
activity and to abnormal imports of corn following bad harvests
both in England and France.

The most interesting feature of the period is the attempt of
Gurneys to coerce the Bank into abandoning the rule of 1858,
by which the brokers were refused a discount account, and
restricted to the usual quarterly advances made during the
"shuttings". The rule provoked much controversy when it

was announced, and it was a standing source of dispute between the discount houses and the Bank. In order to bring the force of their arguments before the public, Gurneys, in April 1860, withdrew all at once £1,650,000 in £1000 notes from the Bank. If their object was to obtain publicity, they certainly succeeded, for Mr Gladstone made a statement in Parliament and the papers teemed with comment and criticism. But that was the extent of their success, for the Bank was quite unshaken, and most of the press comment condemned the action; for instance, *The Economist* featured it under the heading of "Injurious Conduct of a Great Discount House".[1] After a short while, Gurneys replaced the money, and there the matter ended save that ill-temper had been aroused on both sides and a satisfactory solution thus made more remote than ever.

The Economist suggested that the Bank should give the discount houses facilities for discounts up to an agreed limit, in return for their keeping always a certain minimum deposit with it. Instead, however, the larger houses practically boycotted the Bank by refusing to borrow even during the "shuttings", and so, for some years, there was very little co-operation between the Bank and the market. In some quarters the increased number of changes in Bank rate which occurred in the 1860's were attributed to this lack of co-operation, but I incline rather to the view of *The Economist*, which held that the most important causes were the Bank's growing consciousness of the power of Bank rate and the exceptionally disturbed conditions through which we were passing.

THE AMERICAN CIVIL WAR AND THE COTTON FAMINE, 1860–5

For the reasons which we have seen, both the Bank of England and the Bank of France were losing gold in 1860, even before the situation was aggravated by the slavery crisis in America. The election of Lincoln in November produced a financial panic in New York, and America, from having been a great gold-exporting country, became a gold-absorbing one.

1 *The Economist*, 21 April, 1860.

America normally had a credit balance with this country, which she used to pay for imports from the East; these imports now virtually ceased, and America withdrew her balance in gold.

The only two large gold reserves in Europe were those of the Bank of England and the Bank of France; any strain thus tended to fall on them jointly, and any action by the one profoundly affected the other. The Bank of France was already in difficulties owing to its reluctance to raise the discount rate in order to meet an efflux of gold and to the workings of the bimetallic system, which was then tending to drain the bank of gold and leave it with silver only. In November 1860 the Bank of England exchanged £2 mn. of gold for £2 mn. of silver with the Bank of France, at the market price. During 1861, however, the Bank of France was again in difficulties, and rather than raise the rate of interest, it bought gold in London, even though the exchanges were much above gold export point. In June 1861 *The Economist* refers to this "peculiar and anomalous action of the Bank of France".[1] Its difficulties still continuing, that body, in October, contracted with Barings and Rothschilds to draw £2 mn. of bills on London. Then at last it raised its rate of discount and, during 1862, rates remained higher in Paris than in London.

With the beginning of the cotton drain, however, Bank rate rose, and we again hear much of these anomalous transactions of the Bank of France. If the Bank is to lose gold anyway, it may be argued that it does not much matter whether the loss occurs through a rise in the rate of interest in a foreign centre turning the exchanges against sterling, or through a foreign bank buying gold at a loss, while the exchanges are still favourable. The only way in which the latter transaction can be more injurious to the Bank is that it may be more sudden and less predictable.

Bank rate was raised to 6% in November 1860, to 7% in January 1861 and to 8% on 14 February, at which point it remained for five weeks. The reserve was then only £6·3 mn.

1 *The Economist*, 8 June 1861.

On 9 February *The Economist* remarks that the Bank has reduced its holding of government securities by over £1 mn. in a year, and comments on the effect of this in reducing bankers' balances and raising the rate of interest. The same article also refers to extensive "borrowing on securities" by the Bank. Bank rate remained high during the spring and summer, and it was not until 15 August that it was reduced to 4%, with the reserve at £8 mn. By this time the American demand for gold was being largely offset by exports of fugitive capital, and it finally ceased with the suspension of cash payments and the issue of the first "Greenbacks" in the New Year. Hence 1862 was a year of cheap money; Bank rate never rose above 3%, and was at 2% for fourteen weeks, yet the reserve rose to £11 mn.

Meanwhile the spell of dear money had produced some effect on home activity. There was very little change in prices, but the Trade Unions unemployment figure rose from 1·9% in 1860 to 5·2% in 1861, and to 8·4% in 1862. The high level of the latter year was due to the cotton famine, but the famine was not felt in 1861.

The year 1862 saw the most acute stage of the cotton famine, for, after that, imports came in greatly increased volume from India and Egypt. This, of course, meant a disturbance in the normal course of international trade and the development of a new import business against which there were no immediate counter-balancing exports. Further, payment had to be made in advance, as the Indian grower needed capital to finance planting. The result was a considerable drain of silver to the East. The silver was taken from the Bank of France and paid for either in gold or in bills on London. The drain on the reserves, of course, tended to operate jointly on both the central banks. The demand for silver was intermittent, and the situation was further complicated by the policy of the Bank of France in again delaying to raise its discount rate until the last possible moment, and then doing so suddenly and violently, and at the same time making anomalous purchases of gold in London. It is in this that we may find the explanation of the so frequent changes in Bank rate, for which the directors have often been condemned.

The cheap money of 1862, and the new provisions of the limited liability acts of that year, led to a new crop of company flotations in 1863 and 1864. "Never since the days of the railway mania, or the great joint-stock speculation of 1824–5, has there been so universal a disposition to encourage public enterprise", says *The Bankers' Magazine* of February 1864. In 1863, activity in all industries except cotton was increasing rapidly, and in the next two years prices, wages and employment were all rising. There was thus an increasing demand for money at home, in addition to the cotton drain.

The drain of silver to the East was first noticed at the end of 1862. In 1863, Bank rate fluctuated between 3 and 5 % until November, and then rose to 8 % on 2 December, with a reserve of only £6·7 mn. It fell to 6 % in February 1864, but rose to 9 % in May, and this time the reserve was reduced to £5·6 mn. By June, however, the reserve had gone up to nearly £9 mn., Bank rate was reduced to 6 %, and *The Economist* commented on "the almost magical power of the recent policy of the Bank of England" [1] But the reserve again fell, and for some weeks from 8 September Bank rate again stood at 9 %, while at times the Bank was borrowing on securities. A temporary check to prices brought lower rates in 1865; the reserve at one time touched £10 mn., and rates varied from 5½ to 3 %. But in October there was a renewal of the cotton drain, the reserve was reduced to £5 mn., Bank rate rose to 7 %, and the Bank again borrowed on securities.

THE CRISIS OF 1866

It has often been said that the crisis of 1866 was purely a crisis of credit. This is true in the sense that there were fewer commercial and industrial bankruptcies than in the previous great crises, but it is certainly not true that the effects were confined to the money market. On the contrary, there were the same movements, not only in interest rates, but also in prices and activity, as we have noticed in all the previous panics.

1 *The Economist*, 18 June 1864.

The crisis is always remembered by the failure of Overend, Gurney & Co., the great house which at one time controlled more than half the business of the discount market, and which had been turned into a limited liability company the previous year. For some years past the company had been pursuing a policy of almost criminal recklessness. Vast amounts of accommodation bills had been discounted, and when they could not be met, money had been advanced on mortgage. When the firm was forced to foreclose on some of these mortgages, instead of liquidating the assets, it took some of them over itself, and at one time the company was even running its own fleet of steamships at an enormous loss. Much of this did not come out until the court proceedings, but the City had its suspicions, and *The Economist* commented acidly that "the failure of Overend, Gurney & Co. Ltd. has given rise to a panic more suitable to their historical than to their recent reputation".[1]

In January 1866 Bank rate rose to 8% owing to the continued drain of silver to the East, and the firm of railway contractors, Watson, Overend & Co., stopped payment. The unfortunate resemblance between the names threw suspicion on Overend, Gurney & Co., and their shares fell on the stock exchange, though in fact the two firms were quite unconnected. Bank rate fell to 6% in March, but then came the failure of Pinto, Perez & Co., Spanish merchants with whom Gurneys were largely involved, and Bank rate went up again to 7%. Finally, a court ruling of 9 May that the acceptances of the Mid-Wales Railway were *ultra vires* threatened the whole mass of railway paper, which Gurneys were known to hold, and so a run on the house was precipitated. Gurneys approached the Bank, which appointed a confidential committee to enquire into the accounts, and on the basis of its report very naturally refused assistance. So, on 10 May, the "corner house" stopped payment.

The panic which followed was described as more wild than anything since 1825. The Bank reserve was reduced by £3 mn. in a single day. Bank rate was at once raised to 9%, and the rate for advances to 10%. At these rates the Bank made ad-

1 *The Economist*, 12 May 1866.

vances quite freely, save for a moment of hesitation during the afternoon of 11 May, when it was doubtful whether loans could be had on government securities.[1] On 12 May there was issued a Treasury Letter, in the now familiar terms, and Bank rate was raised to 10%. During the five days after the failure of Gurneys the Bank advanced £2,874,000 on securities and £9,350,000 in discounts.[2] It was not, however, necessary to break the law; the reserve stood at £1,200,000 when the rate was raised to 10%, and the lowest recorded amount was £860,000 on 30 May.

A point of difference from previous crises is the weakness of the reserve and the long continuance of high rates of interest. The 10% rate was maintained until 16 August, when it was reduced to 8%, and even then the reserve was only £4·6 mn. This was explained partly by the added caution of country bankers, who were holding banknotes in reserve, and partly by the fact that people on the Continent failed to distinguish between the Treasury Letter and the abandonment of the gold standard; thus their confidence in the stability of sterling was impaired, and the high rate of interest failed to produce its usual effect in attracting foreign funds. But even in view of the weakness of the reserve, the Bank was widely attacked in the press for having maintained the high rate for so long.

The crisis had one interesting sequel. At the next Court of Proprietors, Governor Lancelot Holland, referring to the crisis, said:

We could not flinch from the duty which we conceived was imposed upon us, of supporting the banking community, and I am not aware that any legitimate application for assistance which was made to this house was refused.

This was welcomed by *The Economist* as an unqualified admission that the Bank ought always to lend on good security at times when it was impossible to borrow elsewhere. *The*

1 *The Economist*, 12 May 1866.
2 Statement of Chancellor of the Exchequer, quoted by *The Bankers' Magazine*, June 1866.

Economist article provoked a vigorous rejoinder from one of the more reactionary of the directors, Mr Thomson Hankey, who criticised both the Governor's speech and Bagehot's interpretation of it, and denied that the Bank had any such obligations. The controversy was quoted at great length by Bagehot in *Lombard Street*. Public opinion, however, was on the side of the Governor and Bagehot, and the episode may be said to mark another and final stage in the assumption by the Bank of the responsibilities of lender of last resort.

THE FRANCO-PRUSSIAN WAR AND THE FRENCH INDEMNITY

The crisis was followed, as usual, by low rates of interest and falling prices. The price indices reached the lowest point, and the Trade Unions unemployment figures their peak, in the year 1868. The Bank was distinctly cautious in its reduction of the discount rate, and it was not until December, when the reserve was £11·7 mn., that 3½% was reached; but in July 1867 Bank rate fell to 2%, where it remained for sixteen months. 1869 saw the beginning of recovery, and under the influence of a revival of trade and a renewed export of capital, the reserve fell to £7·5 mn., and Bank rate was raised to 4½% in May 1868. *The Economist* criticised the Bank for its tardiness in checking this decline, and suggested that a reserve of £10 mn. should be regarded as the normal minimum. After only seven weeks, however, the reserve had recovered to £12 mn., and Bank rate was reduced to 3½%. Thenceforward, conditions remained very quiet until the outbreak of the Franco-Prussian war.

The immediate effect of the political crisis was to bring fugitive capital to London. Soon after the outbreak of war, however, there was a strong demand for gold from the banking centres of Northern Europe. On 21 July, while the reserve was still over £12 mn., Bank rate was raised from 3 to 3½%, and by 4 August the reserve had fallen to £9·3 mn. and Bank rate was 6%. The Bank, it will be seen, had acted with notable promptness and caution. The suspension of specie payments by the Bank of France came as a relief, in that the Bank had no longer to face competition for new supplies of gold. It also meant that the Bank of England was now the only central Bank which was bound to buy and sell gold at a fixed price.

With the cessation of the precautionary demand for gold from Europe, and the arrival of new supplies, the reserve was again rapidly augmented. 6% lasted only for one week, and by the end of September Bank rate was down to 2½% again, with the reserve at over £14 mn. A very slight drain in the spring of 1871 was promptly met by a rise to 3%, but in July the rate was reduced to 2%, and at the end of that month the reserve reached the unprecedented figure of £17·4 mn.

It had been expected that the return of peace would bring an efflux of European capital, but this was retarded by the political troubles of France. New complications were, however, created by the indemnity payment imposed by Germany, and which was made largely through London.

The indemnity was fixed at five milliard francs, and after allowing for interest payments on the one hand, and for the value of French railways taken over in Alsace and Lorraine on the other, there remained 4,990,000,000 frs. or approximately £200 mn. to be paid. Payments had to be made in definite instalments and at a date announced beforehand, and could not simply be paid into a current account. They might be made in a number of specified currencies, in gold or silver coin, banknotes, or bills of exchange. Payments made in foreign currencies were only credited at the rate at which the German government actually converted them, and bills were subject to discount. Naturally the French government preferred to handle the exchange operation itself, and so the greater part of the payments were made in German currencies. The first payment of 1,837,000,000 frs. was made in instalments between 1 June 1871 and 12 March 1872, and the second payment of 3,154,000,000 frs. in instalments between 28 August 1872 and 9 September 1873. 742,000,000 frs. was paid in coin and notes, and 4,248,000,000 frs. in bills of exchange in various currencies.

For the handling of its exchange business, the French

government set up agencies in London, Berlin, Hamburg, Frankfurt, Amsterdam and Brussels. That in London was set up in June 1871. It bought £60 mn. and held it until required, employing it meanwhile largely on the London discount market. £31 mn. was converted into German bills before payment, and the rest, apart from small purchases of gold and silver, was paid in sterling. Figures for the balances of this agency are available from December 1871 to August 1873. They were about £5 mn. in December 1871, rising to £6¾ mn. in February 1872, and falling to only £500,000 in May; they then rose to £8 mn. in August, and remained at over £7 mn. until the turn of the year, after which they gradually declined. When we compare these figures with a Bank reserve which varied, during the same period, from rather over £15 mn. to rather under £9 mn., it is obvious how important an influence the indemnity payment exerted.[1]

The transfer of funds to Germany did not at once mean the loss of so much gold to London. The object of the German government was ultimately to obtain gold, either for hoarding in their war chest at Spandau, or for the new imperial gold currency, but they realised that it was in their own interest to make the withdrawals gradually. Gold was seldom taken directly from the Bank, but the German government bought up new supplies as they came into the market. The Bank reserve was, none the less, diminished by the transaction, since the Bank normally relied on new supplies to balance the efflux which took place for other purposes. The German government continued to hold large balances in London for some years and to make large but intermittent purchases of gold.

The first efflux began in August and continued until November 1871. Net exports totalled over £6 mn., and this at a time coinciding with a seasonal decline in the Bank reserve. From £17·4 mn. in July, the reserve fell to only just over £8 mn. on 11 October. Bank rate was raised only to 5%, and even this not until the reserve was below £9 mn. The 5% rate was not entirely effective, owing to the large volume of foreign

1 Léon Say, *Rapport sur le paiement de l'indemnité de guerre*, 1875.

balances employed in the discount market, and *The Economist* criticises the Bank for not borrowing on stock. The efflux of gold ceased at the end of the year, and a large reflux from the provinces raised the reserve to over £15·5 mn. On 14 December Bank rate was again reduced to 3%.

During the first six months of 1873 the German demand rather less than absorbed new supplies, but occasional sudden withdrawals caused oscillations in Bank rate. In the autumn there was again a fairly large net export, and the reserve had fallen to only £9 mn. when the rate was raised to 7% on 9 November. Again there was difficulty in making Bank rate effective owing to the large foreign balances in the market. *The Economist* again criticises the directors, both for raising the rate tardily and for not making it effective, and comments that the rise from 5 to 6%, which was not followed by the market, did more harm than good, in that it promoted an effective rise in Continental centres. As usual, however, the high rate checked the export of gold and brought supplies from the provinces to the Bank; by 12 December the reserve was nearly £14 mn., and Bank rate was reduced to 5%.

THE END OF THE BOOM

The year 1873 was marked by major financial crises both in Europe and the United States, the European one in May, the American in September. In England both these crises had a serious effect on the money market, there were no less than twenty-four changes in Bank rate, and there was a general reversal of the upward trend of prices. But there was no financial panic, no abnormally large number of commercial bankruptcies, and only a very slight increase in unemployment. There is a marked divergence between the Sauerbeck raw material index and that of *The Economist*; the former shows a rise and a fall in prices almost as marked as that culminating in 1866, the latter very much less so. The absence of panic is probably to be attributed in part to the cautious policy of the Bank, and partly to the fact that the boom in England had not reached its full height, but had been prematurely checked by the high interest rates of 1872, coupled with a bad harvest and a sharp rise in the price of coal and iron.[1]

Bank rate fell to 3½% at the end of January, with a reserve of £15 mn., but it was raised to 4% at the end of March. It was not until 7 May, with a reserve of just under £11 mn., that there was a further rise to 4½%. *The Economist* is very critical of this. But if the Bank had been somewhat slow, it now made up for it by acting very firmly. The European panic created a new demand for gold, and the reserve continued to decline slightly. Bank rate was raised to 7% in June, when the reserve was over £10½ mn. With this compare the position in 1866, when the rate was reduced from 7 to 6% on 15 March, with a reserve of only £8·8 mn., and was not raised to 7% again until 3 May, when the reserve was only £5·6 mn.

The German currency demand ceased during the summer, while their mint was coining gold received from France, and the cessation of the panic in Germany brought some improvement in the reserve. Bank rate fell gradually to 3% on 21 August, with a reserve of £13·3 mn. So large a fall was again the subject of adverse criticism from *The Economist*. At the beginning of September came a renewal of the German demand, followed shortly by news of the American crisis. Between 3 August and 7 November there was a net export of £2·7 mn., again coinciding with the seasonal internal demand. Bank rate reached 7% on 18 October, with the reserve just under £8 mn., but this figure represented an exceptional reduction consequent on the payment of the dividends. The same cause made money plentiful in the market, and it was not until the beginning of November, after continued borrowing on stock, that the 7% rate was made effective.[2] The Bank then raised its rate to 8% on 1 November, with a reserve of £8·4 mn., and to 9% on the 7th, with the reserve at 8 mn.; again we may note how much more cautious was this than the policy of 1866. At this moment, the German government, whether from charity or desire for profit, suspended its gold withdrawals, and

1 *The Economist*, 4 Jan. 1873.   2 *Ibid.* 25 Oct. and 1 Nov. 1873.

gold came in from abroad. Bank rate was reduced to 8% on 20 November, and this was ineffective, although the Bank still held the money which it had borrowed on stock.[1] The New York panic rapidly passed, and by the end of the year the atmosphere was again calm, Bank rate was only 4½%, and the reserve nearly £12½ mn.

In retrospect it would seem that the directors came through a very difficult year in a manner worthy of praise; in their day, however, they received much criticism. We have noticed that they kept a reserve much larger than in 1866, though still not large enough for some of their critics. The chief cause for doubt was the speed with which Bank rate was reduced, once the immediate threat to the reserve had passed. This was inspired by a very commendable desire not to press too hardly on trade, when it already showed signs of flagging, combined with the difficulty, which we have noticed, of making a high rate effective in face of competition from large foreign balances.

1 *The Economist*, 22 Nov. 1873.

Chapter Nine

THE GREAT DEPRESSION
1873–96

GENERAL CHARACTERISTICS

The period from 1850 to 1873 had been one in which cyclical fluctuations had been superimposed on a marked upward trend in prices. Wages had been rising, unemployment low, and international trade rapidly expanding. The stock of monetary gold was rapidly increasing, yet in spite of this interest rates were generally high. Between 1873 and 1896 all these features were reversed. The various price indices all showed a markedly downward trend, the drop over the whole period being about 40%, or rather more than double the normal cyclical fluctuation of the nineteenth century. It was not until the 1890's that Mr G. H. Wood's wage index rose above the 1874 level, and the rise over the whole period was only 5%, compared with over 40% between 1858 and 1873. In spite of the great increase in food imports the value of our international trade rose by only a moderate amount—the highest import figure recorded is only 16% and the highest export figure only 10% above those of 1873; the volume of trade, however, increased by more than this, owing to the fall in prices. The Trade Unions unemployment figure shows an average of 5·3%, compared with just under 4·7% for 1856–73. From 1874 to 1879 there was a virtual cessation of foreign investment, and our favourable balance of payments shrank to nothing; there was a recovery to a very high level in the late 1880's, but a fall again in the 1890's.

The world production of gold showed a slight decline, but one which was very small in relation to total stocks. Much more important was the increased demand for gold, as a result of the resumption of cash payments by the Bank of France, and the adoption of a gold standard by Germany, America and a number of smaller countries. Net imports of gold into this country were £74·5 mn. between 1858 and July 1871, but between then and the end of 1888 they were no more than 4·7 mn.[1] A more detailed analysis of movements between 1871 and 1886 will be found in Table XVII. It will be seen that London was carrying on her former business of distributing the world's

Table XVII

MOVEMENTS OF GOLD BETWEEN GREAT BRITAIN AND OTHER PRINCIPAL IMPORTING AND EXPORTING COUNTRIES, 1871–86

Imports from or exports to (−)
£ thousands

Year	France	Germany	Australia	U.S.A.	All countries
1871	2139	−7566	6899	6379	921
1872	7077	−7698	5983	8287	−1280
1873	877	−7144	9444	757	1540
1874	−4694	−47	6721	4500	7439
1875	−3228	−5997	6620	7681	4493
1876	−2762	−1520	4947	848	6960
1877	−5275	−7913	6655	894	−4932
1878	1309	−3445	5671	37	5902
1879	2209	−2833	3185	−6561	−4210
1880	1516	90	3602	−5457	−2374
1881	1041	−168	4470	−7364	−5536
1882	−1458	−547	2997	6008	2353
1883	1194	−32	2256	−928	665
1884	1688	−216	−211	2888	−1269
1885	1669	−2942	3737	610	1446
1886	169	−595	2586	27	−392

new supplies of gold, but was doing much more distribution and retaining much less herself. Yet in spite of this growing scarcity of gold in relation to the demand for it, Bank rate, and interest rates in general, were unprecedentedly low.

THE GROWING SENSITIVITY OF THE MARKET

It was a constant subject for comment in the financial press that the money market was much more sensitive to international influences than it had been in the past. For this there were several reasons.

Most of the gold absorbed between 1858 and 1871 was taken

1 Hawtrey, *A Century of Bank Rate*, p. 47.

into circulation, so that a vastly increased trade was being conducted on the basis of an only slightly increased central reserve.

London's position as the centre of the international gold
market made the Bank reserve liable to considerable fluctuation,
for though, over the whole year, imports of new gold might
more than balance exports, the two would not by any means
coincide in time. When, on balance, arrivals largely exceeded
withdrawals, these fluctuations did not much matter, but when
gold was going away almost as fast as it came they assumed
considerable importance. The liability of the Bank to sudden
demands was further increased between 1871 and 1878, as none
of the other important central banks were paying in gold.

More important still was the growing influence of international capital movements. England had been making long-
term loans to foreign states since the beginning of the nineteenth century, and it was recognised that a low rate of interest
at home tended to stimulate such transactions, while a high rate
checked them. But the effect of changes in the rate of interest
on the movement of short-term funds was not seriously felt
until the 1850's. We find references to it in the evidence before
the Committees of 1857 and 1858, but even then it is only in
times of crisis, when fluctuations in the rate of interest are very
violent, that short-term funds move on a large scale. It is not
until the 1860's and 1870's that such movements become an
everyday occurrence, and that comparative rates between
London and other centres attract the attention of the press, not
only in times of disturbance, but as part of the ordinary routine
of commercial life.

Short-term capital movements were greatly assisted by the
international telegraph, which gave instant information about
comparative rates, and later actually served as a means of
transfer. But the essential thing, without which large-scale
transfers of credit could not take place, is ease in the movement
of gold. The most important items in the cost of sending gold
abroad are insurance and the loss of interest during transit; the
steamship and the railway reduced both these items, by adding
both to the speed and safety of carriage. Thus the gap between
gold import and export points was materially lessened, and the

possibility of loss on the exchanges as the result of a short-term foreign loan correspondingly reduced.

We have already referred to the growth of London as an international banking centre and to the short-term balances kept in London by foreign governments. But it was not only foreign governments who did this. The crisis of 1866 had left gaps in our financial equipment which were filled up by an influx of foreign firms, mostly engaged in contracting for international loans.[1] Foreign banks either set up London offices or opened accounts with London banks, and bills of exchange bearing a London acceptance were a favourite security for foreign bankers. As early as 1864 Goschen remarks on this:

In Paris, Berlin, Frankfurt, Hamburg and other Continental cities, the bills on England held by the bankers and other joint-stock companies often amount to many millions sterling... the immense importance of this circumstance cannot be overlooked. If at any time the rate of interest here falls below that which rules on the Continent, it is inevitable that all the whole mass of these bills will at once be sent to London, and will be discounted there at the cheaper rate, so that the proceeds may be remitted in gold to the Continent, to be invested there in local securities at the supposed higher rate.[2]

It was estimated that a difference of 1% in the rate for three months' bills between London and Paris was sufficient to stimulate the movement of gold.[3]

The Bank was thus in a position in which, more than ever, it needed a sure and firm control over the market, yet at this very time circumstances were making this control weaker than it had ever been. But before we discuss these circumstances we must note one or two changes in the nature of the market.

CHANGES IN THE DISCOUNT MARKET— THE TREASURY BILL

From the 1850's the importance of the bill of exchange in domestic trade was steadily declining. One of the chief advantages of bills of exchange compared with the overdraft

1 W. T. C. King, *History of the London Discount Market*, p. 267.
2 Goschen, *The Foreign Exchanges*, pp. 136–7.   3 *The Economist.*

system was that the banks could re-discount them on the London market, and there was thus provided a convenient means of evening up the position of banks which had either more demands for discounts than they could meet, or more funds than they could employ. But the abuses of accommodation paper threw even this legitimate use of re-discounting into discredit, and with the extension of branch banking the need for it passed away. By the 1890's domestic trade was carried on almost entirely by means of the cheque, and the bill of exchange had become an anachronism.

The volume of bills coming into the market was, however, maintained by the increased number of foreign bills, consequent upon the growth of the London accepting houses, and by the new issue of Treasury bills.

The old Exchequer bill was issued only twice a year, in March and June, and its currency was five years. Interest was paid half-yearly, but at a fluctuating rate to be decided, in the case of each payment, by the government. If the holder were dissatisfied with the rate paid he might, after the first half-year, tender his bill in payment of taxes at par. Otherwise, he had the right to ask for repayment, but only on the anniversary of the bill's issue could he demand it; at all other times the Treasury had the right of refusal. In these circumstances it is not surprising that Exchequer bills were not a very popular security. The new Treasury bill was first issued in 1877, on the advice of Walter Bagehot, and was, in all essentials, the same as an ordinary commercial bill of exchange. It soon became a favourite security with the market, and enabled the government to borrow at a much reduced rate of interest, but its use was somewhat limited by the fact that, until 1902, it could only be used for payments falling on the Consolidated Fund.

THE INEFFECTIVENESS OF BANK RATE

Since the beginning of the nineteenth century there had occurred a great change both in the importance of the London money market in determining international gold movements and in the relationship of the Bank and the market.

At the beginning of the century gold movements depended almost entirely on the visible balance of trade—that is, on the relative prices, here and abroad, of goods entering into international commerce. In determining this, the London discount market was an important influence, but by no means the only one. A great deal of international trade was financed by provincial banks enjoying a measure of independence of London, and one of the chief problems of the central bank was to control the lending policy of these provincial banks. By 1870, however, the fundamental influence of the balance of trade was being profoundly modified, as regards the short period, by movements of short-term capital, and in determining these the London market was all important.

At the beginning of the century discounts were the only way, other than advances to the government, in which the Bank employed its funds, and the Bank supplied by far the greater part of the resources of the market. Thus a decline in the resources of the Bank naturally led to a decline in the resources of the market and so, even though the rate remained unchanged, to a decreased facility of obtaining discounts. But this quantitative supremacy was impaired by the 1850's, and quite lost by the 1870's. In the early 1870's Bank discounts show a considerable decline, and in 1875, the last year for which figures are available, they were only £4·4 mn., including a considerable amount made at the branches. From that time onwards, though figures were not published, it was generally believed that the Bank made few discounts in normal times.

The decline of the Bank's discounts was in part a consequence of the growth of other sources of funds for the market. For this there were several reasons. The first is simply the growth of general banking business. In 1833 the Bank held £13 mn. of deposits, while those of the other London bankers were estimated at £22 mn., and those of the country bankers at from £16 to £20 mn. In the early 1870's, the Bank held about £28 mn., and other bankers probably more than £600 mn., so that the ratio of Bank deposits to those of other bankers had fallen from a third to less than one-twentieth.[1] This growth

1 *The Economist*, 27 Oct. 1877.

of deposits demanded an increase of liquid assets, and these were found either in discounts or loans to the bill brokers, though the liquidity of both really depended on the belief that the Bank would always be willing to discount. Competition among banks led to high rates of interest on deposits, and this produced a reduction in cash reserves and a strengthening of the "second line of defence" to make up for it. Thirdly, there was the influence of foreign deposits. Often they were directly employed in the market by their owners, but even if they were left on deposit with a bank they would indirectly affect the market, as a cautious banker would place them in a different category from ordinary deposits, and would hold a more than usually high proportion of liquid assets against them.

So far from being the largest lender in the market, the Bank was now practically out of touch with it, save only during the first quarter of the year, when the revenue was being collected. How, then, could a diminution of the bank reserve be made to be felt in the market? Ordinarily such a diminution would be associated with a diminution of bankers' balances, but even if that were so, the banks might respond, not by contracting their loans to the bill market, but by contracting other forms of lending, and actually strengthening the "second line of defence". But if a diminution of the reserve arose through the withdrawal of balances held by the foreign governments themselves, or of firms not keeping their accounts with a commercial bank, no such effect on bankers' balances would be produced at all.

The only methods, of diminishing the resources of the market, which tradition allowed the Bank were either selling securities, or "borrowing on stock", i.e. selling for cash and buying back for the account. Both were highly expensive, and it might be necessary to push them to a very great extent before they proved effective. The attempt to find a method of control at once less costly and more certain was the subject of constant thought and experiment and led to a number of changes in Bank technique.

SEASONAL AND OTHER FLUCTUATIONS
IN THE RESERVE

The Bank reserve, under the provisions of the Bank Charter Act, is simply the difference between the coin and bullion in the Bank, plus the fixed fiduciary issue, and the notes in the hands of the public. It is, therefore, subject to three influences, the demand for gold for export, the demand for gold for the domestic circulation, and the demand for notes for the same purpose. In all of these there are more or less regular seasonal fluctuations, on which other and less predictable fluctuations are superimposed.

These are naturally least apparent in the demand for gold for export, but there was a distinct seasonal variation in our trade balance, the most adverse period being in the autumn. There was a regular increase in the demand for gold coin in August and September, for holiday payments and for the harvest, and in May and November there was always an efflux of gold to Scotland. The Scots banks were obliged to cover all their note issue above a fixed amount in gold; their note issues increased largely to meet the half-yearly payments falling due, in Scotland, in May and November, and the Scots banks therefore drew upon their London agents for gold. There was also a seasonal variation in the note issue of the Bank, the highest point being in August and the lowest in February. A further cause of variation in the note issue was the payment of the dividends, of which we have already written. Payment took place in the first weeks of January, April, July and October, the January and July payments being the heaviest. At these times, payments were made not only on British government securities, but also on many foreign ones, and on the shares of railways and other joint-stock companies. It was estimated that some £30 mn. was paid in January, and a similar amount in July.[1]

It will thus be seen that, between July and November, all these influences combined to reduce the reserve. After the budget of 1869, government balances were also especially low, and the resources of the market especially abundant at this time. Hence it is that we so often have a low reserve accompanied by

1 *The Economist*, 29 Dec. 1883.

a high but ineffective Bank rate, and that at this time the problem of the control of the Bank over the market is most acute.

Besides the seasonal fluctuations, there is a fairly clear cyclical fluctuation in the demand for coin and notes. Other things being equal, the demand for both would vary with the level of activity and prices, but the correlation is obscured in the statistics by the effect of changes in Bank rate. A high rate of interest would lead to a reduction of provincial reserves, and so would attract gold and notes—especially gold—to London. The effect of this was, of course, particularly marked when there was a sudden rise in Bank rate after a period of low rates and rapidly increasing circulation. These variations in "interior demand" are traced in great detail by Mr Hawtrey in *A Century of Bank Rate*. Their nature was well understood at the time, and they form the subject of frequent press comment, but they appear, nevertheless, occasionally to have misled the directors. At times they raised the rate when the reserve had been depleted by the export of gold, and reduced it again when the reserve was increased by the reflux from the country, only to find that the forces making for the export of gold were still in operation and that yet another rise was necessary.

CHANGES IN BANK TECHNIQUE

Among the Bank's many difficulties there were one or two new features that were favourable to it. First, the growth of government expenditure increased the power of the Bank over the market during the first quarter of the year. Incidentally, there was a strong tradition that the Bank ought not to use this power to inflict high rates on the country, and it was only in special circumstances that the directors took advantage of their position to the full. Secondly, there was the growth of banker's balances. These had been only about £1 mn. in 1844, but had risen steadily since that time, and averaged over £10 mn. for 1875-7, the last years for which separate figures were published.

Market rate could be made to conform to Bank rate if either the market drew an appreciable proportion of its resources in discounts or advances from the Bank, or if the resources of the market were so fully occupied that a small increase in demand, or a small subtraction of funds, would force dealers to re-discount.

After 1858, as we have seen, the Bank refused advances to the brokers, but tried to maintain contact with the market through extending its own discounts. For the decade 1860–70, discounts averaged £7 mn. Then, in 1871, came the first of those wide divergences between Bank rate and market rate which were later to become so marked. As the gap between the rates grew wider and more permanent, so the Bank's discounts grew less until, by 1875, discounts in the London market were very small indeed. Mr W. T. C. King ascribes this to an act of conscious policy on the part of the directors in refusing any longer to follow the market. I think, however, that Bank rate policy was always decided by two things, the supply and demand for discounts and the state of the reserve. The directors were always anxious to bring Bank rate into as close a relation as possible with market rate, and on many occasions *The Economist* chides them with being too tardy in raising the rate, or too hasty in reducing it, when market rate is below Bank rate.[1] The reason why the Bank did not obtain more discounts was simply that, conditions being as they were, at whatever level Bank rate stood the market would underbid it, until a point was reached at which fear for their reserve prevented the directors from going any lower.

A consequence of the wide gap between Bank rate and market rate was to inflict hardship on a few regular customers who still did their discount business with the Bank, and in June 1878 it was announced that the Bank would discount at market rate for customers who did all their discount business with it. In some quarters it was thought that this change would again bring the Bank into more active competition with the brokers, but this does not appear to have been so, for, two years later, *The Economist* wrote:

The impression of the outer market is that, so far as the action of the Bank can be traced there, the alteration has produced very little effect. There is no reason to believe, as far as the transactions of the

[1] *The Economist*, 12 Jan. 1874, 12 Jan. 1878, 12 June 1886, etc.

outer market show, that the amount of bills held by the Bank of England is now very large.[1]

The concession to regular customers was further extended in 1890, when the Bank agreed to discount for regular customers at Bank rate, even though market rate, and the rate charged by the Bank on other transactions, was above the minimum.[2]

At the same time, the rule of 1858, though formally unchanged, appears to have been a good deal relaxed, for in April 1883 the brokers were charged 4% for advances, though Bank rate was only 3%, and the Bank intimated that, in future, the rule would be more rigidly enforced. *The Economist* commented that "There can be no doubt that, of late, the brokers have come to rely too much upon the Bank".[3] *The Bankers' Magazine* also welcomed the change, and hoped that it would result in the brokers and banks keeping a larger reserve with the Bank.[4] The change does seem to have produced the desired effect of increasing the reserves kept with the Bank, but in so far as it made the brokers more independent, it must have weakened rather than strengthened the Bank's control over the market. It is significant that the difficulty of making Bank rate effective was even more acute after the change than before.

The practice of raising Bank rate by stages of 1% rather than $\frac{1}{2}$% when it was desired to check a foreign drain of gold was first adopted at the suggestion of Goschen in the 1860's, and was now the usual course. Variations in Bank rate other than on Court days had also become so common that, on the occasion of one of them, *The Economist* comments: "We may now consider the traditional rule which used to bind the Bank not to make any change in its rate except on a Thursday, as entirely set aside."[5] Nevertheless, such changes were still exceptions to the usual rule and, consequently, they usually produced a more than normal effect on the market.

Another small change made for the convenience of the Bank was that loans to the stock exchange were made for a minimum period of ten days instead of five.

1 *The Economist*, 18 June 1880.
2 R. S. Sayers, *Bank of England Operations*, 1890–1914, p. 16.
3 28 April 1883.   4 June 1883.   5 4 Feb. 1882.

The new issue of Treasury bills provided the Bank with further assistance in controlling the market, since it meant that money which had formerly been taken from the Bank by means of deficiency bills could now be raised in the market. Often the Bank allowed this to happen as a means of absorbing the surplus resources of the market. But Treasury bills were also a desirable investment from the point of view of the Bank, and the desire to possess them for their own sake seems sometimes to have outweighed more far-sighted considerations. Thus, the Bank bought Treasury bills, while still maintaining Bank rate considerably above market rate. This "holding the rate up with one hand, and beating it down with the other", drew frequent reproaches from the press.[1]

The governorship of the enterprising William Lidderdale, coinciding with the troubles of 1890, produced another crop of changes, some of them very important.

At the beginning of January 1890 Bank rate was 6%, but although the Bank had been borrowing at the end of the previous year, market rate was only $4\frac{1}{2}$%. In these circumstances, the Bank entered into an arrangement with the Hampshire County Council by which that body should keep its balances with the Bank, and any amount over £20,000 should be lent, under the Bank's guarantee, to the market. These loans were to be made by the Bank on such terms as it thought fit, and the interest, less a trifling commission, credited to the council. The Bank was at pains to emphasise that the arrangement involved no departure from the rule that interest was not paid on deposits.[2] At first the manœuvre had only limited success, but during the summer arrangements were made with a number of other public bodies, including the India Council, and first the rate for short loans, and then discount rate, were levered up to Bank rate. A further accession of strength came after the Baring crisis, when the Russian government transferred the balances, which it had formerly kept with Barings, to the Bank.[3]

Meanwhile, on 22 July, the Bank had taken the important

1 Cf. *The Economist*, 17 Nov. 1883 and 17 Dec. 1887.
2 *Ibid.* 22 Feb. 1890, and *The Bankers' Magazine*, March 1890.
3 *The Economist*, 13 Dec. 1890.

step of re-admitting the bill brokers to the discount facilities which they had not enjoyed since 1858. It was announced that, henceforward, the Bank would discount good bills having not more than fifteen days to run. This was at last a recognition that the Bank could not hope both to control the market and to remain altogether aloof from it.

The Bank also initiated a more active gold policy. There were precedents for this in the 1880's, but it was only in 1889–90 that it gained widespread attention. The Bank was bound by law to buy gold bars at the rate of at least £3. 17s. 9d. per oz., and to pay its notes in gold coin at a rate equivalent to £3. 17s. 10½d. It was, therefore, free to raise the buying price of gold bars above £3. 17s. 9d., and to fix as it chose both the selling price of gold bars and the buying and selling price of foreign coin. In December 1889 the Bank refused to sell bar gold at all,[1] and in February 1890 it raised its buying price for bar gold by ½d. per oz.[2] In October 1890 it also resorted to a policy which we have noticed earlier, of discriminating against the discount of bills presumed to be for the financing of gold exports. Gold-market operations became much more important at the beginning of the present century, and we shall have more to say of them in the next chapter.

THE FIRST DEPRESSION, 1874–9

The decline in trade after 1873 was not rapid. The sharp fall in prices from 1873 to 1875 was checked in the next year, and only resumed in 1878–9, while it was not until those years that unemployment reached what could be called depression level. Neither was there the long spell of very cheap money which followed the crisis of 1866. Bank rate fell to 2½% in June 1874, but rose to 4% in October. The Bank of France was trying to accumulate gold and interest rates in Paris were high. The Bank delayed raising the rate any further, as market rate was lagging some way behind, but at the end of November it had to go to 6% and borrow on stock, with the reserve at little over £9 mn. 1875 was a year of cheaper money; Bank rate varied from 4 to

1 *The Economist*, 4 Dec. 1889.　　　2 *Ibid.* 15 Feb. 1890.

2½%, and even so the Bank often lost touch with the market. In August Bank rate dropped to 2%, but the market rate was still so far below it that the joint-stock banks held a meeting to try to arrange some alternative method of fixing the London deposit rate; they failed, however, to reach any agreement. In April 1876, in spite of occasional purchases of gold by France and Germany, Bank rate again fell to 2%, and remained there for over a year, while, in September, the reserve touched the unprecedented height of nearly £22¼ mn. At the beginning of 1877 there was a great efflux of gold, but the reserve was allowed to fall below £11 mn. before Bank rate was raised to 3% on 3 May. In the autumn the reserve was further weakened, and Bank rate rose to 5%. This rate was quite ineffective, and this time the joint-stock banks agreed to allow 1½% below Bank rate, instead of 1% below Bank rate, for deposits.

By now British prices were out of alignment with those of the rest of the world, and in 1877 our adverse visible trade balance was £142 mn., practically double that of 1874. Yet, at the beginning of January 1878, the reserve rose to £13 mn., and Bank rate was reduced to 2%, in an attempt to keep in touch with the market. It remained at that level for eight weeks, although the reserve fell to no more than 37% of its liabilities, "a figure more usually associated with 5 or 5½% than 2%".[1] The reserve was very weak during the summer, but the Bank was reluctant to raise the rate because of the difficulty of making it effective. In August 5% was imposed, but the Bank had to sell £2·4 mn. of securities between 1 August and 2 September in order to make it effective. In October came the City of Glasgow failure. The Bank showed praiseworthy judgement in not raising rates above 6%, although the note issue reached an unprecedented height, and the reserve fell to £8·5 mn., only 28% of the liabilities. The failure did not create a crisis in the money market, but it was followed by all the usual consequences of one. Prices fell rapidly, unemployment rose to 11·4%, and there was a rapid recovery of the Bank reserve. In April 1879 Bank rate fell to 2%, and in July the reserve again exceeded £21 mn.

[1] *The Economist*, 23 March 1878.

RECOVERY AND RENEWED DEPRESSION, 1880–7

The year 1880 saw a slight recovery in prices and a general improvement in trade, and for the next four years unemployment averaged only 3·4%. Then the downward trend was resumed, and the succeeding four years showed an unemployment figure of no less than 8·8%.

During 1880 and 1881 the Bank reserve was abundant, and, for the most part, market rate was below Bank rate, yet the directors pursued a markedly more conservative policy. In June 1880 Bank rate was reduced to 2½% only when the reserve reached £17·4 mn., or 48% of the liabilities, and it was raised to 3% in December, with the reserve still nearly £14 mn. (45%), and to 3½% in January 1881, with a reserve of over £12·5 mn. (40%). By now the market was in the Bank owing to the collection of the revenue, and it was a tradition that the rate should not be kept unduly high at such times. Yet it was not until the reserve had reached £16·5 mn. (47%), on 17 February, that Bank rate was reduced to 3%. Compare this with the reduction from 3 to 2%, with a reserve of less than £13 mn. (44%), in 1878.

There was a short spell of 6% at the beginning of 1882, as a consequence of the Union Générale failure in Paris, but otherwise the years 1881–3 were uneventful. The problem of the market and the Bank was, on the whole, less acute; market rate was often below Bank rate, but the gap was less than formerly, and not infrequently the Bank found itself in complete control of the situation.

The reason for the renewed industrial depression of 1884 is far from obvious. It was not the result of any monetary crisis, or even of a period of very high interest rates, for during 1883 Bank rate ranged only from 3 to 4%.

Whatever its causes, the effect of the depression was to reduce the demand for discounts, and to make the gap between the market and the Bank more marked than ever. Consequent on the panic in New York in May 1884, there was an export of gold to America. Bank rate was only 2%, and the Bank waited until that rate was effective before raising it to 3 % on 9 October, though the reserve, partly owing to the dividend payments, had fallen to only £10·4 mn. (33%). Further rises followed, to 5% on 5 November, but the market still lagged behind, in spite of the Bank's borrowing on stock, and at the end of the month market rate was 1⅜% below Bank rate.

The reserve improved rapidly in the spring of 1885, but now the Bank pursued a cautious policy, and allowed it to reach over £18 mn. (52%) before finally reducing Bank rate to 2% in May. There was again a drain in the autumn, and again the Bank waited until the 2% rate was effective before raising it and borrowed on stock to make it so. Bank rate was raised to 3% on 12 November, and further borrowing raised market rate to 2½%, but as soon as borrowing ceased, market rate fell back to 2⅛%. *The Economist* speaks of this effort as "Demonstrating the futility of attempting permanently to influence rates by such exceptional means as those recently adopted".[1] When Bank rate was raised to 4% in December, it was unaccompanied by market operations, and market rate rose only to 3½%.

In the spring of 1886 market rate remained well below Bank rate in spite of the collection of the revenue. A 2% rate had a brief moment of effectiveness, but there was a wide gap again in the summer, and further market operations were necessary to make a 4% rate effective in October. Again market rate fell away as soon as the operations ceased. Events in 1887 followed almost exactly the same course. Again the reserve improved in the spring and, as the Bank reduced its rate, the market continued to underbid it. Again there appeared that autumn weakness in the reserve, and again a rise in Bank rate was followed only after a long interval by the market. This time there is no record of borrowing on stock being attempted; its inadequacy had already been too clearly shown.

1 *The Economist*, 28 Nov. 1885.

THE BARING CRISIS

From the depth of depression reached in 1887 there was soon
a recovery. Between 1887 and 1890 the Sauerbeck raw material
index rose from 67 to 71, *The Economist* index from 94 to 102,
and the Board of Trade one from 99·6 to 104. It is noticeable,
however, that these movements were much less than those
which had preceded former crises. Meanwhile, unemployment
fell from 7·6% in 1887 to 2·1% in 1889 and 1890.

Improving trade produced the usual adverse effects on the
Bank reserve, but failed to increase the Bank's control over the
market, so that this problem now became more acute than ever.
In January 1888 Bank rate was reduced to 3%, though the reserve was only £13 mn. (42%), and *The Economist* commented:

It has, however, been forced upon the Bank by the keenness of
outside competition, and is another instance of the altered relation
in which the Bank now stands to the market. Formerly it was the
leader, whereas now, too often, it has to be the follower.[1]

Throughout the summer the continued ineffectiveness of Bank
rate hindered the effort to prevent gold withdrawals. In
the autumn withdrawals increased, and Bank rate was raised
to 5% in October and kept there to the end of the year. Yet
before the end of the month market rate was down to 3%, and
it was only the effect of further borrowing by the Bank, and
continued gold withdrawals, that it was raised to something
like 4½% in December.

The year 1889 opened with the Bank holding only a very
small gold stock. Trade was still reviving, and there was a spate
of new loans, both to English industry and to foreign countries,
notably Argentine and Brazil. Bank rate was only intermittently
effective during the spring and summer. The rise to 5% in
September quickly brought a rise to 4½% in market rate, but
this level was not maintained. In November the Treasury co-
operated by repaying advances to the Bank out of revenue,[2] but
shortly afterwards the Bank was again believed to be borrowing

1 *The Economist*, 21 January 1888.   2 *Ibid.* 2 Nov. 1889.

on securities.[1] In December the Bank refused to sell bar gold. But in spite of all these efforts the reserve fell to only £9·5 mn. (33%), and Bank rate was raised on 30 December to 6%.

By the middle of January 1890, however, market rate had fallen to only 4⅛%. Under the able guidance of William Lidderdale, the Bank now adopted a much more vigorous policy. While keeping its rate as low as possible so as not to penalise domestic industry, new and energetic steps were taken to make that rate effective. Bank rate was reduced by stages until it reached 3% on 17 April. In February came the arrangement with the Hampshire County Council, to which we have referred, and similar arrangements were made with other bodies. In June *The Economist* reports that the Bank has gained control of the India Council balances, and describes it as working energetically on the market.[2] As a result, the Bank found itself in complete control by the early summer. In its general purpose it received temporary assistance from the great finance houses, who were engaged upon trying to float a Russian loan. In January it was reported that £1 mn. of Russian gold was sent to England in order to keep down interest rates, and later it was believed that the finance houses were trying to prevent the export of gold for the same purpose.[3]

Gold exports did, however, take place, and there was also an interior demand. Bank rate was raised to 4% in June, and in July the foreign exchanges became adverse and market rate actually rose above Bank rate. Bank rate was raised to 5% on 21 July, but this was largely a strategic measure, as the adverse exchange had already been corrected. Gold imports were expected from America, and it was to make sure that this gold was sent to London that the rate was temporarily raised. The influx of this gold reduced market rate to 3%, and after three weeks the Bank reduced its rate to 4%, and then borrowed on stock to make it effective.[4]

The autumn brought renewed gold exports, and Bank rate was raised to 5% on 25 September. The 5% rate was im-

---

1 *The Economist*, 16 Nov. 1889.   2 *Ibid.* 14 June 1890.
3 *Ibid.* 25 Jan. 1890 and 28 June 1890.   4 *Ibid.* 18 Oct. 1890.

mediately effective, and the market, for a change, was so much
indebted to the Bank that even the payment of the dividends
made little difference. *The Economist* believed that the joint-
stock banks were assisting by realising the need for caution,
and increasing their balances with the Bank.[1]

London now reaped the fruits of the new issues mania of the
past few years. Many English firms, especially breweries, had
been converted into joint-stock companies at inflated prices, but
the most notable excesses had been in South American loans.
The London issuing houses had acted as underwriters for these
loans, and they now found themselves left with large amounts
on their hands. Their saleability was greatly impaired by a
revolution in the Argentine in the summer, and still further
diminished by the stringency in the money market in the
autumn. The great house of Barings was foremost in the issue
of South American loans, and had also been doing an extrava-
gant volume of acceptance business. In an attempt to meet the
demands upon them, Barings sold securities to the value of
£4 mn., but on 8 November they were forced to place their
position before the Bank, and to appeal for assistance.

Investigation convinced Governor Lidderdale that, given
time, Barings would prove solvent, but the liabilities of the
firm were enormous—they were subsequently revealed to be
£28 mn.[2]—and there was the risk of serious loss if the opinion
proved unfounded. The Bank, therefore, did not feel justified in
giving direct assistance, but, at the same time, it was obvious
that the failure of Barings, with their great acceptance business,
would provoke a major crisis. Lidderdale approached Goschen,
the Chancellor of the Exchequer, and suggested a government
guarantee of Barings' liabilities, but Goschen refused this,
though he promised the issue of a "Treasury Letter" if this
should prove necessary.[3]

Lidderdale next approached the leading bankers, and invited
them to subscribe to a guarantee fund. The response was

1 *The Economist*, 18 Oct. 1890.
2 Lidderdale to the Court of Proprietors, Sept. 1891.
3 Elliott's *Life of Goschen*, quoted by Hawtrey, *op. cit.* p. 108.

amazingly generous; £9 mn. was promised within a week, and the fund eventually reached over £18 mn. The Bank did not subscribe to the fund itself, but simply acted as liquidator, making any advances which might be required for that purpose. Lidderdale thus secured his end without the smallest risk.

At the same time, he took special precautions to protect the reserve; £1·5 mn. of Treasury bonds were sold to Russia for gold, and a loan of £3 mn. in gold was arranged with the Bank of France through the agency of Rothschilds.

The plight of Barings was not generally known until the 15th, when all these measures had been taken, and all possibility of a panic removed. Bank rate had been raised to 6% on 7 November, with a reserve of 11·2 mn. (33%), and it was not raised any higher, though some business was charged at higher rates.[1] The other securities rose by £7 mn., and the private deposits by £6 mn., but the influx of borrowed gold raised the reserve to £14·5 mn. on 19 November. There was, of course, never the smallest question of invoking the promised Treasury Letter.

By the end of November market rate was no more than 4¼%, and on 4 December Bank rate was reduced to 5%, with a reserve of £16·6 mn. (45% of the liabilities).

AMERICAN GOLD EXPORTS AND CHEAP MONEY, 1891–6

After the crisis, the secular downward trend of prices was resumed, though the fall was far from violent. The Sauerbeck raw material index fell from 71 in 1890 to 60 in 1894, and then remained stationary for three years. The other indices reveal falls similar in magnitude, though slightly different in timing. Unemployment rose to 3·5% in 1891, 6·3% in 1892, and 7·5% in 1893, but had fallen again to 3·3% in 1896 and 1897.

From the banking point of view the period divides sharply into two parts. Up to the autumn of 1893 the gold position was still precarious, and the Bank's efforts to protect the reserve were still hampered by its inability to control the market.

1 Lidderdale to the Court of Proprietors, Sept. 1891.

Recourse was therefore had to all the expedients which we have already discussed. But after the American crisis of 1893 the influx of American gold coincided with increased world production and falling domestic prices. The reserve rose to unheard of levels, Bank rate fell to 2%, and when this became quite ineffective, the Bank temporarily abandoned all attempts to keep in touch with the market.

One effect of the crisis was to induce, for the moment at least, greater co-operation between the Bank and the joint-stock banks. Goschen's plan for a second reserve found no favour, but he notes with satisfaction that the banks are increasing their balances with the Bank.[1] In 1891 *The Economist* estimated that this increase in cash reserves amounted to £5 mn. An instance of the altered feeling between the parties occurred in 1891, when the Bank was finding difficulty in making its rate effective; *The Economist* refers to "a combination of half a dozen or so of the larger joint-stock banks" in support of the Bank. Precise details are not known, but the movement appears to have been temporary, and not very effective.

It was naturally expected that the Bank would respond to this increase in the reserves of the joint-stock banks by itself holding a larger reserve, but here the old difficulty recurred. In January 1892 *The Economist* remarks that the reserve is less proportionately than in 1890, and comments:

It (the Bank) has been trying to take money off the market, but the floating supply is so large that it cannot operate in this way with any effect, and the result is that, while, for the protection of the reserve, it is maintaining a rate higher than is justified by internal requirements, the reserve is not protected.[2]

But after the American crisis of 1893 this situation was completely changed. For some years America had been coining a fixed quantity of silver annually; at first this was offset by the withdrawal of notes, but after 1888 silver began to displace gold. The outflow of gold was interrupted by the 1893 crisis, but at the end of that year it was resumed in increasing volume.

1 Goschen, *Essays and Addresses*, p. 129.
2 *The Economist*, 30 Jan. 1892.

Table XVIII

BANK RATE AND MARKET RATE OF DISCOUNT FOR
THREE MONTHS' BILLS, *BANKERS' MAGAZINE*
AVERAGES, 1884–96

Year	Bank rate (%)			Market rate (%)		
	£	s.	d.	£	s.	d.
1884	2	19	4	2	8	0
1885	2	18	2	2	2	6
1886	3	1	2	2	2	7
1887	3	6	11	2	8	1
1888	3	6	4	2	7	8
1889	3	12	0	2	13	0
1890	4	10	0	3	13	3
1891	3	6	8	2	12	6
1892	2	10	0	1	8	6
1893	3	2	0	2	2	6
1894	2	2	4	0	19	3
1895	2	0	0	0	15	11
1896	2	9	0	1	9	5

At the same time, the world production of gold was increasing,
and falling prices and industrial depression were exerting their
usual influence towards augmenting the reserve.

On 23 August 1893 Bank rate had been raised to 5% with
the reserve at £15 mn. (45%), and for once the rate was effective.
By 3 October the reserve had risen to £16·6 mn. (45% in spite
of the dividend payments) and Bank rate was reduced to 3%.
There followed reductions to 2½% and then 2% in February
1894, the latter with a reserve of £22·6 mn. (60%). 2% was
continued until September 1896, and at one time the reserve
rose to no less than £149 mn. The Bank was quite out of touch
with the market, market rate being 1% or less. But now the
directors had not the problem of protecting the reserve, but
rather of finding profitable employment for all their resources.
This difficulty was aggravated by the presence of a large deposit to the credit of the Japanese government, arising from the
payment of the Sino-Japanese war indemnity. The directors
frankly abandoned any attempt to make Bank rate effective, and
instead of taking advantage of this deposit to raise market rate
they largely added to their securities. Thus the problem of protecting the reserve was not solved but shelved—for the solution
we must wait until the beginning of the present century.

Chapter Ten

THE LAST YEARS OF THE GOLD STANDARD
1897–1913

By contrast with the period of depression culminating in 1896 the closing years of the pre-war period are a time of comparative prosperity. The general trend of prices was markedly upward, though there were checks in 1900–2 and 1907–9. Over the whole period the Sauerbeck index rose from 59 to 88, *The Economist* index from 89 to 113, and the Board of Trade one from 90·1 to 117·2. Unemployment averaged 4·7%, compared with 5·3% for 1873–96. Our overseas trade, which had been nearly stagnant in value, now showed a marked expansion, and foreign lending, after having been rather small during the first few years, showed an unprecedented expansion between 1903 and 1905.

The increase in the world output of gold can be appreciated from the following figures:

Year				Output in tons
1886	...	...	...	160
1893	...	...	...	227
1896	...	...	...	300
1904	...	...	...	500
1913	...	...	...	700

One consequence of this was that, whereas central bank reserves had previously been small in comparison with the total volume of monetary gold, and during the 1880's had even shown a tendency to decline, they now increased largely and, for the first time, absorbed a considerable proportion of the world's gold stock. The increase in the reserve of the Bank of England in 1894–5 was partly due to exceptional circumstances, and was only temporary, but it will be seen from the table in Appendix I that the Bank was now raising its rate when the proportion of reserve to liabilities was considerably higher than that which would have induced a corresponding rise in the 1880's.

THE AMALGAMATION MOVEMENT

The amalgamation movement in banking had been proceeding all through the century, but it was not until the 1890's that the pace and size of amalgamations increased so as to revolutionise the whole structure of the banking system. In 1886–7 there was a total of some 370 banks with about 3700 branches; of these some 250 were private and 120 joint-stock companies. Four of the joint-stock banks had more than 100 branches, and seven from 50 to 100. Twenty years later there were twenty joint-stock banks with over 100 branches (three of them had over 500) and about a dozen smaller joint-stock banks doing ordinary banking business in a restricted locality, while the 250 private banks "had shrunk to little more than a dozen".[1]

This change modified the relations of the banking system with the central bank in a number of ways. It meant that there were now a number of firms wielding resources vastly greater in amount than the Bank. Had these firms chosen to be refractory, the task of control would have been rendered impossible. On the other hand, the fewness of the important banks made communication much easier and so facilitated the growth of understanding and co-operation between the parties.

The amalgamation movement brought a greater degree of uniformity into banking practice and generally led to the keeping of larger cash reserves. The provincial banks formerly treated their deposits with their London agents as cash; the agents, however, treated these balances as ordinary deposits, and held only a small proportion of them in actual cash. The ratio of cash to deposits for the system as a whole would thus be less than that for its individual members, and the abolition of this "pyramiding" of deposits by amalgamation tended to promote the holding of larger reserves. This tendency was further accentuated by the increased caution which prevailed after 1890.

Part of these reserves were, of course, kept in the form of balances with the Bank of England. Bankers' balances were

[1] J. H. Clapham, *An Economic History of Modern Europe*, vol. III, pp. 278–9.

growing both because of this increase in the proportion of reserves, and because of the general expansion of banking
liabilities. In 1875 the Bank had ceased to publish bankers'
balances because they had grown so large as sometimes to exceed the reserve, and it was feared that this would cause alarm.
The balances were then about £10 mn. After 1890 they increased greatly, and Withers estimates them at about £22 mn.
in 1908.[1]

In the early twentieth century the joint-stock banks also
increased their holdings of gold and began to hold cash considerably in excess of their normal requirements for till money.
Sir E. Holden revealed that, in 1914, the Midland Bank held no
less than £8 mn. of gold.[2]

But the most important effect of the amalgamation movement
was in changing the nature of the discount market. The decline of
the inland bill, the reasons for which we have already described,
was greatly accelerated. In 1869, when bank clearings were
£3,626 mn., the duty on bills of exchange yielded £731,000.
In 1904, when bank clearings amounted to £10,564 mn., the
proceeds of the duty had fallen to £700,000.[3] By this time the
discount market had become of negligible importance in the
finance of purely domestic industry.

This meant that the market was no longer the powerful force
which it had been in influencing prices. Formerly, if the Bank
brought about a rise in discount rates, that, in itself, tended to
cause a fall in domestic prices. Now, however, expansion and
contraction could not come about through the market, but only
through a change in the whole lending policy of the banks. The
Bank's power to influence prices depended, therefore, entirely
on the joint-stock banks' reaction to a diminution in their cash
balances. The Bank's power would be more or less according
as the other banks kept a more or less constant proportion between cash and total liabilities.

1 Withers and Palgrave, The English Banking System, for U.S. Monetary
Commission, p. 9.
2 Clapham, op. cit. p. 287.
3 Hawtrey, A Century of Bank Rate, p. 57.

Table XIX

RATIOS OF CASH AND MONEY AT CALL AND SHORT NOTICE TO DEPOSITS

A. The London clearing banks.
B. Other English joint-stock banks.

Year	A (%)	B (%)	Year	A (%)	B (%)
1889	27·1	18·4	1899	29·1	18·9
1890	26·8	18·3	1900	27·4	18·6
1891	26·8	18·4	1901	27·7	19·6
1892	26·8	19·1	1902	29·9	19·5
1893	27·2	18·7	1903	31·0	20·2
1894	26·2	18·0	1904	28·5	18·5
1895	28·5	22·0	1905	30·7	20·7
1896	28·2	20·0	1906	31·6	21·6
1897	26·7	18·8	1907	30·7	20·5
1898	26·9	19·6	1908	29·5	20·7*

* U.S. Monetary Commission, Banking Statistics.

The discount market remained, however, of unique importance in determining movements of short-term capital. The funds for the market were supplied partly by the joint-stock banks, and partly by a number of foreign and colonial banks and private firms. But it was the funds of the joint-stock banks which were the most important and the most sensitive to open market operations, and it was universally agreed that the Bank's power over the market lay ultimately in its power over bankers' balances. The effectiveness of this power depends, of course, not on the banker's keeping a fixed ratio of cash to total liabilities, but on the way in which his short lending is influenced by a change in his cash balance. If the cash balance diminishes, and the banker wished to maintain a fixed ratio of cash to total liabilities, he will be able to do so only by immediately recalling some of his short loans, and so adding again to his cash. But after a time, there will be the alternative of calling in loans of longer duration, and a weakening of the cash reserve may thus be offset by an actual increase in short lending.

It is very hard to obtain a statistical check on any of these things. The half-yearly balance sheets of banks, even when they are not vitiated by window dressing, are not a reliable guide to

Table XX

LONDON AND COUNTY BANK AND LONDON AND WESTMINSTER BANK

A. Ratio of cash to deposits.
B. Ratio of money at call and short notice to deposits.

Year	A. Cash		B. Call money	
	L. and C.	L. and W.	L. and C.	L. and W.
1878	15·5	15·3	10·0	7·4
1879	16·0	16·0	10·1	15·1
1880	16·0	17·3	11·2	17·5
1881	14·6	14·0	11·6	18·5
1882	14·3	13·6	11·7	16·2
1883	14·5	13·3	11·0	16·4
1884	13·7	13·4	11·4	17·0
1885	13·7	12·1	10·8	16·3
1886	13·4	13·3	13·0	23·3
1887	13·1	13·2	9·9	17·9
1888	11·5	13·8	11·0	19·3
1889	13·5	13·5	9·0	25·9
1890	14·8	15·4	7·9	25·6
1891	14·0	16·9	9·4	20·5
1892	13·6	16·0	8·9	19·8
1893	14·5	16·6	7·7	17·9
1894	13·8	16·8	8·9	19·5
1895	14·0	17·7	8·6	16·7
1896	12·4	15·7	9·1	20·0
1897	13·1	16·7	8·4	26·3
1898	15·7	17·7	8·3	23·4
1899	17·1	17·3	7·3	21·0
1900	18·5	16·0	6·5	22·8
1901	18·6	17·6	6·4	23·0
1902	19·6	17·6	6·7	23·9
1903	18·5	16·6	5·8	23·5
1904	19·4	15·9	7·7	23·0
1905	18·2	14·0	8·2	26·5
1906	18·0	13·5	7·3	24·5
1907	16·1	16·0	7·9	18·3
1908	18·4	16·3	9·4	27·3

short-period changes. Further, many banks still lumped together cash and money at call and short notice in their published statements. The U.S. Monetary Commission obtained only a statement of cash and call money jointly, in relation to deposits, and I quote these figures (Table XIX). The London and Westminster and the London and County Banks both gave cash and call money separately after 1878, and I quote their figures from that date until their amalgamation in 1908 (Table XX).

Table XIX shows a slight upward trend for the period as a whole, but comparatively little deviation from it. In Table XX the most noticeable thing is the very big difference in the call-money ratio between the two banks, and the fact that, whereas the trend for the London and Westminster was upward, for the London and County it was markedly downward. The cash ratios show considerable variation. For both banks, they fall during the middle 1880's, and rise markedly in 1890 and the years immediately following. The London and County then shows a marked fall in the middle 1890's, which is shown much less by the London and Westminster. Both banks show a rise at the turn of the century, but that for the London and County is much the greater, and that bank, for the first time, now attains the higher ratio. Thenceforward the London and County ratio is kept fairly constant at the higher level, whereas there is a marked fall in that of the London and Westminster. There is very little correlation between changes in the cash ratio and in that of call money. Comparison with the tables of interest rates reveals, as we should expect, a fairly strong correlation between the amount of short loans and the market rate of discount.

These observations do not enable us to throw very much new light on the situation, but they suggest that the control of bankers' balances was a precarious method of controlling the market. This is fully borne out by experience. Market operations were generally effective for a while, corresponding to the immediate calling in of short loans by the banks, but very often the market fell away again after quite a short while as bankers redistributed their assets. Hence the fact that market operations were regarded as an emergency policy only. The Bank itself must have been conscious of the inadequacy of control through the bankers' balances, as it developed other measures, operating directly. Thus funds were borrowed by the Bank from other bodies which would have directly lent them in the market, and even, on rare occasions, from the banks themselves.

THE BANK AND THE MARKET

With the increase in activity, and the end of the cheap money period in the autumn of 1896, the problem of the Bank's control over a market again came into prominence. By now the Bank had quite abandoned the policy of forcing the market to become independent of it, which had been issued between 1858 and 1890. The re-discount facilities offered in 1890 were gradually extended. In 1894 the Bank offered to take parcels of bills whose average échéance did not exceed 30 days, and in 1897 the maximum currency was extended to three months. The Bank informed the U.S. Monetary Commission that the maximum usance was four, or exceptionally, six months.

It was an established convention that the Bank did not buy bills in the market, and that bills once discounted should be held to maturity. The Bank did a considerable re-discount business for foreign and colonial banks, but it told the U.S. Monetary Commission that the large joint-stock banks "Do practically no discount business with us".[1]

The crisis of 1890 was a landmark in the development of co-operation between the Bank and the joint-stock banks, but traces of the old jealousy still lingered. It was a standing grievance of the joint-stock banks that the Bank used their balances in the market, and some of them at least still looked upon the Bank as a rival. For instance, Sir Felix Schuster, of the Union of London and Smiths' Bank, complains of the use of bankers' balances in the market, accuses the Bank of trying to regain the business which it had previously lost to the joint-stock banks, and states that Bank competition is "a source of very great complaint by the other banks".[2] On the other hand, Charles Gow, of the London Joint Stock Bank, says: "The Bank of England is our ally, and our best possible ally, and, speaking for myself, I will do nothing contrary to the general desires of the Bank of England."[3]

Until nearly the end of our period there was no formal means

1 U.S. Monetary Commission, Interviews, p. 22.   2 Ibid. p. 48.
3 Ibid. p. 91.

of communication between the Bank and the other banks. In 1860, the Governor of the Bank had been made an ex-officio member of the Committee of the Clearing House, but he never attended ordinary meetings.[1] It was rumoured that the Bank had, on occasions, conveyed informal hints to individual banks, though the U.S. Monetary Commission, in spite of careful questioning, obtained no evidence of this. A most important change took place, however, in 1911, when it was decided that the Committee of the Clearing House should meet once a quarter at the Bank.

The Bank was growing increasingly reluctant to impose a high Bank rate, not only on account of the difficulty of making it effective, but also because the rates charged for commercial advances throughout the country were coming to depend more and more on Bank rate. It is significant that the Bank was becoming much more tender in its attitude towards trade and industry than in the earlier years. We therefore see experiments with methods of protecting the reserve, other than by raising Bank rate.

The most notable of these methods were direct operations in the gold market. We have already noticed the Bank raising the buying price of bullion, and raising the selling price of gold bars, or even refusing to part with them at all. These measures, which had been only occasional in the 1890's, became a matter of ordinary routine in the early years of the twentieth century.[2] The buying price of gold was not, however, raised above £3. 17s. 10d. per oz.[3] The Bank also frequently manipulated both the buying and selling price of foreign coin, and occasionally made interest-free advances to gold importers.[4] A further method of hindering the export of gold was by sorting sovereigns and paying demands believed to be for export in coin which, though heavy enough still to be legal tender, was below the mint weight. Lord Swatheling says that the Bank

1 Palgrave and Withers, Memorandum, pp. 282–3.
2 R. S. Sayers, *Bank of England Operations*, 1890–1914, p. 76.
3 U.S. Monetary Commission, Interview with Lord Swatheling.
4 U.S. Monetary Commission, Interviews, pp. 28–9.

"sift out the minimum legal weight of the sovereigns, and heap them up for the exporters". The greatest difference which could be made by this method was, however, only one per mille.[1]

Another method of protecting the reserve without raising Bank rate was the forcing of market rate above Bank rate.[2] This could be done by the Bank refusing to work at its minimum rate, or by charging a higher rate for advances than for discounts. The latter was common in the 1890's, but, after 1903, advances for one week were generally made at $\frac{1}{2}$% above Bank rate, and deviations from this rule were rare. Further, the Bank might, in accordance with long-standing tradition, discriminate against certain types of bills. In October 1890 it discriminated against bills "having the appearance of being offered with a view to gold export", and in the autumn of 1906 against American bills. The Bank told the U.S. Monetary Commission that it always discriminates against finance bills, but that, in time of crisis, it would consider each case on its merits.[3]

In one important respect, however, the Bank's task was made easier. In the third quarter of the nineteenth century England had been a debtor on short-term account; now she became a creditor. It was, therefore, only necessary to bring about a rise in short-term interest rates sufficient to check new borrowing in order to bring an automatic influx of gold as existing assets matured.

But the effect which could be produced by these measures was limited. They might suffice to tide over minor fluctuations, but the only remedy for a major drain of gold remained an effective rise in Bank rate. The old problem of making Bank rate effective was, therefore, still as important as ever, and this period witnessed notable changes in market technique.[4] The old practice of outright sales and purchases of securities had practically died out, and the U.S. Monetary Commission is informed that the Bank now buys or sells securities only "on rare occasions".[5] As for the time-honoured practice of selling stock for cash and buying it back for the account, there is no evidence

1 *Ibid.* p. 98.   2 Sayers, *op. cit.*   3 *Ibid.* p. 68.
4 U.S. Monetary Commission, Interviews, p. 28.   5 *Ibid.* p. 29.

for it in the proceedings of the U.S. Monetary Commission, or in the works of Withers or Palgrave. The press often described this and other processes indiscriminately as "borrowing on stock", so no real evidence is to be found there. Sayers, however, believes the practice to be extremely rare. It had, in fact, been superseded by the pledging of securities to brokers as collateral, these securities being then deducted, for purposes of accounting, from the assets of the banking department. It is not known when this was first done. It was treated as a new development by the press in 1897, but Sayers suggests that it may have been used in 1890–3.

The borrowing from special depositors, such as the County Councils and the India Council, which we noticed in 1890, was continued. Sir F. Schuster tells the U.S. Monetary Commission that the Bank does not pay interest on deposits, but "In some cases they act as intermediaries for the making of loans; it is a very subtle distinction".[1] In December 1905, when Bank rate was made ineffective by the repayment of a large amount of Treasury bonds, the Bank took the novel step of borrowing directly from the clearing banks, and in 1910 the clearing banks further co-operated by themselves making purchases of gold.

Finally, as the understanding between the Bank and the banks grew better, all these measures were supplemented, and to some extent superseded, by "the hint from H.Q." It was generally believed in the City, in the early twentieth century, that such hints were not infrequently given and accepted, but they must have been of a very confidential nature, for though there were many rumours, I have found no concrete example. As we have seen, the means of official communication between the parties were very poor, but the views of the Bank, in a general way, must have been apparent, as is suggested by the remark of Charles Gow, which we have already quoted. After the innovation of 1811, of course, the possibility of this sort of thing was greatly extended.

1 U.S. Monetary Commission, Interviews, p. 41.

Table XXI

BANK RATE AND MARKET RATE OF DISCOUNT FOR THREE MONTHS' BILLS, *BANKER'S MAGAZINE* AVERAGES, 1897–1913

£ per cent

Year	Bank rate			Market rate		
	£	s.	d.	£	s.	d.
1897	2	13	2	1	15	8
1898	3	3	0	2	13	3
1889	3	14	1	3	3	7
1900	3	18	10	3	13	2
1901	3	14	6	3	3	2
1902	3	6	7	2	19	5
1903	3	15	10	3	8	3
1904	3	6	0	2	13	7
1905	3	0	0	2	11	3
1906	4	5	1	3	19	9
1907	4	18	6	4	9	4
1908	3	0	3	2	6	4
1909	3	1	11	2	5	9
1910	3	14	6	3	3	3
1911	3	9	6	2	18	5
1912	3	15	5	3	12	0
1913	4	15	5	4	7	5

TRADE RECOVERY, AND WAR, 1897–1902

The Board of Trade price index reached its lowest point in 1896, but the Sauerbeck index continued to fall until 1897, and *The Economist* until 1898. Then all three show a marked rise to 1900, followed by a fall in 1901 and 1902. Unemployment fell from 3·3 % in 1896 to 2·0 % in 1899. The peak of industrial activity was reached in the spring of 1900, and unemployment for the next three years was 2·5, 3·3 and 4·0 %, respectively.

In the autumn of 1896 there was an export of gold to America, and a further demand as the Japanese government withdrew its indemnity balance. The Bank pursued a very cautious policy, raising its rate to 2½ % on 10 September, while the reserve was still £32·3 mn. (56%), and to 4 % on 22 October, with a reserve of £25·9 mn. (50%). In the spring of 1897 matters improved, and the rate fell to 2 % again in May, but was raised to 3 % in October to check a renewed export.

There were considerable market operations, and market rate was kept in very close touch with Bank rate.

The years 1898–1900 were a time of net gold imports, but of internal demand owing to rising activity and prices. 1898 was uneventful, the Spanish American trouble in April, and a stock-exchange crisis in Berlin in October, both producing rises in Bank rate only to 4%. The reserve was considerably depleted in 1899, but the Bank was reluctant to raise its rate, and, instead, it raised its buying price for gold and offered interest-free advances to gold importers. But rumours of war in October reduced the reserve to £20 mn., and the rate was raised to 5%, while in November further gold withdrawals for the Argentine raised it to 6%. Market rate kept fairly close to Bank rate, and *The Economist* refers to the increasing co-operation on the part of the joint-stock banks.

The Boer war, which broke out in October 1899, was far from being the dominant influence on the national life which war is to-day. Government borrowing, as will be seen from the following table, was only on a very moderate scale in relation to the national income.

Table XXII

GOVERNMENT BORROWING, 1899–1903

£ millions

Financial year	1899–1900	1900–01	1901–2	1902–3
Funded	−30·6	− 1·4	58·4	30·5
Annuities	24·0	1·4	1·5	− 4·7
Unfunded	8·0	62·0	− 3·0	—
Total	1·4	62·0	56·9	25·8

But the Treasury was naturally anxious to borrow as cheaply as possible, and the Bank therefore endeavoured to keep rates at a moderate level. Thus the demands of the government were, for some time, the most important feature in what would otherwise have been, for the money market, an uneventful period.

In September 1902 the law was amended so as to allow the

issue of Treasury bills to meet payments arising out of revenue account as well as Consolidated Fund services. Treasury bills thus became an alternative to Ways and Means advances from the Bank, but there was not, in the early years of the century, any great decline in the Bank's advances to the government.

In 1900 the reserve improved, and Bank rate was quickly reduced, 3% being reached in June with a "proportion" of only 43%. From the summer of 1900 to the end of 1902 the dominant feature was government borrowing, and this made the Bank very reluctant to raise its rate. There was no very great demand for gold, but some pressure at the end of 1900 was met by discriminating in favour of American applicants in the allotment of Treasury bills. The "Proportion" was noticeably lower than it had been, for corresponding rates, in the immediate past. Apart from a short and long delayed spell of 5% at the beginning of 1902, Bank rate varied only between 3 and 4%. There was little trouble in controlling the market, and, at times, market rate was appreciably above Bank rate.

THE BOOM AND CRISIS OF 1907

The fall in prices was checked after 1902, and from then until 1905 the various indices remained practically stationary at the lower level. Then, from 1905 to 1907, there was a very sharp rise. The Sauerbeck index moved from 72 in 1904 to 86 in 1907, though the others showed a somewhat less marked rise. The unemployment figure rose to 6·0% in 1904, but then fell to 3·6% in 1906, and 3·7% in 1907.

The years 1903 and 1904 were both uneventful, with Bank rate varying only from 3% to 4%, and the Bank keeping in fairly close touch with the market. In 1905 Bank rate was raised from 3 to 4% to check an export of gold in September, but in December the rate was made ineffective by the repayment of £14 mn. of Treasury bonds. The Bank, therefore, invited the joint-stock banks to lend directly to it, the first time that such action is known to have been taken. At the same time, a number of joint-stock banks are reported to have held discussions on means of improving co-operation with the Bank.[1]

In the early summer of 1906 the market broke away from the Bank, and Bank rate was reduced to $3\frac{1}{2}\%$. But in the autumn there were large gold exports, due in part to the discount of American accommodation paper. Bank rate was raised to 5% on 11 October, with a reserve of only £18·2 mn. (35%), and to 6% on the 19th, with a reserve of £18·6 mn. (37%). At the same time, the Bank discriminated against the discount of American bills. The Bank of France, wishing to avoid too great a rise in London rates, relaxed its restrictions on the export of gold and discounted English bills.

With the spring of 1907 easier conditions prevailed, and Bank rate was reduced to 4% in April. The peak of domestic activity and prices was reached in May, and by the autumn there was a definite, though still slight, downward trend. Bank rate was raised to $4\frac{1}{2}\%$ in August, though the "Proportion" was still 50%. On 22 October there occurred the failure of the Knickerbocker Trust, followed by the suspension of cash payments practically throughout the American banking system. There was an immense drain on the Bank of England, and Bank rate was raised to $5\frac{1}{2}\%$ on 31 October, 6% on 4 November, and 7% on 7 November. The 7% rate was effective in bringing gold from many quarters, and the governor told the U.S. Monetary Commission that gold was imported from twenty-four countries. By far the greater part, however, came from the gold-producing countries, Africa and Australia, and from Germany and France.[2] Again the Bank of France relaxed its restrictions on gold export and discounted English bills. The Bank had no difficulty in controlling the market, and the episode was associated with no panic, and no major failures, in London. Bank rate remained at 7% for eight weeks, but then dropped rapidly to 3% in March 1908.

Much was subsequently made of the assistance given by the Bank of France in 1906 and 1907. Some writers have suggested

1 *The Economist*, Commercial Review of 1905.
2 Hawtrey, *op. cit.* p. 117.

that the assistance was sought by the Bank of England, and that, without it, the Bank would have been seriously embarrassed. This, however, seems hardly tenable. The total gold imports from France in November and December were only £3 mn., compared with £7 mn. from Germany and a grand total of £19 mn., while, when Bank rate was raised to 7%, the Bank had still a reserve of £17·6 mn. (35%). Sayers points out that there was no evidence for the Bank of France having done more than remove the obstacles which it normally put in the way of gold export and intimate its willingness to discount English bills. Possibly this intimation was made direct to the Bank of England, possibly not. Sayers shows that it was to the advantage of the Bank of France to avoid too great a disturbance in the London money market, as this would have involved a considerable rise of interest rates in Paris, if gold was not to be lost anyway.[1] It is very doubtful whether the Bank of England did in fact take the initiative in asking for assistance, and had the assistance not been forthcoming, it is probable that the consequences would have been no more than a slight further depletion of the reserve, and possibly a further 1 or 2% rise in Bank rate.

THE CALM BEFORE THE STORM, 1908–13

The crisis of 1907 is the last outstanding monetary event of the pre-war years. The dear money of 1907 hastened the downward trend of activity. Unemployment rose to 7·7% in 1908, and the Sauerbeck price index fell no less than twelve points to 74 in 1908. The other indices again showed a rather less fluctuation. But the depression was shortlived, and prices and employment continued to rise from 1909 to 1913, by which time all the price indices were well above their 1907 level, and unemployment was only 2·7%.

From the point of view of the Bank these years were uneventful; international gold movements were never of a pressing character, and Bank rate never rose above 5%. It fell to 2½% in June 1908, and remained there until the end of the year.

1 Sayers, *op. cit.* pp. 102–15.

In the autumn there was a large export of gold owing to the policy of accumulation which was being pursued by the Bank of France, and the proportion was allowed to fall to only 31$\frac{5}{8}$% without a rise in the rate. Perhaps this was by way of return for the French permission of gold exports in the previous years. Even if there was no deliberate agreement, such incidents mark the growing realisation that central banks must co-operate, and that the penalty of a scramble for gold is rising interest rates in all important centres, with nobody any the better off.

There was a rise in Bank rate to 3% in 1909, followed by a period of cheap money in the summer, and a sharp rise to 5% in the autumn. A very similar pattern was followed in the succeeding four years, 5% being reached in October of 1910, 1912 and 1913, but in each case there was a speedy improvement in the reserve. Otherwise the last years of our period were calm and uneventful.

CONCLUSION

The last quarter of a century before the outbreak of the Great War was much more serene than any period which had gone before. The control of the Bank was at once firmer and more gentle; fluctuations were fewer and less violent; and there was never anything which could be called a financial panic; the reserve was, on the whole, larger, and the Bank had developed a fairly effective working technique for its protection.

The effectiveness attained by that part of the technique which depended on the control of the market can be seen by comparing the tables of market rate and Bank rate in this chapter and the previous one. But these figures are averages, and therefore do not show the whole truth. Market rate would normally be far below Bank rate when gold was coming in and there was no need to protect the reserve, and closer to it when there was a drain. When the Bank had real need to control the market, therefore, its power was greater than the mere average figures suggest.

But the problem of protecting the reserve did not yield to

any simple and logical, still less any automatic solution; we have seen in many and varied expedients, some of them undignified and petty, to which the Bank frequently resorted. In the eighteenth century a run had been checked by paying notes entirely in sixpences; by a return to the same idea, we now have the ludicrous spectacle of the most powerful monetary institution in the world picking and sorting its sovereigns so as to pay its obligations in coin of the lightest weight. The effectiveness of that control depended in part on the changed circumstances of international trade, which had made London a creditor instead of a debtor on short-term account, and so made it easier for the Bank to attract gold by means of a rise in interest rates not sufficient to be severely felt by home industry.

Moreover, the Bank did not gain control entirely through its own power. Also it depended on the co-operation, or at least the acquiescence, of a number of persons and institutions, both in England and without.

First, it depended on the acquiescence of foreign central banks. Too much can be made of the actual direct offers of assistance by one bank to another in times of crisis, but as part of the ordinary routine of international transfers a measure of passive co-operation was essential. If one bank needed to attract gold from abroad, it could do so, in the first place, only by depleting the reserves of other central banks. If, therefore, one bank raised its discount rate, it was necessary, sooner or later, for other banks to resign themselves to a loss of gold, and to refrain either from raising their own rates by an equivalent amount, or placing other obstacles in the way of gold export. The alternative was an international tug of war in which no one would be any better off, and which must go on until such time as credit restriction brought trade depression, and so transferred cash from circulation to bank reserves in every country. In the case of a general rise in world prices, such contraction might be inevitable, but as a means of making temporary adjustments between countries it would be unnecessary, and highly inconvenient. A measure of acquiescence in gold withdrawals was, therefore, a duty owed by every central bank to every other but, because the London gold market was so much more free than any other, the Bank of England was more dependent on foreign central banks in this respect than they on it. Such international co-operation was, and still is, only rudimentary, but we have seen several examples of its growth, and of the growing realisation of the need.

Secondly, the Bank depended on a measure of co-operation from the government, which was easily secured through the Bank's traditional role as the government's financial agent. After 1902 the influence of government borrowing in the market, in ordinary times, was greatly increased. The issue of Treasury bills at an opportune moment might give the Bank the control of the market which it needed, while if they fell due for repayment at an unfortunate time, this control would be seriously impaired.

Then the Bank depended largely upon those bodies, such as the County Councils, the India Council, etc., which entrusted to it funds to be lent at its own discretion in the market.

Lastly, the Bank depended to an ever-increasing extent on the co-operation of the joint-stock banks; not merely on their keeping their balances with it, and varying their liabilities, both short and long term, in response to a change in these balances; but also on their being willing to follow the lead of the Bank without its having to resort to such coercion, and even at times on their lending their short funds to it rather than to the market.

In all these matters, personal relationships were highly important. The giving or withholding of co-operation depended on a personal decision, and the help to be expected from each source would constantly vary in response to personal as well as external factors. The directors had, therefore, not only to attend to matters of minute detail, but also to cultivate numerous personal relationships. On their success or failure in this way might depend the smooth working of the whole system. For an example of what could be achieved by personal tact we need go no further than the governorship of William Lidderdale. About all this there was nothing automatic, no simple and obvious rule by which all decisions could be tried. Some of the sponsors of the Bank Charter Act of 1844 thought that they were reducing the art of central banking to a rule of thumb; how great would have been their surprise if they could have sat in the bank parlour on a Thursday morning sixty years later.

Chapter Eleven

MONETARY THEORY OF THE SECOND HALF OF THE NINETEENTH CENTURY

After 1844 monetary theory comes to have progressively less connection with the practical problems of central banking. The major practical issues of the first half of the century had concerned the working, first of an inconvertible, and then of a convertible note issue, in both of which the central bank was immediately and directly concerned. But in the second half of the century the things most in the public eye were the secular movements in prices closely associated in time with changes in the output of gold. It is the connection between the two which forms the most important point of discussion in monetary theory, and which was responsible for the development of such new ideas as there were. By the letter and the spirit of the act of 1844 the Bank was made only the passive agent in transmitting the effects of changes in the supply of gold to the economic system as a whole, and the theorists were quite right in paying little attention to its activities in this respect. The problems of the Bank were of a more technical nature—the size of the reserve, the behaviour of the bankers' balances, and so on —and they received comparatively little theoretical discussion.

The ideas involved in the gold controversy, though only indirectly relevant, will take up a good deal of our space, but first we must clear away the legacy of dispute left by the Bank Charter Act itself.

THE POST BANK CHARTER ACT DISCUSSION

The surprising thing about the Bank Charter Act is its persistence. Within a generation of its passage it had been three times suspended by the arbitrary action of ministers; it was ridiculed by leading bankers, and condemned by eminent theorists; yet only once was a bill introduced into Parliament to make any serious modification of it. This one bill, introduced by Lowe in 1873, proposed a legal means by which the fiduciary issue could be exceeded so long as Bank rate was 12%; it was felt that this was too high a rate, and that the machinery proposed by the bill was too complicated, and it failed to find any support. Perhaps the reason for this inertia was that the public had been so wearied by the constant repetition of the arguments of the Currency and Banking controversy.

In evidence before the Parliamentary Committees of 1848, 1857 and 1858 the old arguments were still bandied to and fro. Overstone obstinately maintained that, so far from aggravating, the act had diminished the intensity of the great commercial crises of 1847 and 1857; Tooke and Newmarch, with equal obstinacy and superior reasoning, asserted the contrary. Opinion was, however, coming more and more to the side of the Banking School. The Lords' Committee of 1848 unequivocally condemned the act:

> Enough has been said to prove, in the judgement of this Committee, that the inflexibility of the rule prescribed by the restrictive clauses of the Act of 1844 is indefensible when equally applied to a state of varying circulation; and that its enforcement in 1847 was an aggravation of the commercial distress....[1]

The opponents of the act found a redoubtable supporter in J. S. Mill. Mill argues that, since a loss of gold will now fall both on the banking department, as a loss of deposits, and on the issue department, the Bank will, therefore, have to keep a double reserve. This, however, is a fallacy, for the duplication is only a matter of accountancy and, just as the loss appears in duplicate in the accounts, so the gold had previously appeared in duplicate; under its own name in the issue department, and as notes in the reserve of the banking department.[2]

Apart from this, however, Mill gives a very penetrating analysis. He agrees that the act has a beneficial effect in forcing

1 House of Lords' Committee on Commercial Distress, 1848, pp. 28–9.
2 J. S. Mill, *Principles of Political Economy*, p. 671, and Select Committee on the Bank Acts, 1857, Q. 2011.

the Bank to contract credit at an earlier stage in a boom, but he believes that this advantage is gained at too high a price. When a crisis comes the act delays that monetary expansion by which, alone, it can be alleviated. He points out that the expansion of credit when the exchanges become favourable is implicit in the doctrines of the Currency School, but "The machinery of the system withholds, until in many cases it is too late, the very medicine which the theory of the system prescribes to be the appropriate remedy".[1]

Mill pointed out that, in a purely metallic system, some drains, at least, would be met out of hoards, and that, therefore, if the system were to work "as if it were purely metallic", it should be possible for the gold in the issue department to vary without producing any corresponding variations in the note issue. In this connection, he specially emphasised the distinction, made by Fullarton, between various types of drains:

There is a distinction to be drawn between two types of drain; one may be called an unlimited, another a limited drain. A drain occasioned by a revulsion from a state of over speculation is, in its nature, unlimited; unless there is something done to stop it, it will go on. If the high state of prices, occasioned by an inflated state of credit, continues, the drain will continue, and it can only be stopped when the high prices have ceased by a diminution of the currency, or a diminution of loans. But the case is different with all other drains; for instance a drain occasioned by payments for the import of corn or by foreign payments by government, or by the exportation of capital for foreign investment. This drain stops of itself as soon as the purpose is effected which caused it; and, therefore, it seems to me that the reserve should always be such as may be equal to the probable demand of a drain of this sort; and that, in the case of such a drain, bullion may be allowed to run out from the reserve, without any violent action on credit to stop it.[2]

Many other eminent economists, including Marshall, took a similar view. But no amount of sound reasoning seemed to bring any nearer a change in the law, and as the Bank grew more skilful in its operations public interest in the matter

1 *Principles*, p. 664.   2 Committee of 1857, Q. 2073.

waned. The argument went on, to be a source of annoyance to the author of *Lombard Street* and to form one of the main themes of Palgrave's *Bank Rate and the Money Market*. But the old acrimony, and the old freshness, had gone, and Palgrave's academic thesis consists of an elaborate statistical comparison between England and other countries, designed to show that fluctuations in interest rates have been greater in England than on the Continent, and that this is due to the operation of the act of 1844. It is not here that we have to look for any interesting new development in monetary theory.

GOLD, INTEREST AND PRICES.
WILLIAM NEWMARCH

We have already described in some detail the economic conditions associated with the influx of gold from California and Australia in the 1850's. The ground for discussion was how far these conditions were a consequence of the influx of gold, and how that influx operated to produce the effects which might be attributed to it.

The discussion provoked an investigation by Jevons, who combined the mass of undigested information on prices furnished by Tooke, to form an index number. But the best theoretical treatment of the subject in England came from Tooke's collaborator, William Newmarch, in the last volume of the *History of Prices*.

The two collaborators were both strongly opposed to any rigid form of the quantity theory, and Newmarch's analysis takes the form of a refutation of the extreme propositions—which few would have been so bold as to propound—that an increase in the stock of gold will lead simply to a proportionate rise in general prices, and will make no addition at all to the real wealth of society. Following Adam Smith's simile, he likens money to a road. To say that an increase in money will at once produce a proportionate increase in prices is as absurd as to say that the widening of a road will at once produce a proportionate increase in traffic.

Newmarch insists on the effect of new gold in stimulating demand, first in the countries in which it is found, then in those having trade relations with them, and so on, in less degree, throughout the world. It is this stimulation of demand which leads to the distribution of gold throughout the world:

The distribution has taken place in the precise proportion in which the extended demand for commodities, originally proceeding from the earliest labourers who picked up the gold, has gradually set in motion increased numbers of labourers, and increased amounts of capital to supply the requirements, not only of the populations of the gold countries, but also, more or less, of the populations of all the countries producing raw materials or the manufactured goods upon which incomes are at present expended.[1]

This increase in effective demand leads to an increase in real wealth, most notably in the gold-producing countries, but, to a lesser extent, in other countries as well:

In the United Kingdom, for example, the continuance, year by year, of an effective demand for commodities has led to improvements and extensions to the means of production—has led to accumulations of capital *as savings out of the larger incomes of capitalists and labourers*—and has diminished within the country the pressure of unemployed and destitute persons.[2]

Newmarch emphasises this effect of new gold in stimulating effective demand, and lays much less stress on the increase in investment, either from the increase in demand or from a reduction in the rate of interest. This is doubtless because capital accumulation is believed to proceed from the act of saving rather than from the act of investing.

Interest is assumed to be determined principally by the supply and demand for capital, and monetary factors are believed to produce only temporary fluctuations about the level thus determined. Newmarch refers at one point to "the absurdity of any doctrine which connects the rate of interest merely with the

1 *History of Prices*, vol. VI, p. 190.
2 Newmarch, *History of Prices*, pp. 192–3. My italics.

amount of the circulating medium".[1] Nevertheless, he agrees that the initial effect of the gold discoveries was to raise bank reserves, and so reduce both discount rates and "through the rate of discount to reduce the rate of interest on advances made for long periods on mortgages and other similar securities". Such a reduction of interest rates would stimulate production:

The most immediate consequence of the extreme reduction of the rate of interest was to lessen the cost of producing commodities, and to increase the profits of all persons requiring the accommodation of advances for short or long periods. In other words, the low rates of interest of 1852 set in motion in some important degree the extended trade and enterprise of 1853; and that extended trade and enterprise rapidly raised the demand for capital beyond the supply....[2]

Thus interest rates were raised again.

Though he still clings to the orthodox nineteenth-century view of capital and investment, Newmarch was in many ways strikingly in advance of his time. In abandoning the merely algebraical approach of the quantity theory, and enquiring *how* each change took place, he introduces an element of realism which was lacking in many later discussions.

THE GOLD AND SILVER COMMISSION

The rapid increase in the world stock of gold had been accompanied by a high level of employment, rising wages and prices and, after the first few years, low bank reserves and high and fluctuating discount rates. When, after 1873, the output of gold slightly diminished, and the demand for it largely increased, all these phenomena were reversed. Prices and wages fell, bank reserves rose, and discount rates were on the whole lower and more steady, while unemployment was rather higher than before. This change aroused much more attention than did the previous one. There was a revival of the bimetallist agitation, which had been dormant since the 1820's, Parliamentary Com-

[1] Newmarch, *History of Prices*, p. 201.   [2] *Ibid.*

mittees were appointed on the depression of trade and on the relative prices of gold and silver, and practically all the leading economists of the day took part in the discussion.

The part of the argument which principally concerns us is that on the mechanism by which gold affects prices. There was a general acceptance of the quantity theory, qualified by the inclusion of bank credit, and the recognition of possible changes both in the volume of transactions and the velocity of circulation. But when put in this refined form the quantity theory becomes very uninformative. It tells us that a change in one of the variables must be offset by changes in one of the others, but we have no means of telling upon which of them it will fall, or what will be the actual process of change. It was here that important differences of opinion arose.

One school of thought minimised the influence of gold supplies, pointing out that the diminution of production was small in relation to the total stock, emphasising the improvements in banking technique by which cash had been economised, and finding explanations of the fall in the prices of commodities—silver included—in the conditions of supply and demand for each. This was the view of the majority report of the gold and silver commission, and was supported, among others, by H. D. Macleod. Macleod emphasised the importance of credit, and denied the existence of any shortage of gold in England. He attributed the fall in prices to technical improvements, which had reduced the cost of production of commodities, and to the lack of speculation. He maintained that the volume of credit depended on commercial transactions, but, when pressed, he admitted that a certain minimum of gold would be necessary in order to sustain a given volume of credit, and that the amounts of gold and of credit tended to move together.[1]

Some authorities, who believed that gold produced a more positive effect than this, thought that it operated through the retail market, where gold coin was still the principal means of payment. This explanation was given to the Commission by

[1] Gold and Silver Commission, Q. 7196 seq.

J. B. Robertson, though the precise mode in which it operated was never made very clear.[1]

Another explanation was that gold affected prices through international trade, either with the "unbanked" countries, or with countries on a silver standard. In an "unbanked" country using gold, it was generally agreed that there was a direct connection between an increase in the quantity of the metal and a rise in prices, and vice versa. If prices in these countries fell, then prices in other countries must fall too, in order to preserve equilibrium in international trade. With regard to countries on a silver standard, e.g. India, it was argued that a fall in the gold price of silver would enable the Indian exporter to sell more cheaply in gold in England. The English exporter, on the other hand, would be unable greatly to raise the silver price of his goods in India, and so he too would have to sell for a lower gold price. Thus the gold price both of imports from the exports to silver-using countries would be lowered, and other prices would fall in sympathy.[2] This is very similar to the modern theory of exchange depreciation applied to free currencies, and it would be true if neither party held any appreciable quantity of the metal used as money by the other. Marshall, however, pointed out that, in fact, the fall in the gold price of silver led to the export of silver to the East until Indian prices were raised to an extent sufficient to offset the depreciation of gold, and that there was a bounty on Indian exports only so long as the export of silver continued.[3]

But the most popular view was that gold influenced prices through bank reserves and discount rates, the most distinguished exponents of which were Marshall and Sir R. Giffen.

Marshall accepts the quantity theory with qualifications as to the velocity of circulation and the volume of transactions, and he defines money as "everything which passes from hand to hand as a means of purchasing, without requiring any special or trade knowledge on the part of those who handle it". He believes, however, that the theory is valid whatever definition

1 *Ibid.* evidence of J. B. Robertson.
2 *Ibid.* evidence of R. Barclay and others.
3 *Ibid.* evidence of Alfred Marshall.

of money is employed, provided that that definition is adhered to.

He attributes to money only a subordinate influence in determining discount rates:

The average rate of discount is permanently determined by the profitableness of business. All that the influx of gold does is to make a sort of ripple on the surface of the water.[1]

And again:

I conceive that the average rate of discount during the past ten years has had nothing to do with the supply of the precious metals, except in so far as a fear of a further fall in prices has deterred people from new enterprises.[2]

To a limited extent, however, an increased demand for gold will bring about higher discount rates, and this will produce forced sales, and cause people to delay purchases, thus leading to a fall in prices. Marshall confines this analysis entirely to the effect of short-term interest rates on wholesale markets.

When asked to explain the coincidence of reduced supply and increased demand for gold with larger bank reserves and lower discount rates, Marshall distinguishes between a fall in the rate of discount due to an influx of gold and one due to "the thinning out of the field for the investment of capital relative to the supply of capital". As a result of the demand for gold from America and Germany, other things being equal,

They (the Bank) would have to raise the rate of discount when otherwise they might have kept it stationary; they would have to keep it stationary when otherwise they might have lowered it. The result would be a check to speculative investments, a diminished demand for commodities, and a fall in prices.[3]

A more unequivocal statement of the same view is given by Giffen.[4] He takes it for granted that, in a country where gold was the only circulating medium, changes in the quantity of gold would lead directly to changes in prices, and also in discount rates, as "the amount of cash kept by capitalists is an

1 Gold and Silver Commission, Q. 9651. 2 *Ibid.* Q. 9661.
3 *Ibid.* Q. 10,178. 4 *Essays in Finance*, Second Series, 1886.

unusually important item in that portion of capital known as circulating capital".[1] In a complex system, however, gold comes into use only for small change, and as bank reserves. Cash ceases to be any large part of circulating capital and as, he maintains, the rate of discount is the price of circulating capital, permanent changes in discount rates must be due to changes in the supply and demand for capital. Changes in the quantity of gold may, however, have important temporary effects through bank reserves. The banker must always maintain a certain minimum proportion of cash to liabilities, and so

Refined and complicated as the system may be, there must be cash somewhere, which sets an impassable limit to the amount of nominal capital which may be circulated by banks; and consequently, as we shall see, to the whole amount of nominal property in a community at a given time. Like a small weight on the long arm of a lever, the cash reserve of a banking system has enormous force.[2]

We thus reach the conclusion that

In the long run, and on the average, matters are settled by the relation of the supply of capital and the demand; but minor fluctuations must be settled by the varying relations of the cash reserve to the liabilities of the banks, and through them, to the nominal capital of the country.[3]

The influx of gold will reduce discount rates, which will tend to stimulate borrowing and cause people to make purchases and avoid sales; thus prices will be raised, and the rise "will add to the nominal capital, and particularly to the nominal capital represented by the loans and deposits of banks".[4] Wages will also rise, and this will mean a greater demand for gold as small change; thus bank reserves will be trenched upon, and the process of expansion checked:

What appears to happen is that when cash is added to the banking reserve it acts first on the rate of discount, and tends to produce the addition required to the circulating capital of the country; but

1 *Essays in Finance*, Second Series, 1886, p. 40.   2 *Ibid.* p. 45.
3 *Ibid.* p. 47.   4 *Ibid.* p. 49.

the supply of cash for small change being only obtainable from the banking reserve, the reserve in turn is trenched upon, and the addition to the bank's liabilities is checked.[1]

Conversely, when there is an efflux of gold. If, however, prices are to be maintained in an expanding society, it is necessary that the output of gold should not only be sustained but increased. The growth of population and of output creates an increasing demand for cash for small change, and in the absence of increasing supplies, bank reserves would be reduced, and all the results described would follow.

J. B. Robertson also alluded to the effect of gold on interest rates, besides the more direct effect on prices through retail trade. As well as stressing the effect of discount rates on wholesale markets, he makes the point—ignored by Marshall and Giffen— that long-term interest rates will move in sympathy with discount rates, and so investment in fixed capital will be affected.

In all these discussions, it will be noticed that the effect of new gold in directly stimulating demand, which was so important in the analysis of Newmarch, is conspicuously absent.

THE FUNCTIONS OF THE CENTRAL BANK

When we quit the field of abstract monetary theory and descend to specific problems of central banking, much the most important work which we have to consider is that of Walter Bagehot. Bagehot's *Lombard Street* is the synthesis of all the central banking wisdom which had accumulated up to the 1870's, and it remained as the epitome of sound principle for many years after: Bagehot was less an innovator than a publicist. He made no great developments in theory, and suggested no startling changes, but he supported, on almost every problem, the most advanced opinion of his day, and supported it with balanced judgement and powerful argument. He was thus often instrumental in changing a speculative opinion into an accepted doctrine.

1 Giffen, *op. cit.* p. 51.

It was Bagehot who, more than anyone else, insisted that the Bank was different from any other bank, that it had special duties and responsibilities, and it was he who gave the clearest analysis of their nature. Yet, in theory, he was not a supporter of central banking at all. Were it possible to start afresh and construct a banking system based entirely upon principle, he believed that the best system would be one in which each bank kept its own reserve. The dominant position of the Bank of England arose from a combination of historical accident and government interference, and Bagehot never tired of pointing out that the Bank was an anomaly. But it was an anomaly which was so firmly rooted that it could not reasonably be changed, so the only thing was for the Bank frankly to accept and faithfully to discharge the responsibilities of its position.

The first of these responsibilities arose from the fact that the Bank was the only body in England, and when Bagehot wrote, in Europe too, which kept a large and readily available reserve of gold. It was an undeniable fact that there was no other source of gold for export in the country, yet some of the directors continued to deny that they had any special obligation to provide gold for that purpose. For instance, Thompson Hankey states that

The only duty of the directors of the Bank of England as bankers is to take care to maintain their reserve at a sufficient amount to meet all wants of their banking customers, knowing quite well that the gold question can take care of itself.[1]

Why then, asks Bagehot, does the Bank keep a reserve of some 40%, compared with the 13% of the London and Westminster? In fact "the gold question" is itself the most important determinant of the needs of the Bank's "banking customers". This fact was partly obscured by the provisions of the Bank Charter Act and the theories on which it was based, and one of Bagehot's greatest services was to throw penetrating and remorseless light upon it.

The second duty of the Bank which Bagehot stresses was to

[1] *Principles of Banking*, 1873 edition, p. xi.

act as lender of last resort. We have seen that, during the first half of the century, the Bank was gradually assuming this responsibility in face of strong opposition from the theorists. This opposition was continued by Hankey, among others.

The trading community (says that worthy director) must be taught at some time or other, that no such establishment as the Bank of England can provide ready money beyond a clearly established limit, and that limit is the money left in their hands by their depositors.[1] It was to the violation of this principle that Hankey attributed the need for the suspension of the act of 1844. In 1866 the Bank was very liberal in its lending, and the governor, in his address to the proprietors, acknowledged that the Bank regarded such lending as a duty. Bagehot, in *The Economist*, commented that "the Bank agrees in fact, if not in name, to make unlimited advances on proper security to anyone who applies for it". This provoked the comment from Hankey that "*The Economist* newspaper has put forth what, in my opinion, is the most mischievous doctrine ever broached in the monetary or banking world in this country".[2] Public opinion, however, was swayed by the force of Bagehot's argument, and I am not aware that any well-known writer has since suggested that there was anything improper in the Bank's lending freely in time of crisis.

Arising from these two responsibilities of the Bank is its peculiar liability in respect of bankers' balances. The directors insisted that the accounts of the bankers were just like any others, and indeed, more stable than any others, as the bankers always kept a certain minimum of funds with the Bank. Hankey states that the Bank knows this minimum level, and that "when these deposits are so found in excess, the Bank knows that they cannot be made use of as ordinary deposits",[3] and H. H. Gibbs also emphasises the stability of the bankers' accounts.[4] But Bagehot points out that these accounts might, nevertheless, form the channel for an indefinite drain on the reserve. For, as their balances were depleted, the bankers might present bills for

1 Hankey, *op. cit.* p. viii. 2 Quoted, *Lombard Street*, pp. 170–1.
3 Hankey, *op. cit.* p. viii.
4 Printed in B. Price, *Practical Political Economy*.

discount to the Bank, or call in their loans from the market, in which case the market would borrow from the Bank. In its capacity of lender of last resort, the Bank would have to make these loans, even though they went only to replenish bank reserves and enable further gold withdrawals: "The Bank must always lend to keep them up to the necessary minimum, and so they furnish a channel for making indefinite withdrawals."[1]

The moral of all this was that the Bank ought to keep a larger reserve. Bagehot suggested that it ought to have a minimum below which it tried to prevent the reserve ever from falling. H. H. Gibbs describes this as "only a dream"; Bagehot himself, however, held no brief for a fixed cash ratio, and fully realised that what was adequate at one time would be far from adequate at another. His idea in suggesting the minimum was merely to prevent the reserve being depleted to what he considered the dangerous extent to which it had been on a number of occasions. Here, as in other things, the arguments of Bagehot bore fruit in the more cautious policy of the Bank in the last years of the century.

With regard to the means by which the reserve was to be protected, Bagehot, like most of his contemporaries, had complete faith in the efficacy of Bank rate, and he gives the familiar analysis of its operation, first through movements of short-term capital, and then through changes in prices.

In the 1850's and 1860's it had been fashionable to deny that the Bank had any power at all over interest rates, and to state that in fixing Bank rate it ought simply to follow the market; in other words, the rate should be fixed by the supply and demand for discounts. This had been the policy of *The Economist* at one time, but it was going out of favour in Bagehot's day. In its place was the view that Bank rate ought to be fixed with reference to the reserve, of which H. H. Gibbs provides an admirable statement:

The sole principle which actuates us in fixing the rate of discount —that is to say the price of our loans—is the state of our reserve,

[1] *Lombard Street*, p. 317.

the amount which we have in our coffers, wherewith to pay our debts, and meet demands upon us.

And in judging of the amount so disposable, we have, of course, to take into account the probability of those demands, and many other circumstances present or foreseen, that is to say the mood of our depositors, the condition of our borrowers, the state of trade, of the harvest, of home and foreign politics, everything, in short, which can affect the case.[1]

Bagehot, himself, strongly supports the view that Bank rate must be fixed with reference to the state of the reserve, and without regard to market rate. He points out that the only way in which a drain of gold can affect the market is through Bank rate. In the case of such a drain, therefore, the Bank must raise its rate, even though it is not followed by the market, and, in the absence of any stronger action, it must be willing to see its discounts shrink for a time, until that shrinkage causes a scarcity of money in the market, and Bank rate becomes effective again.

Bagehot followed Mill and Fullarton in distinguishing between an internal and an external drain. He also gave the generally accepted diagnosis of a crisis, as an internal drain superimposed on an external one, and prescribed the generally accepted remedy, a rapid rise in discount rates, followed by large loans at high rates.

In Bagehot's time the problem of making Bank rate effective, and of the relation between the Bank and the market, had not become really pressing, and he takes it for granted that Bank rate can soon be made effective merely by a temporary shrinkage of the Bank's discounts. When the problem did become acute, it received hardly any theoretical consideration, and the quotations from the press with which we illustrated earlier chapters say all that was said about it.

1 *Practical Political Economy*, p. 551.

THE LIMITATIONS OF NINETEENTH-CENTURY MONETARY THEORY

The history of nineteenth-century monetary theory is the story of the emergence from controversy of an orthodox body of doctrine commanding general acceptance. This acceptance was first obtained for the theory of international trade developed by Hume and Ricardo and the theory of the distribution of the precious metals advanced by Senior. These were developed, with only minor modifications, by later economists.

In the theory of money and prices, we begin the century with a crude quantity theory on the one hand, and, on the other, an equally crude denial of any connection between money and prices. After the tortuous windings of the Currency and Banking controversy we emerge with a refined quantity theory, taking account of the existence of bank credits, the velocity of circulation, and the volume of transactions, which was accepted by almost everyone at the end of the century. When it came, however, to translating the static theory into dynamics, we have seen that there was still difference of opinion, and that none of the explanations offered were, of themselves, entirely convincing. The great weakness of the theory here was in its neglect of the importance of effective demand. Effective demand might be stimulated by monetary factors, as Newmarch pointed out with reference to new gold, for instance, but it might also change as a result of changes in technique or sentiment, quite independently of monetary phenomena. The quantity theory thus led its adherents to attach too much importance to money as the *initiating* factor in price changes.

Thus in discussing how money affected prices, they made for themselves a problem greater than actually existed. At the same time, their efforts to solve it were hampered by their conception of money and interest rates. Here we begin the century with the Ricardian doctrine that interest was the marginal yield of capital on the one hand, and the "City man's" view that it was the "price of money" on the other. Again, there emerges a compromise. In the long period the rate of interest, both for long- and short-term loans, is regarded as depending on the profits of capital, but it is recognised that changes in the quantity of money produce temporary fluctuations at least in short-term rates. It is in these temporary fluctuations that most economists sought the connection between money and prices, but if one regards the rate of interest as not primarily a monetary phenomenon, this view is not very convincing, and so we find a number of writers groping for other explanations.

With regard to the functions of a central bank, we again have the emergence of a body of orthodox doctrine. The superiority of unitary note issues, the duty of a central bank to keep the country's gold reserve, and to act as lender of last resort, the need to distinguish between internal and an external drain, all these, by the end of the century, commanded general assent. But the role assigned to the Bank was too negative. Its function was still regarded as the transmission of the effects of gold movements to the economic system as a whole, save that it was recognised that, in certain special cases, the Bank ought to bear the brunt of such movements itself, and shield domestic trade from their effects. But these special cases were more evident in theory than in practice. Even the quite regular and predictable autumn drain was still allowed to cause a rise in interest rates, and I know of no suggestion that the Bank ought to allow its reserve to be depleted and prevent a rise in rates. Indeed, in this respect the end of the century was hardly in advance of the period before the passage of the Bank Charter Act. The greatest need, in the pre-war system, was for a greater measure of international co-operation to stabilise interest rates, and to insulate domestic trade from the effects of temporary international fluctuations. There were signs, at the end, that the need was felt, and had monetary systems not been thrown into chaos by the World War, the development of such co-operation might not have been long delayed.

Appendix

CHANGES IN BANK RATE, 1876–1913, WITH THE AMOUNT OF THE RESERVE OF THE BANKING DEPARTMENT AND THE "PROPORTION" ON THE PRECEDING WEDNESDAY

UPWARD MOVEMENTS

Date	Proportion %	Reserve £000	Date	Proportion %	Reserve £000
2 to 2½%			**3 to 3½%**		
10/ 9/96	56	32,380	4/ 7/78	32	9,082
23/ 9/97	50	24,350	13/ 1/81	40	12,578
			7/ 2/84	40	12,213
2 to 3%			16/ 4/91	35	12,997
3/ 5/77	37	10,927	11/ 5/93	39	14,115
28/ 8/77	44	12,120	13/ 7/99	42	20,031
28/ 3/78	33	11,916			
6/ 1/79	46	16,663			
9/10/84	33	10,473	**3 to 4%**		
12/11/85	41	11,773	4/10/77	37	9,721
6/ 5/86	39	11,739	25/ 8/81	41	12,925
4/ 8/87	38	11,121	17/ 8/82	38	10,001
10/ 5/88	36	11,211	10/ 5/83	33	10,307
20/10/92	41	15,105	30/10/84	36	10,062
			17/12/85	46	12,298
			1/ 9/87	42	11,683
2½ to 3%			13/ 9/88	44	12,696
27/ 6/78	37	10,858	29/ 8/89	41	12,301
9/12/80	45	13,983	26/ 6/90	37	13,167
18/ 8/81	43	13,285	29/10/91	38	13,247
9/ 8/88	39	10,958	10/ 8/93	43	14,616
8/ 8/89	36	11,578	22/10/96	50	25,920
24/ 9/91	46	16,759	7/ 4/98	37	18,351
4/ 5/93	41	15,011	13/10/98	46	20,291
3/ 8/93	46	16,813	19/ 7/00	38	18,911
24/ 9/96	55	31,293	21/10/01	46	23,882
14/10/97	44	20,924	2/10/02	45	23,616
22/ 9/98	51	23,495	3/ 9/03	49	24,442
7/ 9/05	45	24,695	28/ 9/04	40	23,808
14/ 1/09	43	21,013	14/10/09	44	22,950
7/10/09	45	23,636	17/ 3/10	49	24,943
			29/ 9/10	50	27,839
2½ to 3½%			21/ 9/11	57	32,573
26/ 8/86	44	12,222	29/ 8/12	49	30,994

Date	Proportion %	Reserve £000	Date	Proportion %	Reserve £000
3½ to 4%			**4 to 5% (continued)**		
1/ 8/78	34	8,903	3/ 1/01	30	16,212
21/10/86	40	10,792	11/10/06	35	18,290
7/ 5/91	33	12,211	21/10/09	54	22,323
18/ 5/93	38	13,323	20/10/10	47	22,802
3/ 5/06	39	21,892	17/10/12	49	27,388
13/ 9/06	48	24,762			
			4½ to 5%		
3½ to 4½%			5/10/99×	39	20,051
3/10/99	39	23,424	2/10/13	53	26,412
4 to 4½%			**5 to 6%**		
15/ 8/07	50	24,959	14/10/78×	34	10,215
			30/ 1/82×	39	10,970
4 to 5%			30/12/89×	33	9,590
3/11/77	36	9,431	7/11/90	33	11,207
16/ 8/78	36	8,603	30/11/99	41	19,336
6/10/81	30	10,322	19/10/06	37	18,862
14/ 9/82	39	11,157			
6/11/84	34	9,517	**4½ to 5½%**		
16/12/86	43	11,644	31/10/07	40	20,834
4/10/88	34	10,302			
26/ 9/89	42	12,392	**5½ to 6%**		
31/ 7/90	38	12,035	4/11/07×	40	20,834
25/ 9/90	41	13,163			
14/ 5/91	34	12,445	**6 to 7%**		
24/ 8/93	45	15,016	7/11/07	35	17,695

DOWNWARD MOVEMENTS

Date	Proportion %	Reserve £000	Date	Proportion %	Reserve £000
7 to 6%			**5 to 4%**		
2/ 1/08	36	21,473	29/11/77	47	11,547
			16/ 1/79	30	11,517
6 to 5%			9/ 3/82	40	13,218
21/11/78	46	12,311	25/ 1/83	44	12,377
23/ 2/82	39	12,418	29/ 1/85	45	13,938
20/ 2/90	50	16,177	3/ 2/87	48	13,235
4/12/90	45	16,673	10/ 1/89	39	12,491
11/ 1/00	39	21,832	21/ 8/90	44	14,287
17/ 1/07	45	22,593	8/ 1/91	40	15,532
16/ 1/08	53	25,867	4/ 6/91	44	17,661
			14/ 9/93	53	17,585
5 to 4½%			23/ 1/08	55	27,523
6/ 3/90	51	16,367			
18/ 1/00	42	23,113	**4½ to 4%**		
7/ 2/01	46	21,514	12/ 3/90	51	16,905
11/ 4/07	44	25,135	25/ 1/00	45	23,922
—/12/09	57	26,006	21/ 2/01	52	24,467
1/12/10	—	25,686	25/ 4/07	45	25,905
17/ 4/13	48	27,929	6/ 1/10	39	23,288
			26/ 1/11	52	27,177

Date	Proportion %	Reserve £000
4 to 3½%		
21/ 3/76	45	13,487
15/ 2/83	45	13,288
13/ 9/83	47	14,481
19/ 3/85	49	18,270
10/ 3/87	49	15,931
12/ 1/88	40	12,326
24/ 1/89	46	13,992
10/ 4/90	44	15,107
22/ 1/91	44	17,054
12/10/91	43	15,169
21/ 9/93	54	18,331
21/ 1/97	52	27,450
25/ 5/98	48	26,545
19/ 1/99	45	22,103
24/ 4/00	44	22,124
6/ 6/01	51	24,687
23/ 1/02	49	24,699
21/ 5/03	51	25,181
14/ 4/04	47	24,143
5/ 4/06	45	26,447
21/ 6/06	49	26,668
5/ 3/08	49	29,518
20/ 1/10	51	26,911
2/ 6/10	53	29,020
8/ 2/12	42	29,402
4 to 3%		
10/ 1/78	40	11,902
30/ 1/79	36	12,850
23/ 3/82	46	15,113
21/ 1/86	40	12,400
18/ 6/91	46	19,436
8/ 6/93	47	17,399
3½ to 3%		
6/ 4/76	45	12,980
17/ 2/81	47	16,580
1/ 3/83	43	14,057
27/ 9/83	44	14,836
13/ 3/84	44	15,109
7/ 5/85	51	17,786
24/ 3/87	49	17,056
19/ 1/88	42	13,050
31/ 1/89	46	14,546
17/ 4/90	45	15,643
29/ 1/91	46	17,599
21/ 1/92	39	14,789
5/10/93	45	16,654
4/ 2/97	52	28,244
2/ 6/98	48	26,046
2/ 2/99	46	22,970
3½ to 3% (continued)		
14/ 2/00	43	21,003
13/ 6/01	52	25,603
6/ 2/02	49	25,184
18/ 6/03	53	26,823
21/ 4/04	47	24,861
19/ 4/08	51	31,279
10/ 2/10	52	27,227
9/ 6/10	51	31,941
9/ 3/11	51	29,847
9/ 5/12	51	29,212
3 to 2½%		
5/ 7/77	43	13,174
30/ 5/78	40	11,338
13/ 3/79	50	19,302
17/ 6/80	48	17,394
28/ 4/81	49	15/897
3/ 4/84	44	15,548
14/ 5/85	51	17,549
10/ 6/86	39	11,399
14/ 4/87	50	15,387
16/ 2/88	46	15,184
7/ 6/88	41	12,647
18/ 4/89	41	13,985
2/ 7/91	43	18,245
7/ 4/92	40	15,449
26/ 1/93	47	17,364
15/ 6/93	50	19,597
1/ 2/94	55	19,739
8/ 4/97	52	27,581
30/ 6/98	49	27,071
9/ 3/05	52	30,856
28/ 5/08	52	27,662
1/ 4/09	48	30,754
3 to 2%		
20/ 4/76	47	13,392
31/ 1/78	44	12,982
18/ 2/86	49	14,904
2½ to 2%		
12/ 7/77	46	13,911
10/ 4/79	49	18,662
19/ 6/84	47	15,687
28/ 5/85	52	18,369
28/ 4/87	51	15,871
15/ 3/88	44	16,507
28/ 4/92	43	15,284
22/ 2/94	60	22,602
13/ 5/97	51	25,611

Index

Printed in the United States
By Bookmasters